The
Detective
and The
He
Investor

ALSO BY ROBERT G. HAGSTROM

Investing: The Last Liberal Art

The
Detective
and The
Investor

**Uncovering Investment Techniques
from the Legendary Sleuths**

Robert G. Hagstrom

TEXERE
New York • London

Copyright © 2002 Robert G. Hagstrom

Published in 2002 by

TEXERE LLC
55 East 52nd Street
New York, NY 10055

Tel: +1 (212) 317 5511
Fax: +1 (212) 317 5178
www.etexere.com

In the UK

TEXERE Publishing Limited
71–77 Leadenhall Street
London EC3A 3DE

Tel: +44 (0)20 7204 3644
Fax: +44 (0)20 7208 6701
www.etexere.co.uk

This publication is designed to provide accurate and authoritative information in regard to the subject matter covered. It is sold with the understanding that the publisher is not engaged in rendering legal, accounting, or other professional services. If legal advice or other expert assistance is required, the services of a competent professional person should be sought.

Library of Congress Cataloging-in-Publication Data has been applied for.

ISBN 1-58799-127-6

Printed in the United States of America.

This book is printed on acid-free paper. ∞

10 9 8 7 6 5 4 3 2 1

TABLE OF CONTENTS

PREFACE

This is a book for investors. That is why it is called *The Detective and the Investor* rather than *The Detective and the Speculator* or *The Detective and the Trader*. So, here at the outset, you should realize that if you are a market speculator or a stock trader, this book will not serve your needs.

But are you a true investor? Over the years I have observed that many people can't answer that question, because they don't know the essential differences between investing, speculation, and trading. Although it is easy to blame this ignorance on the investing public, much of the fault lies elsewhere—in no particular order, I am thinking of academia, the financial media, and the financial services industry. Representatives of these three groups are responsible for educating and informing people about finance, and for navigating the financial markets on behalf of individual investors, but I believe they have done a very poor job of helping people distinguish between these three different approaches.

For the record, investing is the process of calculating the economic return of an asset over the life of the asset. This process has two parts. The first seeks to determine the fundamental return that the asset will yield, based on its underlying economics; the second adds to or subtracts from this return based on the price paid for the asset.

Thus, if you pay fair value for an asset, you will get that asset's economic return—no more and no less. If you are able to purchase the asset at a discount to fair value, you get the asset's economic return *plus* the added return when the market reprices the asset to fair value. Conversely, if you purchase the asset at a price above fair value, you get the economic return of the asset *minus* the price decline when the market reprices the asset to fair value.

Benjamin Graham put it succinctly and memorably: "In the short run the stock market is a voting machine; in the long run it is a weighing machine."

Determining how the stock market will "vote" in the short run is the domain of the speculator. "A speculator," says Warren Buffett, "attempts to forecast what stock prices will do independent of the underlying economics of the business." That is, they do not bother with trying to understand the value of the underlying business, but simply look at today's stock price and make a guess about tomorrow's.

Speculators base that guess on their understanding of market psychology. They try to anticipate changes in market behavior, factoring in what they imagine people will want to buy or sell in the very near future. On any given day the market is the sum total of all the immediate desires, preferences, and personality quirks of all the individual investors. If someone had a good enough viewfinder and could see into their collective minds, that person could anticipate tomorrow's prices and be a very successful speculator indeed. To my knowledge, that magic viewfinder has not yet been invented.

To say this a different way, an investor focuses attention first on the asset and second on the price, while the speculator focuses attention first on the price and then second (or sometimes not at all) on the asset. Investors think long-term; speculators think short-term.

Traders are also short-term thinkers, but unlike speculators, they do not make all decisions on the basis of market psychology. Instead, they attempt to integrate some basic understanding of economics into their trading strategy. They studiously gather information on such factors as interest rates, global commodity prices, changes in government policies and regulations, international trading partnerships, and so on. They then array that information alongside historical stock prices in sophisticated charts and spreadsheets, looking for patterns that they think will repeat in the future and thus offer an opportunity for profit.

The trader's goal, in other words, is to profit from perceived patterns in stock, bond, and market prices. The difficulty is that patterns can be seen only in the past tense. Most traders rely on historical relationships as guideposts for what the future will look like. That is why trading is often referred to as a "rear-view mirror" process: It will work as long as the future resembles the past, but as so many have learned so painfully, the future is not predictable, and so trading strategies have a tendency to work until one day they don't. When suddenly tomorrow turns out to be different from yesterday, those with a trader's mindset are often unable to alter their models and actions.

Understanding the difference between long-term investing and short-term greed is an important dynamic in financial markets, and it is fundamentally important to our understanding of how to make money. Despite a library full of books on how to invest for the long term, people are too easily seduced into speculation and trading. The emotional need to satisfy short-term greed often overpowers the sensibilities for pursuing long-term goals.

To repeat: This is a book for investors, those who are in it for the long term. It is also a book for people who enjoy reading mysteries and detective fiction. I believe it is the first investment book that combines the two. The basic premise is that investors stand to learn a great deal from observing the methods and the mental habits of the best detectives.

In this book you will meet three who are known as Great Detectives, possessed of superior analytical minds. The investigative methods used by C. Auguste Dupin, Sherlock Holmes, and Father Brown to analyze the evidence and solve the mystery are the very same methods that investors should apply when analyzing a business and determining its value.

We don't know (because it doesn't come up in their stories) what any of these Great Detectives thought of the world of investing. But I am absolutely certain that if they were standing on Wall Street today, each of them would instinctively act as an investor and not a speculator or trader. That is simply the way their minds work.

It is my hope that, after reading this book, you will remember the exploits of these Great Detectives and install them somewhere in your mind. Then, when you are back in the stock market trying to decide whether to buy a certain stock, consider how one of them would approach the problem. Ask yourself, *Am I behaving like Dupin, Holmes, or Father Brown would, or am I closer to the bungling police detective with his superficial methods and questionable judgment?*

Once you make the basic connection between detective and investor, you can extend that connection to your own favorite mystery authors and detectives. And the next time you pick up a mystery novel, while you are enjoying a good read, try also to take note of how the mystery is solved. You may discover that the methods used by your favorite detective may help you the next time you invest.

CHAPTER ONE

The Detective and the Investor

Between my freshman and sophomore years in college, I worked as a bellhop in a hotel in downtown Nashville. The pay was good. I was easily making more in tips than my friends who were sweating away their days at landscaping jobs. But the hours were lousy. As the newest bellhop, I got the graveyard shift: 11:00 p.m. to 7:00 a.m.

Now, the work of a bellhop is not all bad. The problem with graveyard is boredom. Most guests had already checked in before I came on duty, although occasional late arrivals kept me occupied the first few hours; the next morning, around daybreak, I was sometimes busy with early-bird checkouts. But for three hours, between two and five in the morning, the hotel was completely, utterly dead. The lobby was vacant, the phones stopped ringing, and the front desk clerk always managed

1

to slip behind a closed door and catch a few winks. But the hotel's trustworthy bellman—me—always had to be ready at the front door to welcome a new guest or assist in an early departure, even if none appeared.

By the end of the second week I had had enough. Even pulling weeds in the hot sun at half my pay had to be better than being bored out of my mind.

When I told my father I was planning to give notice and look for a day job, he didn't argue. He merely reached over, picked up a book, and tossed it to me. "How about reading when it gets slow?" he suggested. "Maybe it would help the time go by faster."

I was as arrogant as any other college kid, and the idea of spending the summer reading, after hitting the books from September to May, didn't sound good. There was no way I was going to rupture any brain muscles before the fall semester started.

But the book my dad gave me wasn't intimidating. By its size— which is how I judged most books I was forced to read—it looked pretty easy. A small paperback, about a half-inch thick. "Stick it in your back pocket," Dad said, "and take it out when you get bored. You might enjoy it."

I went to work that day and forgot all about the book until, hopelessly bored in the middle of the night, I grabbed a stool to sit down and felt something uncomfortable in my back pocket.

The book was *Fer-de-Lance* by Rex Stout. From the title, I first thought it was one of those weird French books I purposely didn't read in high school, but the cover blurb set me straight: "He likes his orchids rare, his beer cold, his food gourmet and plentiful. He's Rex Stout's brownstone-based, one-seventh-of-a-ton, super-sleuthing genius of detection—Nero Wolfe." I wasn't sure about the orchids, but the beer and the food sounded pretty good, so I opened the book and stepped inside the brownstone on West Thirty-Fifth Street and into the world of Nero Wolfe.

I'm not really sure how it happened. One minute I was reading this detective book and the next minute the sun was rising and the phone was ringing. I still had a few chapters to finish so I dog-eared the page, stuffed the book back into my pocket, and rushed to cart luggage down for the guests and load their suitcases into waiting taxicabs. As soon as my shift was over, I grabbed a cup of coffee, walked across the street, sat down in the park, and finished the story.

In the nights that followed, I read a great many Nero Wolfe mysteries. My dad owned almost the entire collection, so there was plenty to choose from. I withdrew my notice to leave and finished out the summer working at the hotel. Although each shift began and ended with the customary duties, the middle hours were for Nero Wolfe and Archie Goodwin. I cooked Wolfe's dinners with his chef, Fritz Brenner, and tended to his orchids with his gardener, Theodore. I laughed out loud each time Wolfe dressed down New York's finest—Inspector Cramer, Lieutenant Rowcliff, and Sergeant Purley Stebbins. I willingly tagged along with Saul, Fred, and Orrie, private detectives frequently enlisted to help with a complex investigation where there was more than one suspect to tail.

After graduation, I began a career in the financial services industry. I started as a stockbroker and later became a portfolio manager. As my professional endeavors broadened, the pile of investment material I was required to read grew into a mountain. But what I read for fun on my own time has remained essentially unchanged. Today, my bedside table always carries a mix of classic detective fiction and contemporary writers.

After Nero Wolfe, I moved on to other detectives. I read the wonderful adventures of Sherlock Holmes and his trusted Dr. Watson. I visited small English villages, peering over the shoulders of Miss Jane Marple and Hercule Poirot. I drank elegant cocktails with Nick and Nora Charles, busted heads with Philip Marlowe, and prowled the late-night streets of San Francisco with Sam Spade. I endured grotesque autopsies with Dr. Kay Scarpetta and chased lunatics with Detective Alex Cross, and I occasionally returned to the English countryside with Commander Adam Dalgliesh.

Why this attraction to detective stories? Several reasons. At the surface level, a well-written detective story is terrific entertainment and provides a healthy escape from the stresses of work and hectic schedules. It's fun to tail a suspect down a sidewalk, ducking and dodging so as not to be noticed; to follow a suspect in a thrilling car chase; to slip into a dark doorway when guns start blasting, bullets ricocheting a few inches from me.

But for all the action that is packed into a detective story, what most grabs my attention is the challenge of solving the puzzle. In the beginning, each case seems baffling and unsolvable, with a long list of suspects. Yet as the story unfolds, the detective takes the pieces of evidence (pieces that were all laid before my eyes but overlooked) and arranges them into a neat patchwork of undeniable guilt. To this day, whenever I start a new detective story I construct a mental list of the suspects and search intensely for clues. For me, the ultimate pleasure of reading a mystery is the chance to solve the crime before the detective does.

Looking back, I have often wondered whether my interest in studying investing is in some way connected to the fascination I have for detective stories. In a fundamental way, solving a mystery is similar to figuring out whether a security is priced accurately. Both are puzzles. The detective gathers clues to determine whether a suspect is guilty or innocent. In much the same way, a security analyst gathers financial data and industry facts to determine whether a company's value is being accurately assessed by the market, in the form of its stock price that particular day.

Over the years, I have learned many things about people, money, and investing. I have also observed, through good times and bad, through bull markets and bear markets, how investment professionals act and behave. What I have discovered is that the professionals, no less than individual investors, have fallen into bad habits. In all likelihood, no one of these questionable behaviors, by itself, would be catastrophic. But in the aggregate, these bad habits have the potential to do real damage both in our ability to think clearly and our ability to manage money smartly.

My intention here is to spread these bad habits out on the table so we can look at them, one by one. (They will reappear in subsequent chapters, in greater depth.) But even though I must of necessity catalog them this way, one at a time, the real world is, as we all know, far less tidy. Most of these actions, behaviors, trends—call them what you will—exist in a tangled snarl that is not easily dissected, much less diagnosed.

Short-term thinking. Starting in the 1950s, more and more Americans had cash to invest, and so more and more professionals jumped into the money-management field to serve them. The competition for new clients became intense, and this new crop of brokers—many of whom had no long-term record to present—instead trumpeted their most recent quarterly results. Investors were quick to catch on: Whoever had the best record from the last quarter became the one who would get their money in the next. Once investors came to expect good short-term results, the managers had to deliver it, or risk losing a significant share of their business. In this way we created a short-term mentality—widespread, insidious, and self-perpetuating.

Infatuation with speculation. This mad rush to produce the highest return in the shortest period of time has dramatically changed the investment landscape. In fact, we now have a nasty kind of double whammy: To beat out the competition, money managers are under extra pressure to make decisions faster, but since fast decisions are not necessarily good decisions, the quarterly race is even more precarious.

The focus on the short term has created a climate that favors

THE DETECTIVE AND THE INVESTOR

speculation rather than investing, and individuals are as susceptible to it as the professional money managers. Speculation is the
activity of forecasting the psychology of the market. People who
speculate are trying to anticipate the change in market behavior,
trying to guess which stocks will most likely be bought in a particular environment and which stocks are likely to be sold. Speculation is all about guessing what people are going to do. Investment,
on the other hand, is concerned with what an asset will yield over
time. Investors are focusing on the value of the business and are
attempting to profit from the difference between its value and its
current market price. Speculators seek to forecast changes in stock
prices. Investors seek to understand business values.

We all know this. We have known it since the days of John Maynard Keynes and Benjamin Graham, both of whom passionately
argued against a speculative frame of mind. Yet we still got giddy
over the soaring prices of high-flying, high-tech stocks in the late
1990s, and itched to get in on the action. And many of us paid a
severe price for that kind of speculative thinking.

Mental shortcuts. Choosing which securities to buy, which to sell, and
when to do either can be incredibly complex—so complex that
individuals try to simplify the process by settling on shortcut methods for making stock decisions. They establish some numeric
threshold for that factor, and take action only when a stock trips
against it. Some of the more popular single-factor metrics are price
to book value, dividend yields, and price-to-earnings ratios. Other
single-factor models have come into favor and gone out again over
the years. It hardly matters what the metric is, for the fundamental
flaw remains the same: When the universe is complex (and here I
mean all the forces that affect companies and drive the market),
using a single factor as the decision point severely understates reality and cripples the ability to make good decisions.

Race for information. The single-factor decision approach has never gone away. In the late 1990s, the single factor most used to predict short-term results was "earnings surprise": the degree to which a company's quarterly results were better than had been predicted, or worse. If quarterly earnings were better than expected, the stock price often rose, sometimes very dramatically. But if the company reported lower-than-expected earnings, the stock price was likely to decline. Any professional investor who could gain access to the quarterly results *before* they were released to the public could turn a nice profit buying or selling shares in advance of this "surprise." The trick, then, became how to get hold of company information early.

So enterprising investment professionals requested private conference calls and one-on-one meetings with company management, ahead of reporting time. If these professionals happened to work for firms that controlled billion-dollar portfolios, the companies often complied with these special requests. Individual investors and money managers from smaller investment firms had to wait for the official quarterly reports.

This selective disclosure of company information had long been frowned upon at the U.S. Securities and Exchange Commission (SEC), and in August 2000 that body made its disapproval official by adopting a new rule known as Regulation Fair Disclosure, which was quickly dubbed "FD." Companies were required to treat all investors equally, distributing the same information at the same time to individual small investors and billion-dollar money managers. This leveled the field dramatically. No longer could Wall Street professionals argue that they were better analysts because they had better, quicker information.

Overload of information. Today, financial information is both instantaneous and ubiquitous due to the combined effects of Rule FD and the Internet, which puts information at everyone's fingertips in nanoseconds. Whether Rule FD will be a good thing for investors in the long run is open to some debate. What is unarguable, though, is that all of us now have a great deal of information available to us, more than ever before, in all kinds of media. This makes it all the more urgent that we learn how to interpret the data and analyze it correctly.

Tainted objectivity. Most investors have heard of the Chinese Wall. It's that intangible separation in a large financial services firm between the brokers, who recommend that their clients purchase a certain company's stock, and the investment bankers, who are eager to woo that company. The potential conflict of interest is serious, for investment banking fees are very lucrative. The brokers are *supposed* to make their recommendations independently and objectively, but in reality the Chinese Wall is often breached—or at least that is the perception on the public's mind.

As of this writing, faced with widespread skepticism from the general public and with congressional hearings on the subject, the industry is working to develop "best practices" guidelines that it hopes will restore public trust, but the fox is still watching the henhouse, and suspicion remains.

Emotional potholes. Although professionals seek to explain the behavior of stocks and the market by purely rational methods, we are very much aware that emotions play a big role in decision-making. Behavioral finance experts have argued convincingly that various psychological missteps—including overconfidence, overreaction, bias, loss aversion, and mental accounting—often lead investors to make foolish mistakes that can have adverse effects on their portfolios. Today, the study of psychology is every bit as important to investing as the study of balance sheets and income statements.

• • •

For years, investment professionals, all competing for clients, have argued that their competitive advantage lies in obtaining better information and demonstrating superior analytical abilities. However, because of Rule FD, information is now available to all parties simultaneously, and thus only one advantage remains: superior analysis. As we have seen, though, the stubborn reliance on single-factor models coupled with the emphasis on short-term thinking has undercut good analysis, bringing us back full circle to the destructive effects of limited thinking and bad habits.

Not to say that bad habits are the exclusive domain of those who are professionally involved with investing in one way or another. There have always been some individuals who prefer to make their own investment decisions, and today they have a lot more company, as more and more people decide to go it alone. Many intelligent people are questioning whether the advice they get from professional analysts is really useful or really objective. And now that information is so easy to come by, people are concluding that they don't need professionals for research and analysis—they can do it themselves.

And what happens? They quickly find themselves entangled in the same predicament that has snared the professional. They have too much information and no clear way to think about it. They are tempted to take shortcuts. They are vulnerable to emotional issues. They are easily seduced into a destructive short-term mentality by high quarterly numbers and hot trends. They have no true understanding of the difference between speculation and investing.

Over the years, as I watched investors make the same analytical mistakes, I often wondered what it would take to break them of these bad habits of short-term thinking and speculation. And what could those of us in the profession, who are supposed to be advising others, do to help them develop the right mental framework to be successful? Then one day the lightbulb turned on as two very different thoughts came together in my mind: On the one hand, my frustration over the entrenched problems people have with investing; on the other, my delight in reading good detective stories, enjoying the exploits of very smart people who managed to untangle complex puzzles and find the truth at their core. Was it possible that one could be the solution to the other? That we could learn to be better investors by following the methods of good detectives?

The core premise of this book is that the same mental skills that characterize a good detective also characterize a good investor. Both of them painstakingly gather information from a wide range of sources, study and analyze data, discard some facts that turn out to be irrelevant and dig out new ones, and ultimately come to the one right conclusion. To say this another way, the analytical methods displayed by the best fictional detectives are in fact high-level decision-making tools that can be learned and applied to the investment world.

At the most basic level, good investing means figuring out whether any particular security is mispriced in the current market. Is it priced too high? Pass. Is it, for some reason, underpriced? That represents a good opportunity. Market pricing is a puzzle to be solved, just as a mystery is a puzzle to be solved.

As investors, we are now standing at the crossroads. In the decades-old attempt to generate the best returns in the shortest period of time, we have developed too many bad habits and we have taken way too many financial shortcuts. Having worn the speculator's hat for so long, we have forgotten how to be analysts. In trying so desperately to predict what a stock price will do next week, next month, next quarter, we overlook (or no longer recognize) the clues that determine a company's long-term value. In a word, we have mislaid our puzzle-solving abilities. Perhaps one way to become a better investor, to learn how to improve our puzzle-solving abilities, is to adopt a detective's habits of mind.

And not just *any* detective.

• • •

Depending on whom you ask, there are anywhere from a half dozen to more than twenty types of fictional detectives. They may be trained professionals (either law-enforcement officers or licensed PIs) or talented amateurs. Mysteries may be solved by doctors, lawyers, clerics, psychologists, academics, journalists, psychics, and any number of quirky "ordinary folks" with a gift for uncovering the truth. But standing in a class by themselves, head and shoulders above all others, are those few who have come to be known as the Great Detectives.

The Great Detectives are defined first and foremost by their superior intellect, possessing extraordinary mental acumen that puts them on a higher plane and distinguishes them from ordinary smart people who may be engaged in the same activities. They are, in a word, mental giants.

In practical terms this means they solve the mystery through intellectual prowess. This sets them apart from most fictional police detectives, who use a combination of dogged investigation and luck—like a tip from an informer or an unexpected confession—as well as from modern tough-guy PIs (male and female), who are willing to use physical intimidation against a suspect or a witness. It also sets them apart from the great panoply of amateur detectives, those friendly folks who display many different skills and personality traits (including terminal nosiness) but who, more often than not, find the solution to the mystery by being in the right place at the right time: overhearing an important conversation, stumbling upon a hidden item, picking up the wrong suitcase at the airport.

Great Detectives, in sum, outwit the criminal not because they work harder, not because they are luckier, not because they can run faster, hit harder, or shoot straighter, but because they *think* better.

Great Detectives are also defined, in a subtle but inescapable way, by time period. All fictional characters reflect the mannerisms and values of the times in which they live, and so as society evolves, the essence of

11

our protagonists changes as well. Modern detectives use modern tools and reflect today's sensibilities. Great Detectives, cerebral and somewhat aloof from quotidian society, fit more comfortably in an earlier time. They are classic and in that sense timeless, but they do seem in some intangible way to be part of an earlier era.

We could, of course, point to certain contemporary detectives who have some of the attributes of Great Detectives, and most mystery fans could name several favorite modern heroes who work on an intellectual rather than a physical plane. But intellectualism by itself is not sufficient to earn the title of Great Detective; it is the high-level quality of thinking—the depth, the breadth, and the sheer brilliance—that transforms a good detective into a Great Detective. At that rarified level, there are only a few.

Literary critics and historians may honorably debate many aspects of detective fiction—and do—but there seems to be general agreement on where the mantle of Great Detective belongs. Two are universally acknowledged: C. Auguste Dupin, the patrician hero of the first true detective story, and Sherlock Holmes, the very epitome of brilliant deduction.

After those two, critical unanimity falters a bit. Other protagonists are sometimes suggested, including my old friend Nero Wolfe, but the one who is most often named as the third Great Detective is G. K. Chesterton's Father Brown, a gentle, unprepossessing cleric who works miracles of detection.

All three have a similar approach to the mystery that is set before them. They gather all the information (evidence), analyze it thoroughly and correctly, and draw the correct conclusion. Others on the scene (along with the reader) have access to the same information, but their interpretation is flawed. Only one person has the dual ability to observe fully and analyze accurately—to sort through conflicting data, incomplete or inaccurate witness testimony, and puzzling physical clues, and tease out the truth.

Though each of the Great Detectives differs in his particular method of searching for the truth, they all have one thing in common: unparalleled skills of observation and analysis. They look at the situation, see everything, and understand what it means, in the process displaying a particular set of mental strengths: superior analytical reasoning; encyclopedic knowledge of all the pertinent facts; the power to enter the minds of others; and an uncanny ability to find a logical explanation for something that at first seems illogical, extraordinary, and unexplainable.

But this is a book about investing, and so the critical question is, can we distill the unique skills of Dupin, Holmes, and Father Brown into a practical menu of concepts for investors to follow? I believe we can. I believe that the mental strengths of the Great Detectives have an immediate, tangible application to us as investors, and so in the chapters that follow we shall spend some time getting to know these Great Detectives and discovering how they think. We will look at some of their greatest cases and the specifics of their methods. As we get to know each of these detectives we may come to understand and adopt their habits of mind.

Each Great Detective is accorded his own chapter (Chapters 2, 4, and 6), and these three chapters are paired with three others (3, 5, and 7) that describe modern-day "financial detectives." These modern practitioners, who are affiliated with the financial industry in one capacity or another, exhibit the same mental traits as the best fictional detectives, both the classic and the more contemporary ones.

One type of new financial detective is the investigative journalist who specializes in writing about finance in general and the market in particular. As a group, these journalists display many of the habits of mind that are familiar to mystery fans: They possess a healthy skepticism that makes them question first impressions and renders them unable to accept at face value what they are told by official sources. Of course, skepticism by itself is only half the formula; it brushes away useless information but puts nothing in its place. So the best journalists pair it with another trait that turns skepticism into a positive: tenacity. If they automatically discount the surface level, they are absolutely relentless in digging beneath the surface to uncover all the facts and tell the full story. Questioning the obvious, digging for the unobvious, and using good deductive reasoning to figure out what it all means—all are mental habits we find in detectives like Auguste Dupin and in top-notch journalists.

We meet such a journalist in Chapter 3, and follow his insightful investigation of a tumultuous Wall Street story of fraud and bankruptcy. We also meet another real-life journalist: reporter turned mystery author Edna Buchanan, who writes a delightful mystery series featuring an intrepid reporter who finds herself involved in deadly situations.

To pair with the incomparable Sherlock Holmes, Chapter 5 introduces the idea that the ideal investment analyst would combine the best skills of two types of Wall Street professionals: security analysts and credit analysts. To this ideal analyst, security analysts would contribute their special strengths of breadth of knowledge and reasoning ability; credit analysts would contribute objectivity and attention to detail. The synthesis of the two would be a modern analyst who very closely matches Holmes's way of operating.

In this chapter, we again see how the Great Detective, and his modern-day counterpart, would investigate a real company—this time one on the way up. And we also meet another modern author: Laurie King, creator of a remarkable series featuring a retired Sherlock Holmes and his brilliant young partner.

The third group of modern-day financial detectives is defined by its members' intellectual approach to the profession. Using a combination of academic training, solid experience, a wide-ranging intellectual curiosity, and an unusual intuitive sense that alerts them when things are not what they seem, these more cerebral individuals serve the entire profession and all investors as a kind of searchlight, pointing the way to new ideas and finding explanations for the mysterious and extraordinary behavior of certain stocks. In this way they are like Father Brown, who has the unique capacity to observe the scene and reach a conclusion using both logic *and* intuition.

In Chapter 7 we meet one such person, someone who might best be described as a Renaissance figure in the world of finance. And we have the pleasure of meeting another contemporary mystery author: Stephen Kendrick, who had the very original idea of putting Father Brown and Sherlock Holmes on the same case.

Finally, in the last chapter of the book we consider an intriguing "what if" question. Remembering that Dupin's analytical talents are somewhat different from those of Sherlock Holmes and that Holmes's talents are not the same as Father Brown's, what if we could somehow combine the abilities of all three? Would we then have the ultimate detective?

Then let us consider what would happen if individual investors adopted the combined analytical skills of the Great Detectives, and approached the puzzle of selecting stocks in the same way as our ultimate detective would go about solving a mystery. Would we then have the ultimate investor? What would this ultimate investor be like? What mental habits would he or she possess? How would his mind work and how would he approach each investment problem?

First, our investor-detective would have to keep an open mind, be prepared to analyze each new opportunity without any preset opinions. He or she would be well versed in the basic methods of inquiry, and so would avoid making any premature and possibly inaccurate assumptions. Of course, our investor-detective would presume that the truth might be hidden below the surface and so would distrust the obvious. The investor-detective would operate with cool calculation and not allow emotions to distract clear thinking. The investor-detective would also be able to deconstruct the complex situation into its analyzable parts. And perhaps most important, our investor-detective would have a passion for truth, and, driven by a nagging premonition that things are not what they seem to be, would keep digging away until all the evidence had been uncovered.

When I began collecting ideas and background information for this book, I found quite a number of pieces about mystery fiction by academicians and serious critics of literature. Some were quite blunt in their disdain, but many others seemed to be engaged in a kind of literary apologia, attempting to make detective fiction, the most popular form of "popular fiction," more respectable. They pointed to certain authors they felt displayed a high level of literary quality, and they listed the names of famous personages past and present who were fans of mystery stories. Often they indulged in social commentary, suggesting that the popularity of mysteries can be ascribed to their ratification of a moral social order, where wrongs are always righted and justice always prevails.

This is interesting to think about on an abstract level, and probably very significant in some circles, but the truth is I don't wish to join the highbrow debate about whether popular detective fiction is worthy of serious literally attention. What I care about is the idea that the methods of the best analytical detectives, and their habits of mind, can be turned to good advantage by investors. It is my hope that, by the end of this book, readers will have not only greatly enjoyed the journey but will find themselves in possession of a new set of mental habits with which to approach investing in the market—the same mental habits possessed by the great detectives.

CHAPTER TWO

Edgar Allan Poe and Auguste Dupin

On the night Mme. L'Espanaye and her daughter were butchered, my wife and I had our dinner on the patio. We had a veal ragout, Persian bread, and a salad of sliced beefsteak tomatoes with basil from my mother-in-law's garden. I don't know why I remember that. After dinner, I read the newspaper while my wife worked on our household accounts, and then around midnight, our usual time, we went to bed.

Sometime around 3:00 we were both awakened by the most horrendous screams I have ever heard, filled with both terror and pain. In our quiet neighborhood, nothing more startling than a fire alarm ever happens in the middle of the night. We rushed downstairs, and from the porch we could tell that the screams were coming from the street behind us, the rue Morgue. Several men from our block were running in that direction and, pushing my wife back inside, I started running too.

As we rounded the corner, other men ran up from the opposite direction. We all rushed to the front of a four-story building that seemed to be the source of the screams, and found ourselves blocked by a locked gate. The men from the neighborhood all looked helplessly at each other, paralyzed in momentary confusion, but two policemen quickly broke open the gate with what I believe was a crowbar.

The first thing I noticed was that as soon as we got into the building, the screams suddenly stopped. Then, as we all spread out to search the rooms on the first floor, we heard the sounds of an argument coming from above us, two loud and angry voices. When the police questioned me later, I told them one of the voices was clearly a Frenchman—I heard him shout *sacre*—but I couldn't be sure about the other. There was something very foreign about the up-and-down intonation, and I guessed it might be Italian; I wasn't even sure whether it was a man or a woman.

We continued dashing from room to room, and by the time we reached the second floor the sounds of the arguing voices had also stopped. The eerie silence seemed even more frightening than the horrible screams.

We found nothing on the second floor, nor on the third. On the fourth floor, the first rooms we checked were empty as well. My heart rate was just beginning to slow a little, and I could feel the pinpricks of adrenaline in my fingers, when we came at last to the apartment at the rear. The door was locked. All was silent.

The policemen forced open the door, and from the hallway I saw my first glimpse of the scene that is now burned into my memory and comes in the night to haunt my dreams. The front room of the apartment was completely torn apart. Furniture was turned over, lamps and pictures broken, the mattress pulled off the bed, the drawers of a dresser hanging open with their contents spilling out, papers and jewelry and clothing and money all tangled together in an ungodly mess. The only piece of furniture not upturned was a small chair, off by itself in a corner. In contrast to the chaos in the rest of the room, the little chair seemed almost innocent, except that lying on it was an open straight razor, dripping with bright red blood.

The two policemen moved through the apartment quickly, and now one of them, squatting in front of the fireplace, cried out for help. A body had been wedged into the narrow chimney, feet first. I can only imagine the officer's shock when he looked upward and saw the lifeless face staring back at him. It took the two of them, working with all their strength, to remove the body. It was the daughter, Camille L'Espanaye. All of us crowded around, and we could easily see several dark horizontal bruises and deep fingernail indentations on the throat. Even I, with no medical training, could see the signs of a particularly violent strangulation.

I found myself turning to the little chair in the corner of the room, and the bloody razor. Camille's body was covered with severe lacerations, but they were rough scrapes, not the sort of sharp cuts a razor would make. Where had the blood come from?

I found myself wondering something else too, and as I looked at the puzzled expressions of the police officers, I imagined they were thinking the same thing. No one had passed us as we came up the stairs. The apartment door had been locked from the inside, the windows shut. Where was the killer? How had he managed to escape? And where was Mme. L'Espanaye?

With a renewed sense of urgency, we all went racing back through the building a second time, searching every small nook that might serve as a hiding place for either the killer or another body. The policemen also ordered us to be on the lookout for another way out of the building, such as a second staircase or access to the roof. I believe we as good as tore the building apart, but we found nothing.

Finally, there was only one place left to search—the small backyard. It was here that we made a discovery so gruesome that I will never be able to forget it. There was one aspect so terrible that to this day, I haven't described it to anyone, not even my wife; except by writing them here, I cannot get the words out.

You may have already guessed: we found Mme. L'Espanaye's body in the rear yard. Her face and torso were viciously slashed—so savagely mutilated, in fact, that had I not known her well, I couldn't have sworn absolutely that it was she. Then, to our horror, when the policemen tried to lift the body, the head did not move. Someone had slit this poor woman's throat so deeply that her head was completely severed.

Many of you will no doubt recognize the preceding as a contemporary version of Edgar Allan Poe's famous story "The Murders in the Rue Morgue," recast into a first-person witness's account. Rewriting it this way is not meant as a trick on readers. With apologies to Mr. Poe, and with the very greatest respect, I wanted only to demonstrate that, except for the language in which it is rendered, his story has all the drama, suspense, and horror of today's detective fiction.

What makes this so remarkable is that before the publication of this story, there *was* no detective fiction: "The Murders in the Rue Morgue," published in 1841, was the first detective story ever written. (Notice I do not say the first mystery; there are those who argue that mysteries in the purest sense of that word appear in much earlier works, starting with the Bible. They may be right, but I'm not convinced it makes much difference for our purposes here.)

Think about that. In just one short story, this genius of a writer created an entirely new type of fiction, one that has endured to the present day and in fact is by many measures the most popular form of popular fiction. Even if Poe's hero (who we'll introduce presently) did not have the qualities of a Great Detective, we would still owe him serious attention as a pioneer. But in fact he *is* a Great Detective, and the basic appeal of this first story, written more than a century and a half ago, is so strong that simply by updating the language we can make it a thoroughly modern tale.

The works of even the most adventurous authors, of any era, reflect the language patterns of their time. Even Poe, so far ahead of his time in so many ways, wrote his dazzling stories in the intricate, stately language of the early nineteenth century—how could he have done otherwise? Modern readers, accustomed to a faster pace and crisper sentences, will inevitably label his writing style old-fashioned, and will therefore find it either charming or irritating, depending upon their personal orientation. If you are among the latter, I ask that you make a conscious effort to suspend your irritation temporarily, in order that we may learn what Poe has to teach us. And that is a very great deal.

Let's pick up the story again.

At the time of the killings, a reclusive Parisian nobleman by the name of C. Auguste Dupin reads with fascination the newspaper accounts of the atrocity, a "horrible mystery," the account concluded, "without the slightest clew."

Dupin lives in a dilapidated mansion where daylight is perpetually shut out with heavy drapes and shutters and nighttime is lit only with candles. His housemate is the anonymous friend who narrates the story. Except that he admires Dupin and shares his taste in literature, we are told very little about this man, not even his name. His function is to relate to us what happens, and to serve as a foil for his brilliant friend.

The next day, Dupin and the narrator read the follow-up stories in the newspaper, where considerable new details are added. Summaries of police interviews with eyewitnesses and other people connected to the victims are presented, along with the distressing news that a bank employee who recently delivered a large sum of money to the murdered woman has been arrested. Dupin suspects that the police, who just the previous day had not the slightest clue, have merely found a convenient scapegoat. Dupin feels indebted to the bank clerk, who once did him a favor, and decides he must look into the case to clear his friend.

Dupin asks for, and receives, police permission to visit the scene of the crime. And now, as we watch Dupin in action, and observe how his mind works, we begin to see the full depth of his genius. (Note that in this retelling I am taking mild liberties, describing Dupin's detailed investigation step by step as I imagine it happened, in order to illustrate his methods. Poe, in contrast, has his detective relate his observations and interpretations in a different sequence and completely after the fact, in an armchair summary.)

COLLECT THE FACTS
No thoughtful investor makes a decision in the absence of all relevant information.

Dupin begins by carefully examining the building's exterior. In the rear, he notices a lightning rod next to the wall, extending up to the fourth floor and about six feet away from one window of the L'Espanaye apartment. The shutter on the window is open halfway—that is, at right angles to the wall—so that from the ground, a casual observer would see only the narrow edge and would not realize how wide the shutter is; in any case, the police had no reason to think twice about the shutter. Dupin, however, notes that the shutter is a one-piece design, rather than hinged into sections, and that when fully open, flat to the wall, it would be just two feet away from the lightning rod. He also notices that the bottom of the shutter is an open trellis rather than solid wood. On the ground near the lightning rod, he finds a dirty ribbon tied with a distinctive knot. The police either missed it or considered it insignificant.

Dupin mentally catalogs all these observations but says nothing, as he moves to investigate the interior of the house. All those present on the night of the murder agree that the door to the apartment was locked from the inside; there is no doubt about that. The police also found the two windows securely locked from the inside. So how did the killer escape?

In their search for the answer, the police practically took the house apart. Now Dupin double-checks everything they did, and satisfies himself that they are correct: There is no back stairway, no access to the roof, no way for a person to climb up the very narrow chimneys, no secret passage.

Having eliminated all other possibilities, Dupin concludes there is only one remaining: The killer must have left the building through a window, and it must have been one of the two rear windows, otherwise the crowd of people in the front of the building would have seen something. Dupin now turns his scrupulous attention to the two windows in the back room. The police found them tightly fastened shut; the police must be wrong. The impossible must be possible.

With minute care, Dupin examines the first window. He finds the window sash fastened to the frame with a heavy nail. However, when he pulls the nail out he still cannot open the window, so he realizes there is another locking mechanism. Working slowly, he feels along every inch of the window, and sure enough, finds a hidden spring. When he releases the spring, he is able to lift the window. If the killer had closed the window from the outside after climbing out, the spring-loaded catch would fasten itself once again, and the police would find it securely locked. But the killer did not escape through *this* window, for there would be no way to replace the nail from the outside.

So now Dupin moves to the second window, just behind the bed. It appears to be just like the first in every respect, including the strong nail, and like the first resisted all efforts by the police to open it. Dupin, however, presses forward on his line of thinking. He is convinced the killer escaped through a window, which means unequivocally that this second window must be openable. Running his fingers around the edge, he finds it has a spring catch just like the first. That leaves only one possible point of difference: the nail.

Visually, the two windows appear to be the same; the exact same type of nail is used. But Dupin, certain that the answer is here, picks at the nail with his fingertips and finds that it comes apart easily. Some time in the past the shank of the nail was broken and the nail head placed back in position. Merely looking at the head, one would never know that the nail is in fact useless as a fastener.

LOOK IN ALL DIRECTIONS
Sometimes you find the answer by reasoning backwards.

Let's pause for a moment to consider Dupin's thinking. Faced with an apparent impossibility—how a murderer escaped from a locked room—he realizes that the police are looking at the mystery the wrong way 'round. The question is not how the murderer got out but how he got *in*. One solves the other.

For Dupin, all that he observed at the rear of the building now comes together in his mind: the tall lightning rod, the proximity of the shutter, the trelliswork providing easy finger holes. What if the killer was able to climb up the lightning rod, grab hold of the bottom of the shutter, push off from the wall, and use the shutter to swing into the room through the open window? The killer could then leave the apartment the same way, closing the window on the way out.

But who could do that? It would take superhuman strength and agility. Yet Dupin is convinced his theory is correct. And if it is, then the killer must be superhuman. Dupin sets that one solid deduction aside while he moves to the next phase of his investigation.

Still in the women's apartment, he now looks over the two bodies with meticulous care. He removes small clumps of hair from the mother's fingers, and memorizes the shape of the bruises on the daughter's neck; he will later compare his observations with the sworn statements of the two physicians who examined the bodies.

This examination of the scene, indoors and out, takes the better part of a day. In all that time, Dupin makes no comment, but silently adds one observation onto another. On the way back home, he stops briefly at the offices of a local newspaper.

The narrator tells us what happens next.

Back in their sitting room, Dupin hands his friend a pistol, saying that soon a certain person will arrive who has material information about the case and will have to be detained. While they wait, he begins to explain his theory of the murders. One element at a time, Dupin summarizes for his friend all that they know and all that he has observed.

One aspect that has profoundly puzzled the police is the conflicting reports from witnesses about the voices they heard. All the witnesses heard two voices, very different in character, and all heard one of them speak recognizable French. But the other was unrecognizable, and thus everyone assumed it was a foreign language, but they all supposed a *different* language. One person thought it was Spanish; another, a Spaniard, was certain it was English. An Englishman thought it was German, a Dutchman thought it French, a Frenchman thought it might have been Italian, and an Italian thought he was hearing Russian. Several witnesses also commented on the unusual quality of the voice— uneven, shrill, with none of the discernible intonation that marks all human speech, even when the language is foreign to the listener.

Next, Dupin describes his theory of how the killer climbed into and out of the window, a feat requiring an extraordinary level of physical agility.

Working from his memory of the daughter's body, Dupin has sketched a life-size facsimile of the bruises on her throat, and asks his friend to match his own fingers to the drawing. It is immediately apparent that the strangling could not have been done by any human hand. Finally, he produces the strands of hair that he removed from the mother's fingers, and the narrator recognizes that the hair is not human.

Now Dupin summarizes his observations; we can easily imagine him ticking them off on his fingers. The voice that had no recognizable cadence. The sheer brutality of the slaughter. The lack of any obvious motive, since a great deal of money and valuable jewelry was left in the room. The inexplicable act of stuffing a body in the chimney. The superhuman agility needed to climb into the window and back out again. The throat bruises that fit no man's hand, and the hair that came from no human head. Adding them all together, Dupin draws a spectacular conclusion—bizarre yet believable, and in the end inevitable.

As Dupin points out to his faithful friend, the police are stumped by the unusual circumstances of the case and the utter horror of the slaughter; faced with such an extraordinary situation, they do not know what to think. But, he says, the more extraordinary the circumstance, the more the answer lies in clear thinking. "In investigations such as we are now pursuing, it should not be so much asked what has occurred, as what has occurred that has never occurred before."

Suddenly, the two men hear the sound of someone coming up the stairs; the man for whom they have been waiting, who will perhaps be able to verify Dupin's theories, has arrived.

And who is ultimately revealed as the killer? Ah no, my friends; read the story.

Walking in Dupin's shoes through the scene of horror, what can we learn about his methods, his way of reasoning? And what can we take from watching him that we can put to good use in thinking about investing?

One of Dupin's strengths is his ability to see each detail, down to the most minute, and to understand them in a way that escapes other observers who cannot grasp the whole picture. The police saw everything that Dupin saw, yet they were stymied while he was successful.

And he was successful partly because he was thorough, and took the time to do a complete investigation.

Another key ingredient of Dupin's method is independent thinking. He is not afraid to question what are presented to him as facts, even when they seem at first to be unarguable. Because all the witnesses thought they were hearing a different language, the police wasted time trying to determine which language it really was. Dupin looked at the question from a different direction: Perhaps the sounds were unrecognizable because they were not uttered by a human. Because the windows appeared to be locked, the police assumed no one could have left the room by the windows. Dupin, having eliminated all other possibilities, correctly deduced the only possible explanation: Appearances to the contrary, one window was *not* locked.

THE FOREST OR THE TREES?
Intelligent investors are able to observe all the details (the trees) and the big picture (the forest) simultaneously.

Modern investors can take two lessons from Dupin: First, look in all directions, observe carefully and thoughtfully everything you see, and do not make assumptions from inadequate information. On the other hand, do not blindly accept what you find. Whatever you read, hear, or overhear about a certain stock or company may not necessarily be true. Keep on with your research; give yourself time to dig beneath the surface.

We will visit these lessons again in greater detail in the next chapter.

About a year after "The Murders in the Rue Morgue" appeared, Poe began writing another story featuring Dupin. "The Mystery of Marie Roget" closely follows a real murder mystery. Some months earlier, in a case that attracted a great deal of attention, a young woman named Marie Rogers had been murdered in New York; the circumstances were never fully uncovered. To bring his French detective into the case, and apply his considerable intellectual talents to its solution, Poe transported the story to Paris and gave the victim a new, more French-sounding name.

Poe described his second story as "a sequel to 'The Murders in the Rue Morgue'" and explained to his friend Joseph Snodgrass that his main interest was not so much in solving the Marie Rogers murder as in analyzing the police investigation. Poe was, it seems, less concerned with uncovering the actual killer than with showing what a superbly logical mind could achieve in a puzzling situation.

The story of how Dupin analyzed the investigation into the death of Marie Roget, using only secondhand material, provides a brilliant template for investors faced with a confusing jumble of information about a stock, a particular company, or indeed any financial circumstance where too much data overwhelms common sense.

Marie Roget is a pretty young woman who works in a Paris perfume shop, lives with her mother in Mme. Roget's rooming house, and is engaged to one of her mother's lodgers. On a Sunday morning, she leaves home to visit an aunt for the day. Her fiancé is to pick her up there at dusk, but since it's raining heavily by the time evening arrives he decided against it, assuming Marie will spend the night with her aunt, as she has in the past. Four days later, Marie's body is found floating in the Seine, showing severe bruises and signs of strangulation.

The gruesome murder catches the public's attention and several newspapers begin carrying day-by-day updates of the police investigation, along with the writers' sometimes outlandish interpretations of the findings. The police question many people, find evidence of a struggle near the river, and offer a significant reward, but the mystery remains unsolved and public outcry increases.

Thus, three weeks after the murder, the prefect of police approached Dupin and asked for his assistance. The reward has now reached a serious sum, but that is not Dupin's chief motivation. He agrees to help because he is intrigued by the challenge.

His first act is to send his friend (our narrator) out to collect every newspaper account of the case, starting with the very first report of finding the body. He then arranges the articles in sequence and proceeds to study them one by one, considering each one in light of the whole. In this he has something of an advantage over the individual newspaper writers, for he can see the entire sweep of the situation. And, as he explains to his friend, it is quite useful to look beyond the central event (which in this case has been thoroughly examined, to no avail) and take in the full picture of all the circumstances.

> **CONSIDER THE CONTEXT**
> **Add together all you know, and analyze it within the larger context. Specifics about a company mean little unless you also know something about the industry in which it operates.**

In reviewing the newspaper articles, Dupin quickly finds that many of the writers rely heavily on speculation and farfetched theories, and that their articles contain many factual errors.

After dismantling most of the faulty theories put forth in the newspapers, Dupin undertakes a completely new scrutiny of the newspaper accounts, reassembling the pieces of evidence according to the rules of logic. With remarkable tenacity he goes over the same ground again, developing a chronological summary of events that he believes points in a different direction.

You may remember that earlier I suggested that Dupin's actions in this story are particularly useful for modern investors trying to make sense of a confusing mountain of information. The parallel is that, like most investors today, Dupin had only secondhand information to work with, and had to call on his own good brain to evaluate the worth of that information.

Poe himself was not in New York when Marie Rogers was killed; he worked solely from newspaper accounts. Dupin, for his part, had no access to the body, the crime scene, or any of the witnesses, but formed his conclusions from just one source: newspaper articles. That is, both author and detective relied on secondary information to piece together what they considered to be the truth.

With one big difference, this is exactly what conscientious investors trying to make good decisions must do: assemble all the available material they can find on the subject at hand. Like Dupin, they even include information that seems only marginally relevant, for they remember that sometimes truth lies on the outskirts. Like Dupin, they study the material with great care, keeping a keen eye out for contradictions and specious reasoning. The difference for investors is that the volume of financial information available today is vastly larger than was the information about a murder case in nineteenth-century Paris, and it comes at us from all directions (not just newspapers) instantaneously. How we manage that deluge of information makes all the difference.

"The Purloined Letter," the final story featuring Dupin, was written three years later and is one of Poe's best known, a favorite of critics, anthology editors, and readers. As a piece of literature it is the most sophisticated of the three; as a study in the quirks of human behavior it has few peers. And for us, digging for mental models to help us be better investors, it offers a rich vein of new ideas, since in solving this mystery Dupin displays a set of skills we have not witnessed until now.

The story begins in a familiar way: Dupin and his friend are sitting quietly one evening, each engaged in his own thoughts, when a visitor arrives—the prefect of police, once again asking Dupin's assistance. This time the circumstances of the case are a bit unusual, as there is no doubt as to the identity of the criminal. The difficulty is the extreme delicacy of the situation, as it involves a member of the royal family.

It seems that a government minister, identified only by the initial D, on a visit to the royal apartments, boldly stole a certain letter he saw on a table. He recognized the handwriting and when he saw that the queen (we presume the royal personage was the queen, although it is not explicitly stated) was agitated, realized that the letter contained something embarrassing to her. He knew he had stumbled into a golden opportunity and, through a quick sleight of hand, took the letter and left one of his own in its place. The queen actually saw him do it, but was unable to challenge him as there was another visitor in the room.

We can imagine that Dupin instantly sees the implications, but the prefect continues: The minister now possesses very damaging information about the queen, and for several months has ruthlessly exploited it to his political advantage. Desperate, the queen has asked the prefect to retrieve the letter, and to use the greatest discretion in his inquiries.

The prefect is certain that the letter is somewhere in the minister's home, but despite the most thorough search imaginable, he's been unable to find it. He describes to Dupin the lengths his men have gone to: In addition to searching the minister himself twice, they have investigated every square inch of the entire building, and the buildings on either side, and the outside grounds of all three. They have looked inside cushions and mattresses, underneath floors and carpets, behind the wallpaper, inside the legs of tables and chairs, through every page and every binding of every book, between the cracks of the courtyard bricks—but no letter.

The queen is increasingly distraught, and the prefect is so perplexed he is willing to violate his vow of secrecy by bringing Dupin into the case. Dupin asks for a description of the letter and offers but one piece of advice for the prefect: that he search the minister's home again. Sputtering that it is pointless, the prefect departs in despair.

One month passes. The prefect again visits Dupin and his friend, and reports that the latest search proved as fruitless as the others. He is so frantic that he is ready to pay fifty thousand francs to anyone who can retrieve the damaging letter.

In that case, Dupin says, write your check. I have the letter.

Calmly and with only a hint of smugness, Dupin tells his astonished friend how he managed this feat.

The key to understanding the minister, Dupin explains, is that he is both poet and mathematician and thus combines in one person two quite different aspects: the creative and the scientific. This means he approaches problems from a dual perspective that cannot be guessed at by someone who sees the world from a single point of view. That is why the police can search the minister's apartment forever and never find the letter, while Dupin, who also possesses a dual nature, can solve the puzzle easily.

But where was the letter? Drawing out the suspense, Dupin makes a comparison to two familiar pursuits: looking for a particular shop, and searching a map for a certain name. In both cases, most people will completely overlook the largest sign or the biggest print, because they are "excessively obvious." Thus the police look for the letter in what they consider the most obvious spots (that is, hidden), while Dupin knows that the minister would put it in the least obvious: not hidden at all. The minister, Dupin reasons, has hit upon the daring idea of hiding the letter "immediately beneath the nose of the whole world." Which is precisely where Dupin found it.

To verify his theory and retrieve the letter, Dupin concocted an elaborate ruse. He first visited the minister at home, wearing dark glasses so that the minister could not follow his eyes. While they chatted, Dupin scanned the room, and eventually spotted a letter in plain view in a nondescript card rack; he was convinced, by certain physical clues, that it was the letter in question. After making careful mental note of the appearance of the letter, Dupin departed, deliberately leaving behind a snuffbox, which gave him an excuse to return the next day.

During the second visit, the conversation was interrupted by a skirmish on the street outside (arranged by Dupin, it turns out). While the minister's attention was distracted, Dupin quietly stole the incriminating letter, leaving in its place a copy he had prepared the night before, a copy that looked the same from the outside but contained only a harmless literary quotation.

The quotation itself concludes the story, and Poe makes it clear, without saying so directly, that it subtly points to the identity of the thief. Thus we can imagine, with the same pleasure as Dupin must have, the expression on the minister's face when he opens the letter and realizes he has been tricked in the exact same way that he tricked the queen.

It's a cracking good story, and very enjoyable in its own right. But as background material in our search for new investment guidelines, it is much more.

Here again, we see Dupin use his innate skepticism to good advantage. Listening to the police prefect catalog all the ways his men had searched in vain for the letter, he might have concluded, as they did, that it was nowhere to be found—but he did not. He knew that if the letter was important enough to steal, and if it was useful to a blackmailer, that person would keep it close at hand. Thus, while Dupin solved the first two mysteries through superior deductive logic, he actually found the purloined letter by factoring in his understanding of human nature. He knows that people tend to overlook that which is most obvious.

• • •

Edgar Allan Poe wrote some of the most memorable short stories in the English language. Today we read these stories to admire his mastery of his craft, the ingenuity of his plots, and the stately grace of his sentences ... or for the sheer pleasure of being scared out of our wits. All of this is enormously valuable for its own sake. But for investors, Poe offers an added bonus—that is, the skills we can learn by tracking Dupin's habits of mind.

- As you pore over quarterly reports or articles in the financial press, can you imagine yourself in Dupin's shoes as he read the many newspaper stories about Marie Roget, looking for mistakes, contradictions, overblown assumptions?

- As you listen to a television appearance by a Wall Street analyst or by the CEO of a company whose stock you own, what if you were to consider his remarks with the same cool skepticism that Dupin employed when the police concluded that the windows in the Rue Morgue apartment were firmly locked? Could it be that something here is different from how it appears on the surface?

- If you overhear an acquaintance say he or she purchased a certain stock because it "got a good write-up in the press," try to imagine what Dupin, with his dedication to finding all the details, would say about taking such a shortcut and making a decision based on one small piece of evidence.

In modern times, our clearest analog to this way of looking at the world may be investigative journalists who specialize in the area of finance and investing. To do their job, they must question everything and assume nothing, dig through layer after layer, and double-check and triple-check all the information they receive, even that (or maybe especially that) which purports to be the official truth.

As we see in the next chapter, investors have much to learn from these journalists, not only in the information they provide us but also in the methods they use to uncover it. In this, they—and we—can find a wonderful model in M. Dupin.

CHAPTER THREE

Dupin on Wall Street

In the spring of 1997, it seemed that all of Wall Street was in love with Al Dunlap.

Less than a year earlier, the self-proclaimed "turnaround genius" had agreed to take over as chairman of troubled Sunbeam Corporation. He came to Sunbeam still wearing a halo of success from Scott Paper, where in 18 months he increased the value of the stock 225 percent and then sold the company to rival Kimberly-Clark, with huge profits for all Scott shareholders.

Little wonder, then, that Sunbeam stock jumped almost 50 percent on the day Dunlap took the helm.

Dunlap's plan was to duplicate at Sunbeam the pattern that had already made him wealthy: drive up the stock price by any means necessary, sell the company, and cash in his stock options at the inflated price.

It didn't take long for the familiar Dunlap scenario to take hold at

Sunbeam. Within days, he began talking about the kinds of massive cuts he had used in six earlier restructurings, tactics that had earned him the nickname "Chainsaw Al" and led many to describe him as the most hated man in corporate America. In November 1996, after four months on the job, Dunlap announced that twelve thousand Sunbeam employees would be laid off and two thirds of its plants would be closed. Chainsaw Al had hit his stride.

Wall Street, however, watched in glee as the Sunbeam stock continued its rise. Analysts were tripping over themselves piling up "buy" recommendations. One analyst projected the stock would earn $1.55 per share in 1997 and $2.25 in 1998. Others were already talking about $3 per share by 1999.

But not everyone was convinced. A few observers—a very few—wondered publicly whether Dunlap, a master at self-promotion, could actually pull off what he was promising.

Matthew Schifrin, in a *Forbes* article that appeared approximately one month after Dunlap's arrival at Sunbeam, expressed skepticism that the "ruthless cost-cutter" could repeat his success. In what turned out to be an amazingly prescient observation, Schifrin predicted that earnings in 1997 would come as a result of accounting sleight-of-hand in 1996.[1]

- Four days later, Thomas Petzinger, writing in *The Wall Street Journal,* posed an interesting question: Is Dunlap a leader, or a louse?[2]

- Gail DeGeorge, writing in *Business Week* in November, pointed out that some people were leery of Dunlap's tactics and skeptical of his ambitious claims.[3]

- The next month, Andrew Osterland predicted in *Financial World* that Dunlap would find it hard to deliver on his promise of huge growth in sales.[4]

- In January 1997, in *Money* magazine, Junius Ellis made some very blunt predictions: That Dunlap wouldn't come close to matching his success at Scott; that his three-year growth plan would prove disappointing; that in a year's time, investors would be sick of Dunlap.[5] (He was almost right; it took eighteen months, not twelve, for the Sunbeam board to fire Dunlap.)

- Writing in *Fortune* three months later, Herb Greenberg threw cold water on Dunlap's grandiose promises by pointing out the fundamental weakness of his company and the harsh reality of his industry—an industry crowded with competitors and with minuscule annual growth rates.[6]

No doubt there were others who were skeptical of Dunlap's boasts early on, but these are the ones at my fingertips. All of them followed the Sunbeam story with professionalism and hard work, and although it is not possible to measure such things with any precision, I suspect that the cumulative weight of their reporting eventually sunk in with investors. However, of all these journalists, none had greater impact on Wall Street—and on Sunbeam itself—than *Barron's* Jonathan Laing.

On June 16, 1997, *Barron's* hit the newsstands with a cover depicting a cartoon drawing of Al Dunlap, chainsaw in hand, and a small model of a Sunbeam factory slashed in half, underneath a giant headline: "Careful, Al."[7] Dunlap had been at Sunbeam just under one year, and the stock had tripled in price.

The story inside was titled "High Noon at Sunbeam," and featured the infamous photograph of Dunlap holding automatic weapons in each hand and wearing two ammunition belts in a giant "X" over his puffed-up chest. The photo was originally taken as a publicity stunt for his autobiography, *Mean Business,* but became a lasting metaphor for Dunlap's ruthless management tactics.

Laing's article, however, was less about Dunlap's personal style than it was about his questionable accounting practices.

First, Laing pointed out that Sunbeam took a huge restructuring charge ($337 million) in the last quarter of 1996, resulting in a net loss for the year of $228.3 million. The charges included moving reserves from 1996 into 1997 (where they could later be recharacterized as income); prepaying advertising expenses to make the next year's numbers look better; a suspiciously high charge for bad-debt allowance; a $90 million write-off for inventory that, if sold at a later date, could turn up in future profits; and write-offs for plants, equipment, and trademarks used by business lines that were still operating.

To Laing, it looked very much like Sunbeam was trying to find every possible way to transfer 1997 projected losses to 1996 (and write 1996 off as a lost year, claiming it was ruined by previous management) while at the same time switching 1996 income into 1997. Sunbeam CFO Russell Kersh vigorously denied any accounting irregularities, insisting that Dunlap was "vehement about our doing things the right way" and pointing to Sunbeam's internal audit watchdog, whose job it was "to make sure things are right and proper every quarter."[8]

But Laing was concerned about more than these potential abuses of the restructuring charge. He was also suspicious of Dunlap's very aggressive three-year plan for sales growth: that by 1999 he would double Sunbeam's sales to $2 billion, triple international sales to $600 million, and boost operating margins to 20 percent. Laing knew enough about the small-appliance industry to know that Dunlap's promised sales projections were unreachable.

Even though Sunbeam's first-quarter 1997 numbers did indeed show a strong increase in sales volume, Laing had collected evidence that the company was engaging in the practice known as "inventory stuffing"—getting retailers to place abnormally large orders either through high-pressure sales tactics or by offering them deep discounts (using the written-off inventory from 1996). Looking closely at Sunbeam's financial reports, Laing also found a hodgepodge of other maneuvers designed to boost sales numbers, such as delaying delivery of sales made in 1996 so they could go on the books as 1997 sales, shipping more units than the customer had actually ordered, and counting as sales orders that had already been cancelled.

All this, Laing calmly pointed out, would have one predictable effect: Even though 1997's first-quarter report was positive, the gains were largely artificial. By 1998, all the benefits of the 1996

> "I repeat that it is no more than fact that the *larger* portion of all truth has sprung from the collateral; and it is but in accordance with the spirit of the principle involved in this fact that I would divert inquiry, in the present case, from the trodden and hitherto unfruitful ground of the event itself to the contemporary circumstances which surround it."
>
> —C. AUGUSTE DUPIN,
> "THE MYSTERY OF
> MARIE ROGET"

restructuring charge would vaporize. At that point, Dunlap's only strategy would be to sell Sunbeam or find a "juicy acquisition." Neither prospect, Laing thought, looked especially likely. This was written in June 1997, remember; unfolding events would prove that the dramatic story was only beginning.

What tipped him off? When so many were putting Dunlap on a Wall Street pedestal, how was Laing able to see the shaky foundations underneath? Common sense and a natural skepticism, that's how.

"I knew everybody was in love with this guy," Laing remembers today, "but I was skeptical from the get-go. Because it is just not that easy."[9]

How did he know Dunlap's plan was unrealistic? Because of one other critical element: background knowledge gained through hard work. It was Laing's own knowledge of the market, accumulated over years of study, combined with what he learned about the industry in which Sunbeam was competing, that gave him the confidence to recognize "it's just not that easy."

We can almost imagine Dupin watching from the background, nodding in approval. Dupin, you will remember, frequently set himself in counterpoint to the Paris police. In his very first case, he unhesitatingly rejected the police conclusion that the killer had somehow vanished from a locked room in the house on the Rue Morgue. Ever skeptical of such blanket pronouncements, and holding firmly to a supreme common sense that rejects such an impossibility, he proceeded to solve the mystery precisely *because* of that skeptical frame of mind. He started by thinking, "Since it cannot possibly be that the killer escaped from a room where all doors and windows were locked, there must be some other explanation."

Then, like Laing, Dupin reinforced his skepticism with knowledge. Putting together what he observed at the scene of the murder with what he already knew of the physical characteristics of a certain exotic creature, he was able to construct a theory of the crime that reflected both logic and scientific fact. His theory was unorthodox, to be sure, but in the end it was correct.

The core lesson for investors here can be expressed simply: *Take nothing for granted,* whether it comes from the prefect of police or the CEO of a major corporation. This is, in fact, a key theme of this chapter. If something doesn't make sense to you—no matter who says it—that's your cue to start digging. Where to dig, and how, is what this chapter is about.

For a while it seemed Dunlap could do no wrong. In January 1998 Sunbeam reported record earnings and sales levels for 1997, and Dunlap declared he had been responsible for a major turnaround.

At this point, few people realized that the record numbers for 1997 were artificially boosted by the 1996 accounting maneuvers. John

Byrne, who later expanded his insightful *Business Week* articles into a scathing book detailing Dunlap's days at Sunbeam, suggested that even those few on Wall Street who were becoming uneasy about Dunlap at the time chose to ignore their uneasiness, thinking that investors probably wouldn't understand Sunbeam's balance sheet anyway.[10]

Sunbeam's stock continued to rise, and so did Dunlap's star on Wall Street. Two months after the "turnaround," Dunlap announced that Sunbeam had in one day acquired three companies: Coleman (makers of camping equipment), First Alert (smoke alarms), and Signature Brands (small appliances, including Mr. Coffee coffeemakers). Two days later, Sunbeam stock hit a record high of $53.

That brings us to March 4, 1998. Less than a month later, the Dunlap pedestal started to crumble.

In April, Sunbeam announced that first-quarter earnings would be lower than anticipated. When Paine Webber's Andrew Shore, one of the few brokerage analysts who had publicly expressed doubts about Dunlap, downgraded the stock, the share price dropped by 25 percent in one day. In May, Dunlap told stockholders not to worry; he had momentarily taken his eye off the ball, but it would never happen again.

Jonathan Laing was following all this with his trademark intensity and thoroughness. Dunlap's bombastic pronouncements about turnaround success only heightened Laing's skepticism, so he continued to dig through Sunbeam's financial statements.

On June 8, 1998, his follow-up article on Dunlap appeared in *Barron's*.[11] The carefully researched article, titled "Dangerous Games," posed this question in its subtitle: "Did Chainsaw Al Dunlap manufacture Sunbeam's earnings last year?" Laing's short answer: yes.

In his article, Laing reprised some of his earlier concerns about Sunbeam's accounting tactics and Dunlap's overly aggressive sales projections. Point by point, he presented evidence that some of what he had written about the previous June had actually come to pass by year-end 1997. One item alone—the 1997 sale of inventory that had been written off as a loss in 1996—represented almost a third of 1997's net income. Prepayment of 1997 expenses in 1996 added something on the order of $15 million more to 1997's final income. Other expenses appeared to have been shifted forward into future years; another $15 million in advertising costs was "saved" this way (in spite of bigger ad campaigns in 1997) and shifted straight to 1997 income. Stating bad-debt reserves at an artificially high level in 1996 meant these reserves were artificially low in 1997, added maybe $10 million to net income. And on and on.

> **"The necessary knowledge is that of what to observe."**
>
> —C. AUGUSTE DUPIN, "THE MURDERS IN THE RUE MORGUE"

Laing found new problems too. One was the widespread abuse of the practice known as "bill and hold." Here's how it works: Customers agree to buy a certain number of products (in this case a lot of product, as Sunbeam salespeople were under intense pressure to generate high numbers) far in advance of when they would be needed. They would not actually pay for the orders until as much as six months later. In the meantime, the items would be stored in third-party warehouses, and the sales would go on the books for the quarter in which they were written.

Bill and hold is a legitimate accounting practice under generally accepted accounting principles (GAAP), but only when very precise conditions are met. In almost all cases, Sunbeam violated those standards. Sunbeam's earlier boast that "things are right and proper every quarter" was clearly full of holes.

In sum, Laing figured, all the 1997 profit boosters totaled $120 million. Yet the company's reported net profit for 1997 was $109.4 million. So, Laing asked, did Sunbeam actually make any profit from operations in 1997?

Would the three new acquisitions help? Laing was of two minds on this question. On the one hand, he thought the new companies might help restore some calm, if only because they represented new opportunities for restructuring charges spread over several years (continuing the game). On the other hand, they represented a new debt load: $2 billion.

Looking at the whole picture, Laing bluntly concluded that "Dunlap's days at Sunbeam may be numbered."[12]

Once Laing's article hit the newsstands, Dunlap and his key lieutenants went ballistic. Within hours, they released a statement vigorously denying all the statements. Sunbeam, the press release snapped, "categorically did NOT manufacture its 1997 earnings." Using three other capitalized NOTs, the release insisted that all Sunbeam's accounting practices adhered to GAAP.[13]

Five days later—June 13, 1998—Sunbeam's board of directors fired Al Dunlap.

In early June, Sunbeam stock fell to around $25 per share, less than half its high just three months before. By July, the stock had lost 80 percent of its value; it was now lower than it had been when Dunlap took over two years earlier.

Two weeks after Dunlap's sudden firing, Sunbeam announced that a new accounting firm would be brought in to audit the financial statements from 1997, and that in the meantime those statements should be considered unreliable.

In August, one month later, the company announced it would be required to restate its financial statements from 1997—and possibly 1996 and first-quarter 1998.

In February 2001, Sunbeam Corporation filed for Chapter 11 bankruptcy protection.

On May 15, 2001, the Securities and Exchange Commission filed suit against Dunlap and four senior Sunbeam executives, along with their accounting firm, Arthur Andersen, charging them with fraud. The SEC found that the executives and the auditors had perpetrated "a fraudulent scheme to create the illusion of a successful restructuring of Sunbeam and thus facilitate a sale of the company at an inflated price."[14]

"A fraudulent scheme to create the illusion of a successful restructuring." Exactly what Laing had described three years earlier.

Jonathan Laing has worked at Dow Jones & Company, the publisher of *The Wall Street Journal* and *Barron's*, since 1968. You could say he's a reporter raised in the old school. Long before there was an Internet and personal desktop computers, Laing was honing his reporting skills covering the police beat in Chicago. He learned that getting the story, getting to the full truth that other reporters might miss, means digging deeper and talking to more people than the other reporters.

This experience served Laing well. Today, he is one of the more highly respected investigative reporters on Wall Street. His work on the Sunbeam story is typical: He read more background material, dissected more financial statements, talked to more people, and painstakingly pieced together what many others failed to see.

He might, in fact, be the perfect case study for journalism students intent on learning their craft.

Temple University's Department of Journalism, Public Relations, and Advertising is one of only two accredited journalism programs in the state of Pennsylvania. There, many aspiring young reporters eventually fall under the spell of Professor Linn B. Washington, Jr.

Professor Washington is one of Temple's prized assets. Not only a talented teacher, he is also an experienced reporter who brings to the classroom the lessons learned from twenty-five years of investigative reporting. For many years the metro reporter at the *Philadelphia Daily News*, he is best known for his investigative stories on the city's corrupt housing program. He was later awarded the Robert F. Kennedy Prize for his series of articles on drug wars in the Richard Allen housing project. It is particularly fitting, then, that he is responsible for teaching the department's class in investigative journalism.

Over the years, Professor Washington has taught the basics of investigative reporting to countless students, and has watched many of them move on after graduation to a fine career in journalism. I wondered if he had developed a way to spot those future success stories, to distinguish those students who would become good reporters from those who were only interested in the *idea* of being a reporter.

"Early in the semester," he responded, "I can begin to single out the students who have good potential from those who are simply going through the motions. Those who later became successful journalists possessed two key talents. The first talent they had on their own. The second one I could help them learn."[15] The second talent, the learnable one, is mastery of the process and its techniques. The first talent is a personality trait.

"Investigative journalism is not a nine-to-five job," Washington continued. "All good investigative journalists are first and foremost hard workers. They are diggers. They don't stop at the first thing they come to but rather they feel a need to persist. They are often passionate about the story they are working on and this passion helps fuel the relentless pursuit of information. You can't teach that. They either have it or they don't."

What does this passion come from? I wondered. What motivates a person to keep digging? "I think most reporters have a sense of morality," said Washington. "They are outraged by corruption and they believe their investigations have a real purpose, an almost sacred duty to fulfill. Good investigative reporters want to right the wrong, to fight for the underdog. And they believe there is a real responsibility

> **"My ultimate object is only the truth."**
>
> —C. AUGUSTE DUPIN, "THE MURDERS IN THE RUE MORGUE"

attached to the First Amendment.

"But this passion must be balanced with fairness," he added. "Passion is good, but uncontrolled passion can slant the investigation. The reporter must be accurate, balanced (there are always two sides to every story), and above all fair. People have biases, but good reporters start the investigation without any preconceived notions."

There is an underlying thread to this chapter, and it runs thus: The fundamental way of thinking we see in top investigative journalists like Jonathan Laing is the same that we see in Auguste Dupin, and investors can learn much from both of them. The passion to keep going. The willingness to work hard to uncover the truth. The urge to right a wrong. A deep level of curiosity. The need to keep an open mind, without preconceptions. The skepticism to question official pronouncements, to take nothing for granted. Those qualities that Professor Washington describes, that Jonathan Laing epitomizes, and that Auguste Dupin instinctively employs—these are habits of mind that thoughtful investors would do well to cultivate.

I do not mean to suggest that investors should rush out and sign up for journalism school, only that some thoughtful study of the journalist's techniques would be very useful. And for a good grounding in those methods, I know of no better guide than *The Reporter's Handbook*, written by Steve Weinberg and published under the sponsorship of Investigative Reporters and Editors Inc.[16]

Standard issue for most good reporters, the book is chock full of detailed information to help them dig out obscure information on all sorts of issues and from all kinds of sources in both the private and public sectors. In that regard it may at first seem altogether too specialized to be useful for investors. But wait. Suppose you were contemplating investing in some aspect of the health care industry. Don't you think you could find helpful background in a chapter entitled "Investigating Health Care," with subsections explaining hospitals, HMOs, drug companies, pharmacies, labs, nursing homes, and more, and pointing you to specific sources of information on each one? Suppose you then decided you wanted to invest in a company that manufactured medical devices. In one brief but compact entry, the handbook would give you the names of a watchdog organization and its two publications, and two industry groups that could answer questions. Wouldn't you be glad for that information?

If you as an investor see that there might be value in adopting the journalist's approach, I suggest you start reading this handbook at the beginning. In its early section, "The Basics: How to Investigate Anyone or Anything," Weinberg has put together a valuable primer on how reporters go about gathering information, and the mental outlook that makes their work possible.

Gathering information, the handbook explains, involves looking into two large categories: people and documents. Paper trails, in other words, and people trails. Weinberg asks readers to imagine three concentric circles. The outermost one is "secondary sources," the middle one "primary sources." Both are composed primarily of documents. The inner circle, "human sources," is made up of people—a wide range of individuals who hold some tidbit of information to add to the picture the reporter is building.

Ideally, the reporter works from the outside in, starting with secondary sources. From these the reporter gains a basic understanding of whatever is being investigated, and also finds leads to primary sources.

At these two levels of the investigation, the best reporters rely on what has been called a "documents state of mind." This way of looking at the world has been articulated by James Steele and Donald Barlett, an investigative team from the *Philadelphia Inquirer*. It means that the reporter starts from day one with the belief that a good record exists somewhere, just waiting to be found.

Once good background knowledge is accumulated from all the primary and secondary documents, the reporter is ready to turn to the human sources—the people involved in the story. Generally, we can think of them as belonging to three groups: currents, formers, and experts. "Currents" and "formers" are people who are actively involved in the situation the reporter is looking into, or who used to be involved. Their perspectives are likely to be very different. "Experts" is self-explanatory, I think: outsiders with special knowledge about the circumstance.

As they start down this research track, reporters also need to remember another vital concept from the handbook: "Time equals truth." Doing a complete job of research takes time, whether the researcher is a reporter following a story or an investor following a company—or, for that matter, a detective following the evidence at a crime scene. Journalists, investors, and detectives must always keep in mind that the degree of truth one finds is directly proportional to the amount of time one spends in the search. The road to truth permits no shortcuts.

The Reporter's Handbook also urges reporters to question conventional wisdom, to remember that whatever they learn in their investigation may be biased, superficial, self-serving for the source, or just plain wrong. It's another way of saying "Take nothing for granted." It is the journalist's responsibility—and the investor's—to penetrate the conventional wisdom and find what is on the other side.

The three concepts discussed above—"adopt a documents state of mind," "time equals truth," and "question conventional wisdom; take nothing for granted"—may be key operating principles for journalists, but I see them also as new watchwords for investors.

To validate the importance of a *documents state of mind*, let us turn first to M. Dupin, Poe's eccentric detective.

Once he decided to look into the mystery of Marie Roget, Dupin's first action was to collect every single newspaper account of the notorious case, including all the many follow-up stories. We can imagine him in his room, surrounded by piles of newspapers, reading by the light of a single lamp while his heavily draped windows shut off the distractions of the outside world.

He worked for days, meticulously examining every single document, arranging and rearranging them as he tried out various scenarios. Only then was he willing to offer his explanation of what happened.

> "He makes, in silence, a host of observations and inferences. So, perhaps, do his companions; and the difference in the extent of the information obtained, lies not so much in the validity of the inference as in the quality of the observation."
>
> —C. Auguste Dupin, "The Murders in the Rue Morgue"

Do I hear a squeak of protest? That Dupin had only newspaper articles to contend with, whereas modern investors must start their research in a much larger pool of secondary sources—newspapers, magazines, radio and television commentaries, and a seemingly limitless string of Internet documents? You are correct. It's one difference between the nineteenth century and the twenty-first, and it cannot be wished away. You must learn to deal with the morass of information, to sort out what is relevant, to distinguish the important from the tangential. Chapter 5 offers help in dealing with this sorting process.

By concentrating on secondary documents, Dupin had, to use the modern phrase, worked "from the outside in." He of course had little choice. In his era, official police documents were available to the public only as they were quoted in the newspapers. But as Dupin himself eloquently noted, the truth of the matter is often found on the outskirts.

When Jonathan Laing started digging into Sunbeam, he began the same way, working from the outside in. His first step was to collect all the secondary documents he could get his hands on. It was a very large pile of material: hundreds of newspaper and magazine articles, plus Dunlap's autobiography. He read them all.

Next, Laing undertook a slow and deliberate investigation of primary documents: the company's annual reports, 10Ks, and all the 10Q (quarterly) reports. Right away he spotted something striking in the 1997 10K. Despite the $109 million in profit, the company suffered $8.2 million negative cash flow from operations. When he compared the company's 1997 10K with its 1998 first-quarter 10Q, interesting things began to emerge. That's when Laing recognized the massive accounting shifts that had moved earnings from 1996 forward into 1997, and losses and expenses from 1997 backward to 1996.

> "We will discard the interior points of this tragedy, and concentrate our attention upon its outskirts. . . . Experience has shown that a vast, perhaps the larger, portion of truth arises from the seemingly irrelevant."
>
> —C. Auguste Dupin,
> "The Mystery of
> Marie Roget"

Only after he had collected and carefully evaluated all the secondary and primary sources did Laing move to the final phase of his research: interviewing the human sources. He started by talking with "formers." Since Dunlap had fired half the company, there were plenty of people to call; three of the top five Sunbeam executives had by that point left the company.

Laing also talked with experts. He tracked down people in the appliance industry: retailers, brokers who sold to them, and advertisers and marketers who worked for appliance manufacturers. From all this information-gathering, Laing learned much about the state of the appliance market. The technology of small appliances is not complex, so competing manufacturers pop up overnight. It is a tough industry: Competition is fierce, profit margins are minuscule, and sales growth from one year to the next is paltry, often less then 1 percent. When Laing was doing his research, unit shipments in the United States were actually declining, from 166 million in 1994 to 164 million in 1996. In Europe, U.S. companies were competing against SEB and Philips, and were losing. With all that he learned, Laing knew that Dunlap's aggressive sales targets were wholly unrealistic.

For the final piece of the mosaic, Laing talked with "currents," including senior Sunbeam executives and finally Dunlap himself. His finished articles blended all these elements into a thorough, balanced look at a troubled company and its controversial CEO.

Let's say that you are an investor who is no longer willing to rely on questionable advice from your broker's analysts. You are eager to do your own research. How should you go about it?

First, remember that you have two good models—Auguste Dupin and Jonathan Laing—and one good guidebook: *The Reporter's Handbook.*

Start by gathering all the background information you can find, from all three circles: secondary, primary, and human.

Perhaps we should make a brief detour for definitions. "Primary materials" are those that originate from whatever it is you are investigating. If what you want to know more about is a company, you look at the documents produced by the company itself: annual reports, product brochures, 10K and 10Q reports, transcripts of annual meetings, and so on. If you want to learn more about one individual within the company, such as the CEO, the primary material would consist of articles, speeches, and media appearances by that person, in his or her own words. If you want to know more about the industry, primary sources are the materials disseminated by that industry, probably through the official industry organization.

Secondary materials consist of what *other people* say about the company, the person, or the industry. Simply by the nature of our many-faceted media, you will probably find far more secondary sources than primary. One company will produce only one package of official documents, but its fortunes or misfortunes may be covered by dozens of print reporters, broadcast journalists, and commentators.

"Secondary," however, does not necessarily mean "lesser than." If you were considering buying Sunbeam stock and happened upon Jonathan Laing's articles about the company, for instance, you would have to consider them secondary source material, but they are most definitely not inferior.

Secondary and primary resources are plentiful (see Appendix 1 for a summary of places to start looking). Finding human sources will take some ingenuity, but it can be done. Let your mind roam deliberately over the question and see what connections you can come up with. Do you know anyone who works at the company, or used to? Do you know anyone who knows someone at the company, either socially or professionally? Or at a competing company? Or at a company that sells, repairs, advertises, insures, or regulates the company's product? You might find it useful to remember the techniques you used for spreading the word when you were looking for a job, and cast a wide net in the same way. Or make it your own personal game of "six degrees of separation."

Work from the outside in, and keep your common sense well oiled. Understand the nature of the various types of information that exist, and determine which you can and cannot get access to. You will in all likelihood not be able to get an interview with the CEO of the company you are thinking about investing in, so you will have to read articles about him by people who can.

Once you have accumulated and studied a good amount of background material, the story of the company begins to unfold. What should you be looking for as you study your research materials?

First, be on the lookout for any inconsistencies. Is the information in one set of documents different from what is shown in another set? An inconsistency demonstrates two different opinions. One is likely right and the other wrong, but which is which?

The second thing to look for is information buried deep in one document and not reflected in surface documents like the company's annual report. Information buried deep below the surface has not yet affected the consensus view and hence the market price.

For example, the 10Q and 10K reports that companies are required by law to file every quarter and every year-end, respectively, are more detailed than the quarterly and annual reports they produce for shareholders. If you were to look at a 10Q side by side with a quarterly report, you would probably see that the bottom lines were the same but the individual line items might not be. Perhaps the 10Q breaks out separate income items that the quarterly report folds together. Knowing the details, you may think differently about the revenue line. Or, for another example, a footnote in a 10K may explain the details of something that was glossed over in the annual report.

I do not mean to suggest that either document is deliberately false, or even accidentally false—only that in complex financial reports, the truth often is to be found in the small details. Or, as Dupin would say, sometimes the truth lies on the outskirts. Careful investors must be alert.

Remember that in the heyday of Sunbeam, many on Wall Street weren't too concerned about damaging information that showed up in the fine print of the annual reports, because they were pretty sure investors wouldn't understand it anyway. They were probably right. Don't let that kind of information slip by you.

When you cultivate a "documents state of mind" and take your time doing a thorough investigation of the information you collect, you will eventually develop an accurate and complete description of the company. And if you have the right description of the company, you have a much better chance of predicting what will happen next.

• • •

Time equals truth. For journalists, investors, and detectives, this simple phrase means the same thing: The more time you put into answering the question, the more complete and accurate the answer you arrive at is likely to be. There are no shortcuts.

Think back for a minute to Dupin, investigating the mysterious deaths on the Rue Morgue. When the police granted him access to the house, he examined the building with the most intense care. He went over every inch of the apartment where the murders occurred, and all the other apartments, the exterior of the building, and the surrounding grounds. His companion, the nameless narrator, tells us that he and Dupin were at the house for an entire day.

One small detail of that investigation will illustrate the point. The police, in their search of the apartment, saw a pair of windows in the bedroom but checked only one. They found the first window nailed shut and assumed the other was also, since the second looked just like the first.

Dupin made no such assumption. Working meticulously, he went over every aspect of both windows, sills, and frames—and found the answer.

Jonathan Laing's reporting of the Sunbeam story shows us what good journalists do when faced with a complex situation: They collect all the secondary and primary materials, convince as many people as possible to talk to them, and don't quit until they are satisfied they have found everything there is to be found. Remember what Temple University's Professor Washington said about his best students, the ones who will become the best reporters: "They are often passionate about the story they are working on and this passion helps fuel the relentless pursuit of information."

Detectives, both real and fictional, do the same thing, of course. We may smile at the familiar description of "the plodding detective," the one who doggedly pursues all leads, but at the same time we know that is the person who will ultimately find the criminal.

I asked Jonathan Laing why he thought Wall Street missed the story on Sunbeam. His short answer: Time. "Most Wall Street analysts are too busy," he explained. "They have way too many companies to follow. They can't do a good job of investigating all the companies they follow so they just end up taking dictation from the company's management. They take the path of least resistance and as such become mouthpieces for people like Dunlap. On Wall Street, original investigative research is hard to come by."

Laing also pointed out another aspect of the time problem: the compensation system for Wall Street analysts. "Analysts have to spend most of their time dialing for dollars," says Laing. "They are marketers. Either they are trying to drum up investment banking deals or they are trying to sell their research ideas to institutional investors who pay big bucks in commissions for their research."[17] When would they have time to do any real research?

> "The results attained by them are not unfrequently surprising, but, for the most part, are brought about by simple diligence and activity."
>
> —C. AUGUSTE DUPIN,
> "THE MURDERS IN THE
> RUE MORGUE"

What is the answer for investors, especially those who have in the past relied on the research provided by brokerage analysts? They must learn to do their own research, to become their own watchdog. Yes, it will take time. But time equals truth for investors every bit as much as for reporters and detectives.

• • •

When Sunbeam was flying high in the late 1990s, and Al Dunlap was behaving like Superman, many on Wall Street found it extremely easy to simply accept the company's press releases and not look any further. This is what Jonathan Laing meant by "the path of least resistance." Whatever information the company put out, whatever Dunlap said, was taken at face value and repeated, both by brokerage analysts and also by many financial journalists who should have known better. That is how it became conventional wisdom, something that "everybody knows." As we have seen, Laing was one of the few who took the time to wonder whether the conventional wisdom was truly wise, or even accurate.

Conventional wisdom is a dangerous trap. The safeguard against that trap is a healthy skepticism that perpetually reminds you to take nothing for granted.

For understanding the value of skepticism, let Dupin be our first teacher. Think of his reaction when the police concluded that the murders in the Rue Morgue were unsolvable. Or when the police admitted they had no idea how to find a killer who could escape from a locked room. Or when they assumed the screams and shouts heard by bystanders were an unidentifiable foreign language. All these assumptions seemed logical to a degree, yet all were leading the police away from the truth rather than toward it.

Perhaps the most telling example of Dupin's skeptical mind, and certainly the best known, is his reaction to the mystery of the purloined letter. The police assumed it was well hidden by the thief, either on his person or somewhere in his home. That is their view of humanity: To conceal something of value, a thief would hide it in the most secretive spot he could devise. The cleverer the thief, the more cunning a hiding place he would employ.

The police looked at the question literally, and so they took apart every inch of the minister's home. Dupin looked at the question differently. He knew this particular thief would not behave in the usual way. Acting on his belief, Dupin discovered that the thief had found the cleverest hiding place of all: out in plain sight.

The lesson for us is this: It would have been very natural for Dupin to agree with the police that the letter was stashed in some very good hiding place. That was the logical explanation and the official view. But Dupin's instinctive skepticism led him to reject both.

Wonder what he might have said about Al Dunlap.

Investors are especially vulnerable to the dangers of conventional wisdom because it is the easy route, and rejecting it puts them on a path that is hard. Conventional wisdom is also dangerous because it seems so obviously correct. For example, we can say, with little argument, that the current price of a stock is the conventional wisdom of the market about that company. At any point in time, the stock price of a company reflects the weighted average opinion of all the participants in the market. If a company has one billion shares outstanding and is currently priced at $25 per share, the market's opinion (the conventional wisdom) says the company is worth $25 billion. But is it really?

If you embraced the skeptical mindset of the good investigative reporter, you might look at this company and begin to wonder about the conventional wisdom. How did the company get to be worth $25 billion. And for that matter, is $25 billion the right value? Why is another company, similar in so many respects, priced differently? Those kinds of questions would put you on the track of checking some other sources, talking to a few people with different opinions. You might ultimately reach another conclusion, one that you could turn to your advantage.

> "Let us sum up now the meagre yet certain fruits of our long analysis."
>
> —C. AUGUSTE DUPIN, "THE MYSTERY OF MARIE ROGET"

Good investors think like good detectives. So do good reporters. We shouldn't be surprised, then, to find that several modern mystery authors have created protagonists who are reporters. George Harmon Coxe, writing in the 1940s, introduced "Flashgun" Casey of the *Globe* and Kent Murdock of the *Courier-Herald*. Both characters were newspaper photographers who went about solving crimes just like print reporters would.

More recently, Barbara D'Amato has created Cat Marsala, an investigative reporter in Chicago. Mike Lupica, better known as a sportswriter, has written several fine mysteries starring reporter Peter Finley. Gregory McDonald, who has twice won the prestigious Edgar Allan Poe Award for best novel, has written nine novels featuring Fletch, investigative reporter and semi-amateur detective. The 2000 Edgar for best novel went to Jan Burke's *Bones,* featuring her reporter-protagonist Irene Kelly.

Gerry Boyle, a newspaper reporter in rural Maine, gives us Jack McMorrow, a burnt-out *New York Times* reporter who now mirrors the author's life, writing for a small weekly paper in rural Maine. *The Miami Herald*'s Carl Hiaasen writes hugely popular mysteries (ten, to date) in which serious themes like political corruption and brutalization of the environment are encased in outrageous dark humor. His first, *Tourist Season,* features a private investigator who used to be a reporter and still thinks like one.

One of my personal favorites is the fictional Miami reporter Britt Montero, created by Edna Buchanan, herself a longtime newspaper reporter who came to Miami on vacation and fell madly in love with the city. Edna received a splendid education in journalism, she says, by working for several years at a small newspaper where she did some of everything.[18] She then put those skills to good use at *The Miami Herald,* the city's main daily, where she turned the police beat (which many reporters work hard to avoid) into a vehicle for powerful, dramatic stories of humanity at its worst and best. In 1986 she was awarded journalism's most coveted honor, the Pulitzer prize. After eighteen years, she left her full-time position at the *Herald* to concentrate on writing mysteries, to our great fortune.

In Britt Montero, Edna has created a dynamic character who shows us, over and over (in seven books so far), how investigative reporters go about their job. Britt is dedicated, passionate, resourceful, fearless, and tenacious; whether she's tracking down a story or a criminal, she simply does not give up until she has it all.

Edna says she is not as brave or as strong as Britt, but frankly I don't believe it. Having had the opportunity to hear first-hand some of Edna's professional adventures and exploits, I appreciate even more the holy-cow daring that characterizes Britt's approach to her job. In all the ways that count, Britt *is* Edna. Everything Edna learned about the craft of journalism, she poured into her heroine.

And what Edna Buchanan knows about the reporter's craft is definitely worth knowing—for investors as well as young reporters. Here are some of the principles that she believes should guide the work of all reporters, including Britt. It's absolutely uncanny, I think, how closely they echo the basic methods that investors need to follow.

1. **Do a complete background check on all the key players.** Reporters have computers nowadays to do much of their legwork for them, but the principle is unchanged: Find out everything you can about the main participants in the story. Check the archives of the local newspaper in the person's home town; all the public records, such as property and tax records, licenses, birth and death certificates, and criminal records; and the Internet.

   For investors, I second this idea and suggest only a slight expansion: You should look for information on the company itself as well as on the key executives. In the newspaper research, for example, you would check the hometown newspaper of the CEO and also the cities where the company's corporate headquarters or factories are located.

And what should you be looking for?

"When you're investigating someone," Edna continues, "always try to find out if they're good citizens. You can tell a lot about someone by how they treat employees, women, the environment, and animals. Then you know who you're dealing with, whether it's a murder suspect or the president of a corporation. That can apply to companies too. If the company has a history of sexual harassment complaints, or does experiments on animals, or has been sued for illegal dumping somewhere, that tells you a great deal."

You have probably already recognized this as another take on the basic notion of a "documents state of mind." So, in a slightly different form, is Edna's next suggestion.

2. **Cast a wide net.** "Talk to as many people as possible," Edna says, "because you never know who you will find. The head of a corporation, the janitor, and the guy who parks the cars, they all know stuff and that can lead you to something important." She is, of course, referring to interviewing the "human sources," the innermost circle of information; it is the daily bread and butter for reporters.

As an investor, you may not be able to gain personal access to everyone, but you may surprise yourself at how successful you can be at this if you let yourself think creatively. Even if the bulk of your information gathering is from printed sources rather than one-on-one conversations, the same principle applies: Look broadly across the entire horizon.

"And remember," Edna continues, "there is always more

information out there; you just have to find it. And there's always a way. Use your imagination."

3. **Take your time.** All journalists live under the weight of deadlines. Even those who have the luxury of a long time frame in which to conduct a thorough investigation still come down to a deadline, a definite date on which they must deliver their articles. Under that constant pressure, some are tempted to take shortcuts (such as printing a company's press release word for word) rather than continuing to dig. But the ones with the passion that Professor Washington talked about, the passion that "helps fuel the relentless pursuit," will avoid the shortcuts, will stay on the road to the end.

These reporters understand instinctively that time equals truth. They are the ones who, as Edna puts it, "always ask one more question, knock on one more door, make one more call. It could be the one that changes everything. And always take more notes than you think you need."

Converting that lesson to investors needs only a very short step: Read one more article, study one more financial document, find one more person to talk to. You may learn something that puts an entirely new light on the investment question at hand. Don't take shortcuts; you're just shortchanging yourself. Do the full job.

4. **Use common sense.** Reporters need common sense just as much as any other specialists—perhaps more so. They need to be able to spot when something doesn't hold together, when people's behavior contradicts their statements, when official promises and pronouncements don't fit with what they see with their own eyes.

Even though I am urging you to be thorough and thoughtful

with your investment research, I also know that we should not, in our passion to uncover the whole story, abandon common sense. Not every single investment decision requires you to dig up every magazine article and every company financial report ever produced. At the same time, I want to urge you to get in the habit of looking at sources of information with different points of view. That is the best way I know to get a rounded, objective understanding of what is happening.

5. **Take no one's word. Find out for yourself.** This is the working journalist's version of Dupin's skepticism and the handbook's dictum to question conventional wisdom. In fact, Edna says it straight out: "Stay skeptical, and always read between the lines." For example, she points out that official press releases "are often vetted by lawyers, to avoid lawsuits, and so they leave the best part out." Corporate press releases are often egregiously slanted, or so skimpy as to be worthless.

The true journalist, like the true detective, operates on the principle of "take nothing for granted." Investors should do likewise.

This is one area where investors are particularly vulnerable, especially if they are not used to making investment decisions. People who are moving in unfamiliar territory already feel intimidated, and the fact that money is involved only increases their uneasiness. It is very common for them to grab the first opinion they read or hear and hold on to it fiercely, like it's a life preserver. They make their decision based on that one piece of information, and congratulate themselves silently on having "checked it out." But that is backwards thinking. The more inexperienced you are as an investor, the *more* you should be reading and studying, not less. One article will not suffice. What if it is inaccurate?

Even experienced investors fall into this trap, because it's the path of least resistance. They get a very brief statement from a brokerage analyst, let's say, explaining in one paragraph what has just happened to a certain stock, and they conclude that they now know all they need to know. But a one-paragraph statement cannot explain the whole story; in fact, it usually just marks the beginning.

I don't mean to suggest that the statement is necessarily inaccurate, just that you shouldn't stop there. The real story of what happened to the stock, and why, is buried much deeper and will take a little longer to find out. The fact that the statement was released in the first place means that something has happened, and smart investors will see it as a cue to start looking beyond that one paragraph.

6. **Double-check your facts, and then check them again.** Most reporters look on the need to corroborate their information as something of a sacred duty—that is, if they think about at all; for most of them, it's like the air they breathe. It's taken for granted.

If investors could incorporate just that one principle into their own thinking, it would go a long way toward keeping them out of trouble. Having to double-check means that you can't take shortcuts—you must devote adequate time to doing a thorough job of research—and by definition it means you have to look in more than one place, thereby exposing yourself to varying perspectives, all of which will force you to gather in a good assemblage of information.

Of course that in itself doesn't guarantee you'll make good decisions—you still have to be able to think—but I can most assuredly guarantee you the opposite: If you do *not* have a full range of good information at hand, you can never make good decisions.

Does it strike you that this is work? Well, it is. But take my word for it, it does get easier with practice. In the meantime, you might find some value in seeing your investment work as an assignment, like a reporter's assignment, and taking on Edna Buchanan's tunnel vision. "I always felt that because I was working for the *Herald* and had to get the story, I was on a mission and nothing was going to stop me or get in my way. It was like tunnel vision. That deadline was coming at me like an avalanche and nothing was going to stop it, so I had to do my job."

Making the right investment decisions for yourself and your family is your job. Do it right.

From Dupin and his modern-day counterparts, from reporters/mystery authors like Edna Buchanan, and from investigative journalists like Jonathan Laing, we have learned a few fundamental principles that have value for investors.

The first is the reporter's maxim about the importance of a "documents state of mind." You cannot make good investment decisions if you don't know what is going on with the companies you want to invest in, and the only way to know that is through research. The information isn't going to come to you in your sleep.

And that research takes time. For investors, the phrase "time equals truth" takes on a double significance. For one, it means that you must be willing to put in the time to collect information from a broad spectrum of sources. For another, once you force yourself to look at information from differing sources, you have automatically closed off the shortcuts.

Taking shortcuts—making decisions based on just one factor—may be the most dangerous trap of all. Too many investors make decisions to buy and sell based on single-factor accounting metrics, such as a price-to-earnings ratio. They may be acting out of habit, or laziness, or a misguided sense that they are saving time, or perhaps from embarrassment—the single factor may be the only concept they understand fully, and they are afraid to investigate others. But whatever the reason, this is a habit that must be broken. It costs the investor money.

Finally, the research you are doing will inevitably bring to light differing opinions, and that will lead you to question what you are seeing. The more you learn to recognize conflicting and even contradictory statements, the more you will realize that not all information is equally valid. Conventional wisdom can be faulty.

Remember that Jonathan Laing followed his gut reaction about Sunbeam, even though that put him in the opposite corner from many other reporters and most Wall Street analysts. As it turned out, he was right and they were wrong.

So far, we have covered the investment detective's essential first step: collecting the information, including how and why things happened, and what can go wrong. If you've done your job well, you now have a vast amount of data to absorb. Or, putting it into the detective's framework, you have a vast amount of evidence to study.

Your next step is to spread it all out, analyze it, and decide what is relevant and what is not. To assess the various degrees of accuracy and importance, eliminate the inessential, set priorities, and begin to plan your strategy. That's what a detective would do next, and it is the subject of the next two chapters.

CHAPTER FOUR

Conan Doyle and Sherlock Holmes

Imagine this scene.

It is a blazing hot day in August, sometime in the middle of the nineteenth century. Two men sit quietly in their European apartment, reading. One of them is tall and slender, with something of an aristocratic air about him. The other is stockier, quieter, less flamboyant in manner.

The tall man has developed quite a reputation with the metropolitan police force, and indeed with the general public, as a brilliant if eccentric detective. He is well known for his meticulous way of searching the scene for clues, and for his almost magical ability to find the logical explanation that has escaped everyone else. Often the chagrined police turn to him, a private citizen, to solve a case that has thoroughly baffled them—and he seldom fails. His companion goes along on these adventures; he is eager to help solve the mystery but is usually left on the sidelines, awestruck like everyone else as his friend explains his dazzling deductions.

On this August afternoon, however, the two men are simply passing a quiet hour at home. They are comfortable in their mutual silence, each absorbed in his own thoughts. Then, apparently out of the blue, the tall man speaks.

"You are right. It does seem a most preposterous way of settling a dispute."

His companion absentmindedly agrees, then abruptly stops and stares at his friend. "How on earth," he asks, "did you know exactly what I was thinking?"

"Simple," the other replies. "I merely watched you."

And then he proceeds to reconstruct his chain of observations: that the friend threw down the paper he was reading and glanced up at two portraits; that he became in turn thoughtful, then sad, then wistful as he touched an old war wound. Knowing his friend's personal history of wartime service, knowing his opinions about the two military men in the pictures, knowing his strong feelings toward war in general, it was not difficult to deduce that the friend was thinking how foolish it is to settle international disputes with a method that brings such useless waste of life.

Those who have read "Murders in the Rue Morgue," and know Dupin's uncanny ability to deduce what a person is thinking from his manner and facial expressions, may guess that this scene represents the beginning of another case for the aristocratic Parisian. But this sitting room is in London, not Paris. The astonished friend is not Dupin's anonymous companion but another literary narrator, the loyal Dr. Watson. And the eccentric, brilliant sleuth is none other than Sherlock Holmes, unarguably the most famous detective of all time.

It is no accident that Holmes displays the same abilities as Dupin: Holmes's creator, Arthur Conan Doyle, often acknowledged Poe's influence on his own writing, and sometimes even in it—in Holmes's explanation to Watson that August afternoon he makes direct reference to Auguste Dupin. The parallels between the two sleuths—and there are many—have been noted, analyzed, and thoroughly worked over by literary scholars and mystery fans alike. Alert readers of this book will notice some of these parallels in this chapter, but our primary emphasis will be less on the ways the two detectives resemble each other and more on the ways their approaches differ. Investors will then have two complementary sets of skills to work with.

In the small incident described above, we see the essence of Holmes's method. He approaches every problem with three distinct but closely allied actions:

1. First, he makes a calm, meticulous examination of the situation, taking care to remain objective and avoid the undue influence of emotion. Nothing, not even the tiniest detail, escapes his keen eye.

2. Next, he takes what he observes and puts it in context by incorporating elements from his existing store of knowledge. From his encyclopedic mind, he extracts information about the thing observed that enables him to understand its significance.

3. Finally, he evaluates what he observed in the light of this context and, using sound deductive reasoning, analyzes what it means to come up with the answer.

On this particular afternoon, he first observed the changes in Watson's countenance, then factored in what he knew of his background, and thus had no difficulty in deducing precisely what his friend was thinking.

In practice, Holmes moves so quickly and so invisibly from one process to the next that it seems one unified piece of thinking. Indeed, that is why onlookers are so often utterly astounded at Holmes's conclusions: They cannot see inside his lightning-quick mind to observe the three mental steps. It is only from afar that we can separate them into three discrete threads, and in this chapter we shall do exactly that. We will gently ease them apart and look at each individually, the better to find the lessons for investors.

The modest display of mind reading that we have just witnessed is but a minor example of Holmes's skill, a parlor trick. Most of the time, he is called upon to untangle a much more complex situation. In fact, this very day a visitor arrives at the detective's Baker Street apartment with a plea for help on a vexing problem. Can Holmes work his magic once more?[1]

A young doctor, Percy Trevelyan, relates his story nervously, starting with his own professional history. It seems that some time ago, an older gentlemen named Blessington had offered to set Trevelyan up in practice, subsidizing the considerable expenses of establishing a medical office in return for a share of the profits, living quarters in the house, and constant access to the doctor's care. Trevelyan, who would otherwise have had to scrimp for ten years to achieve the same situation, had agreed readily.

The arrangement had worked splendidly for years. Then, a few weeks before, Blessington had begun behaving oddly, showing signs of some great anxiety he was unwilling to explain. Gradually, however, his fearfulness subsided, and Trevelyan thought all was returning to normal. But just two days ago a new cycle of events had begun, to the extent that Trevelyan was now quite beside himself. This is what brought him to seek Holmes's advice.

It seems that the doctor had agreed to see a new patient suffering from catalepsy, his medical specialty. During the initial examination, the patient was gripped by a cataleptic attack, and the doctor raced from the room to grab his treatment medicine. When he returned, the patient was gone and so was his son, who had brought him to the doctor's office. The following day the two men returned, with a reasonable explanation for the mix-up, and the examination continued. On both occasions the son elected to wait in the waiting room.

Shortly after their second visit, Blessington burst into the exam room, frantically demanding to know who had been in his private rooms. The doctor tried to assure him that no one had, but agreed to go look at Blessington's room, where a strange set of footprints clearly verified the charge. The doctor reasoned quickly that his patient's son had snuck into Blessington's apartment while his father was being examined, but nothing was missing. And why was Blessington so very distraught? In the end it was only by promising to ask Holmes for help that Trevelyan was able to calm his resident patient. So here he was.

Holmes, intrigued by the story, agrees to come and talk with Blessington. But when Blessington claims not to know who is after him, Holmes concludes that the man is lying. Afterward he points out to Watson that the patient and his son were fakes (catalepsy being quite easy to imitate) and had some sinister reason for wanting to corner Blessington. He intimates that the affair is not over.

And he's right. The following morning, Holmes and Watson are called to the doctor's house once more, where they find a police inspector, a horrified Trevelyan, and a dead body. Sometime during the night, Blessington hung himself.

After the briefest look around, Holmes knows it was not suicide. Let us review how he reached that conclusion, since it offers a succinct case study of the methods of the famous detective.

The policeman on the scene found four cigar butts in the fireplace, and concluded that the victim stayed up late into the night smoking and, presumably, agonizing over his decision. But Holmes knows at a glance that they are not the same as the type found in the victim's cigar holder, pulling a bit of data effortlessly from his mental encyclopedia. " [Blessington's] is a Havana," he says, "and these others are cigars of the peculiar sort which are imported by the Dutch from their East Indian colonies. . . . Two have been smoked from a holder and two without." Implication: At least two other people were in the room with Blessington.

In his usual methodical way, Holmes then examines all aspects of the room—the lock, its key, the bed, carpet, chairs, mantelpiece, and the deadly rope. Holmes has also noticed three sets of footprints on the stairs, leading him to conclude that three men crept up the stairs to Blessington's rooms; he even knows, by the superimposition of the prints, which man went first. They forced the lock—he found the scratches to prove it.

They came prepared to commit murder: A screwdriver left behind is a strong clue to one who knows how to read it. And after subduing their victim, they debated among themselves how to proceed. That is when the four cigars were smoked; although it is not critical information, Holmes can even tell where each man sat by the ashes he dropped. Eventually they hung Blessington, using a rope he kept in his room as a fire escape. Two of the killers left the house and the third barred the front door behind them. The third murderer must therefore be part of the doctor's household.

All these signs were visible: the three sets of footprints, the scratches on the lock, the cigars that were not Blessington's type, the screwdriver, the fact that the front door was barred when the police arrived. But it took Holmes to put them all together and deduce their meaning: murder, not suicide. As Holmes himself remarked in another context, "The world is full of obvious things which nobody by any chance ever observes."[2]

The next part of the problem may be trickier: Who committed the murder? Here, Holmes has one advantage over the unobservant police inspector: He knows that Blessington was killed by people well known to him. He also knows, from Trevelyan's description, what the fake patient and his son look like. And he has found a photograph of Blessington in the apartment. A quick stop at police headquarters is all Holmes needs to pinpoint their identity. The killers, no strangers to the police, were a gang of bank robbers who had gone to prison after being betrayed by their partner, who then took off with all the money—the very money he used to set Dr. Trevelyan up in practice. Recently released from prison, the gang tracked Blessington down and finally executed him.

Spelled out thus, one logical point after another, it seems a simple solution. Indeed, that is Holmes's genius: Everything *is* simple, once he explains it.

Sherlock Holmes is so universally known that his very name has become a synonym for "detective." Even those who have not read the stories have a mental image of the famous sleuth with the meerschaum pipe, the deerstalker hat, and the magnifying lens always at hand so that he may examine the details of a scene to his satisfaction. In fact, this careful observation of details—which is only the first step in Holmes's method—is what most people remember best about the famous detective. And so, in our quest to understand how he does what he does, that is where we shall start.

Holmes operates from the presumption that all things are explainable; that the clues are always present, awaiting discovery. As he insists repeatedly, discovering those clues depends on seeing fully what is there to be seen, down to the last minuscule detail—in other words, it depends on keeping your eyes open. And that is the first rule for observing details: To see what is there, one must look with open eyes.

Holmes shows us how it is done. In the story "The Greek Interpreter," we meet Holmes's brother Mycroft, a man Holmes insists is more brilliant than himself, and far more eccentric. Sherlock, Mycroft, and Watson are sitting in Mycroft's club, occasionally looking out the window at the passersby. As usual, Dr. Watson relates what happened.[3]

"To anyone who wishes to study mankind this is the spot," said Mycroft. "Look at the magnificent types! Look at these two men who are coming towards us, for example."

"The billiard-marker and the other?"

"Precisely. What do you think of the other?"

The two men had stopped opposite the window. Some chalk marks over the waistcoat pocket were the only signs of billiards which I could see in one of them. The other was a very small, dark fellow, with his hat pushed back and several packages under his arm. [Note that Dr. Watson has observed chalk marks on one man, and for the other, only his size, his hat, and his packages. So much might ordinary observers note. The Holmes brothers see much, much more.]

"An old soldier, I perceive," said Sherlock.

"And very recently discharged," remarked the brother.

"Served in India, I see."

"And a non-commissioned officer."

"Royal Artillery, I fancy," said Sherlock.

"And a widower."

"But with a child."

"Children, my dear boy, children."

"Come," said I, laughing, "this is a little too much."

"Surely," answered Holmes, "it is not hard to say that a man with that bearing, expression of authority, and sun-baked skin is a soldier, is more than a private, and is not long from India."

"That he has not left the service long is shown by his still wearing his ammunition boots, as they are called," observed Mycroft.

"He had not the cavalry stride, yet he wore his hat on one side, as is shown by the lighter skin on that side of his brow. His weight is against his being a sapper. He is in the artillery."

"Then, of course, his complete mourning shows that he has lost someone very dear. The fact that he is doing his own shopping looks as though it were his wife. He has been buying things for children, you perceive. There is a rattle, which shows that one of them is very young. The wife probably died in childbed. The fact that he has a picture-book under his arm shows that there is another child to be thought of."

This incident is, of course, nothing more than a pleasant diversion for the brothers; the man they are observing is not involved in any crime. Doyle includes it in his story, we may imagine, to demonstrate that no magic is involved; all the evidence is there in plain sight, for anyone who bothers to look closely. I include it in this chapter for the same reason. Investors, take note: The necessary information is at hand, waiting to be noticed.

The Holmes habit of looking closely becomes far more significant when a crime has been committed. Then, cataloging all the details is not a game but a critical step in finding the truth. "Details," as Holmes says, "contain the vital essence of the whole matter."[4] Then, too, the second necessity of observation becomes paramount: To learn the full story, one must be scrupulously thorough.

It is tempting to think that we are done once we have accumulated a certain amount of information, enough to construct a theory or support a hunch we already have. But, as Holmes cautioned more than once, it is a grave mistake to draw a conclusion before all the facts are in. Those who do so may miss "the one little point which is the basis of the deduction."[5] Since it is not possible to know in the beginning which facts will turn out to be relevant, it is necessary to collect everything. The sifting will come later.

That is why we so often find Holmes on his hands and knees, peering closely at the corner of a table or the cover plate of a door lock. Or climbing on top of a mantelpiece to check the frayed end of a bell cord.

Or lying prone on the floor, stretched out to his full length, magnifying glass in hand, examining the fibers of the carpet. He does not mind if others think him foolish, for he knows that justice may depend on his findings.

HOLMES & INVESTING: RESEARCH

To see what is to be seen, look with open eyes.

To find the truth, keep looking until all the details have been uncovered.

How does someone attain that heightened degree of awareness? Partly through conscious effort, ever mindful of the purpose. Holmes once remarked, "I have trained myself to see what others overlook."[6] With practice, this heightened state of alertness then becomes natural, and a detective—or an investor—realizes he is perpetually attuned to gathering the small details that make the difference. He may then find, with Holmes, that "observation . . . is second nature."[7]

One reason Holmes is able to see fully what others miss is that he maintains a level of detached objectivity toward the people involved. He is careful not to be unduly influenced by emotion, but to look at the facts with calm, dispassionate regard. He sees everything that is there—and nothing that is not. For Holmes knows that when emotion seeps in, one's vision of what is true can become compromised. As he once remarked to Dr. Watson, "Emotional qualities are antagonistic to clear reasoning. . . . Detection is, or ought to be, an exact science and should be treated in the same cold and unemotional manner. You have attempted to tinge it with romanticism, which produces much the same effect as if you worked a love story or an elopement into the fifth proposition of Euclid."[8]

Holmes is by nature self-contained, aloof, even antisocial. That personality trait makes it easy for him to maintain objectivity when collecting and reviewing the facts of a case. Modern investors may not have this advantage. Too often they fall under the spell of the two classic emotions that create such havoc when human beings think about money: greed and fear. If you would avoid the same mistake, heed Sherlock's dictum: "It is of the first importance not to allow your judgment to be biased by personal qualities."[9]

This habit of objectivity serves Holmes well. Not only

> **HOLMES & INVESTING:**
> **OBJECTIVITY**
> **Do not allow your judgment to be clouded by emotion.**

does it enable him to see all the facts without prejudice, it also helps him avoid premature conclusions. "I make a point of never having any prejudices," he told Watson, "and of following docilely wherever fact may lead me."[10] He starts, that is, with no preformed idea, and merely collects data. But it is part of Holmes's brilliance that he does not settle for the easy answer. Even when he has gathered together enough facts to suggest one logical possibility, he always knows that this answer may not be the correct one. He keeps searching until he has found everything, even if subsequent facts point in another direction. He does not reject the new facts simply because they're antithetical to what he's already found, as so many others might.

Police investigators are susceptible to this mental error, Holmes would have us believe. So are investors. Ironically, it is the investors eager to do their homework who may be the most susceptible. At a certain point in their research, they have collected enough information that a pattern becomes clear, and they assume they have found the answer. If subsequent information then contradicts that pattern, they cannot bring themselves to abandon the theory they worked so hard to develop, so they reject the new facts.

Gathering information about an investment you are considering means gathering *all* the information, no matter where it ultimately leads you. If you find something that does not fit your original thesis, don't discard the new information—change the thesis.

We know how Sherlock Holmes came to be such a superb observer: He was born with an innate ability, which he then expanded and perfected through self-disciplined practice. But how did Holmes's creator, Arthur Conan Doyle, decide that observation is the essential skill of a detective? Through a logical, if somewhat surprising, personal path.

> **HOLMES & INVESTING: PLANNING**
> **Develop your plan to fit the facts, not the other way around.**

Arthur Conan Doyle was born in Edinburgh in 1859, the third child and first son of Charles Doyle, the black sheep of a prominent, artistic family, and Mary Foley Doyle, the daughter of Charles's landlady. Charles Doyle, bitterly disappointed in his job and feeling a failure compared to his famous father and brothers, turned to alcohol. He was apparently not a violent drunk, but became increasingly remote from his family. Mary Doyle, struggling to hold back the poverty that she blamed on her husband's drinking, fastened her attention and her hopes for the future on her adored son. She was, Arthur always acknowledged, the single most important influence on his life.

Throughout his childhood, Arthur listened in awe as his mother told him tales of the Foley ancestors she insisted were famous. She thrust books on him at a young age and drilled him in the fine points of heraldry. Her love of reading, and her mesmerizing skill as a storyteller, shaped him in ways that would become obvious only later.

Mary Doyle wasn't preparing her son for the life of a writer; she had decided he should become a doctor, like her father. And so, after a fine Jesuit education at boarding schools in Britain and Germany (and heaven only knows how Mary Doyle managed to pay for it), Arthur enrolled in the School of Medicine at Edinburgh University. There he came under the tutelage of another seminal influence: Dr. Joseph Bell.

Dr. Bell, a surgeon, taught young medical students by inviting them to sit in on his weekly clinic at the Royal Infirmary, where they could observe his techniques. A popular, charismatic professor, Bell challenged his students to hone their skills of observation. He believed that correctly identifying a patient's illness involved alert attention to all aspects of the person, not merely the stated complaint. He also believed that people carried clues about themselves in their clothes, their way of walking, and their manner of speech, clues that would help the physician more fully understand the problem.

Watching Dr. Bell with patients was very much like watching a magician at work, and Doyle, like all the students, was duly impressed with his performances. Later in life, in his autobiography, Doyle recorded one of Bell's memorable displays.[11]

In one of his best cases he said to a civilian patient, "Well, my man, you've served in the army."

"Aye, sir."

"Not long discharged?"

"Aye, sir."

"A Highland regiment?"

"Aye, sir."

"A non-com officer?"

"Aye, sir."

"Stationed in Barbados?"

"Aye, sir."

"You see, gentlemen," he would explain, "the man was a respectful man but did not remove his hat. They do not in the army, but he would have learned civilian ways had he been long discharged. He has an air of authority and he is obviously Scottish. As to Barbados, his complaint is elephantiasis, which is West Indian, and not British." . . . It is no wonder that after the study of such a character

I used and amplified his methods when in later life I tried to build up a scientific detective who solved cases on his own merits and not through the folly of the criminal.

But that is getting ahead of our story. Doyle, the young medical student, had no inkling that his future lay in the creation of a fictional scientific detective, rather than in medicine. Yet he was, without being aware of it, gaining an advanced education in the art of observation, for Dr. Bell hired him as his clerk at the clinic, performing the preliminary function we today would call intake. It was his job to note the patients' complaint and all supporting details, and record them for Bell. We can certainly imagine that, challenged by his mentor, Doyle became adept at spotting the bits of relevant information unvoiced by the patients.

Money was always a problem for the young student. He took what interim jobs he could find, including serving as ship's doctor on two vessels, one bound for the Arctic and the other for West Africa; these adventures exposed him to exotic locales and colorful characters that would later find their way into his stories, but they also delayed the completion of his medical education. Eventually, however, he earned his degree and set out, at the age of twenty-three, to begin earning a living as a general practitioner.

It was not easy. After several false starts and disappointing positions with other physicians, he decided to establish his own practice. It was a move of desperation, and it took a while to pay off. In the early days, he had almost no patients.

Young Dr. Doyle filled the extra hours by writing, a pastime he had enjoyed since his days at boarding school, where his facility with the written word had been noticed. His chief interest was historical fiction, and he produced both stories and novels that he considered serious literature, and of which he was quite proud. Financial rewards were meager, however, and his medical practice, while slowly growing, was still thin. Concern for his ability to earn a living deepened in 1885 when he married Louise Hawkins, the sister of a patient.

A year later he wrote a piece that would change everything, though he did not know it at the time. It was a short novel titled *A Study in Scarlet,* and it introduced to the world a private detective Doyle had named Sherlock Holmes. Many years later he explained his inspiration: "I thought I would try my hand at writing a story where the hero would treat crime as Dr. Bell treated disease, and where science would take the place of chance."[12]

Doyle originally named his creation Sherrinford. The final name Sherlock came, depending on whom you ask, from a cricket player, a village in Ireland, a violinist, a school chum, or a police inspector in Portsmouth, where Doyle was living at the time. The surname Holmes was chosen to honor Oliver Wendell Holmes, himself a physician. Watson, Holmes's steadfast companion, was named for one of Doyle's classmates, Dr. James Watson.

Doyle wrote a second Holmes piece, *The Sign of Four,* soon after, then, after a short detour in Vienna for advanced medical study in diseases of the eye, he hit on the idea of writing a series of stories featuring one character—and concluded that Holmes was the ideal candidate. Short stories, he felt, would be a quick boost to his income while he continued writing the historical novels he considered his true calling.

So, writing during "the long hours of waiting in my consulting room," he penned the first two Holmes short stories, "A Scandal in Bohemia" and "A Case of Identity," for *Strand* magazine.[13] The stories were a huge hit with readers, and the magazine's editors promptly asked for four more. Even though he still considered the Holmes stories something to fill in the gaps between his "serious" novels, Doyle agreed. He asked for, and received, a substantial fee.

His medical practice was far less successful. As an eye surgeon, he had not had one patient. It was with a light heart, therefore, that Dr.

Doyle made a stunning decision: He would abandon medicine altogether and concentrate on his writing. Modern-day authors will be floored by the irony: Doyle could make more money as a writer than as a doctor.

In short order, he wrote six more Sherlock stories for the *Strand*, asking for a still higher fee. Holmes was immensely popular with readers, and Doyle's plan to kill off his detective after the original twelve stories brought howls of protest from all sides, including his mother. The magazine begged for more stories. Still hoping to focus on other types of writing, Doyle decided to ask for such a large sum that the editors would leave him alone; instead, they readily agreed, asking only that he hurry up.

All told, over the course of four decades Arthur Conan Doyle wrote fifty-six short stories featuring Holmes and Watson, in addition to the four short novels that had begun it all. They became a publishing phenomenon. Even though Doyle himself was thoroughly tired of Holmes long before the end, his readers were not. It is a measure of Doyle's genius that the stories are devoured as enthusiastically today as they were when first published. Even now, mail still arrives at the London postal service addressed to Mr. Sherlock Holmes, 221-B Baker Street.

In our time, physicians are educated in a different way than was common in Doyle's day. Today's young medical students begin to learn diagnostics in a traditional lecture hall, with a professor standing at a lectern and the students taking notes as fast as they can. Later on, as they make hospital rounds under the tutelage of a teaching physician, they watch and learn the process in a hands-on way. They are taught that diagnosis involves three phases: first, take a complete history; second, do a complete physical examination; third, make a differential diagnosis, noting all the possibilities, and order laboratory tests to narrow things down. Throughout, they are reminded not to skip any steps, even if the problem seems obvious, and not to be influenced by someone else's judgment.

Classroom lecture, then practical learning. This is the method that has been used in our medical schools for decades. Until recently, no one questioned its efficacy. Then Dr. Irwin Braverman, professor of dermatology at Yale University School of Medicine, began to wonder whether there might be a better way.

"Too often doctors learn by memorizing patterns," Dr. Braverman said. "Once they have the patterns down, they know what disease they are looking at. The problem is that the patterns consist of large details, not the fine details. But it is often in the fine details that the answer lies. Most physicians, when they examine patients, see only what is obvious. They don't easily see the fine details. It seemed to me that we needed to improve their fine-detail skills."[14]

To solve this problem, Dr. Braverman hit upon a very original idea: Put the medical students in an art-appreciation class and teach them to how to look at paintings. Using art as a vehicle, students might be able to learn the strong observational skills that otherwise are acquired only through years of clinical practice. Dr. Braverman's thinking was that if the students knew they would have to describe something they were completely unfamiliar with, and therefore had no preconceived ideas about, they would have to pay attention to all the details. They couldn't depend on recognizing patterns, because no patterns existed.

In an experiment conducted over two academic years (1998–99 and 1999–2000), he put one group of first-year medical students into the art class, while the others attended standard medical lectures. Those in the art class studied a preselected painting for ten minutes, then described it in specific detail, based solely on visual evidence. Looking at a portrait of a woman who seemed sad, they could not, for example, simply say she was depressed. They had to explain what they observed about her eyes, mouth, and other features that led them to their conclusion. Open-ended questions from the art professor helped the medical students learn to see more fully.[15]

Dr. Braverman found that even as little as one two-hour art class made a significant difference in students' ability to diagnose patients. "It's critical," he says, "to understand the details. You have to put energy into looking at details. Passive transmission of information—pattern recognition—is just memorization. Active searching allows for more independent work and better analysis."[16] Because of Dr. Braverman's findings, all first-year medical students at Yale are now required to take a class in art appreciation.

Sherlock Holmes is the master observer of details large and small. But he knows, as physicians do, that merely collecting the details is not sufficient. Observing, even Dr. Braverman's "active searching," is only the first step. It falls upon the observer to decipher the meaning behind the details by analyzing them in context.

Earlier I described Holmes's approach as a three-step process: observe, factor in background knowledge, draw a conclusion. Holmes himself described his method more simply: "observe and deduce." He does not specifically include the second element, that vast store of knowledge he carries in his mind, probably because he takes it for granted. But I pull it forward here and call it to your attention, because it is a critical piece for investors.

It is not possible to make a reasoned decision from observed details until you know what those details mean *in context*. You may, for example, find an unusual expense item in the footnotes of a company's annual report, but you cannot make any use of your discovery unless you can put it in perspective. How does this expense compare with prior years? Is it unique to this company, or does it perhaps represent some general event that affected everyone in the industry that year?

Just as he did with showing us how to take note of all details, Holmes can serve us as teacher in this regard as well.

• • •

"My name is Sherlock Holmes. It is my business to know what other people don't know."[17]

Holmes is not particularly known for modesty, but this statement is not mere braggadocio. He knows his stuff, and he knows why it is important.

The list of things Holmes knows about is staggering: the typefaces used by different newspapers, what the shape of a skull reveals about race, the geography of London, the configuration of railway lines in cities versus suburbs, and the types of knots used by sailors, for a few examples. He has authored numerous scientific monographs on such topics as tattoos, ciphers, tobacco ash, variations in human ears, what can be learned from typewriter keys, preserving footprints with plaster of Paris, how a man's trade affects the shape of his hands, dating a document from the appearance of the paper, and what a dog's manner can reveal about the character of its owner.

Why does he take the time to learn these somewhat esoteric subjects? Partly because to an intellect such as his, knowledge is a valuable commodity for its own sake—but more, he believes that it may someday prove helpful. "All knowledge becomes useful to the detective."[18]

Knowledge is useful because it has a very practical value. Note, for instance, what Holmes says about his monograph on the subject of tobacco: "In it I enumerate 140 forms of cigar, cigarette, and pipe tobacco. . . . It is sometimes of supreme importance as a clue. If you can say definitely, for example, that some murder had been done by a man who was smoking an Indian lunkah, it obviously narrows your field of search."[19] Obviously.

In the stories, we find countless situations where Holmes is able to pull from his great store of knowledge the one specific item that is useful in the investigation. To take just one example, he is able to determine how a young boy disappeared from his boarding school by deciphering the tracks left by bicycle tires. "I am familiar with forty-two different impressions left by tires," he says.[20] Clearly, depth of knowledge is critical here; if he knew only two or three types, how likely is it that one of those few would have been involved in this particular mystery?

How does he manage it? Watson describes his method: "For many years he had adopted a system of docketing all paragraphs concerning men and things, so that it was difficult to name a subject or a person on which he could not at once furnish information."[21] Holmes had, in other words, the habit of automatically absorbing and storing all information that passed his way. Most of it, as we know, was stored in his mind, reinforced by the physical filing system that Watson suggests.

HOLMES & INVESTING: KNOWLEDGE

Learn everything you can; you never know when it will come in handy.

Holmes, for his part, gave us a more colorful, more memorable description: "A man should keep his little brain-attic stocked with all the furniture that he is likely to use, and the rest he can put away in the lumber-room of his library, where he can get it if he wants it."[22]

Investors seeking to add to their reservoir of knowledge should adopt Holmes's habit: file away, either mentally or literally, all the investment-related information that they come across. It is easier than you might at first imagine. I believe you will find that as you train yourself to observe the details (the detective's first habit), you will automatically be increasing your store of knowledge.

Have you ever noticed that when you're considering purchasing a certain model of car, suddenly you see that car everywhere? It's a simple matter of bringing the issue forward into your consciousness, and it works the same way with financial information. Once you take an interest in a particular company, or even a particular industry, you will find relevant information everywhere you turn. Then each tidbit you absorb adds to your mental encyclopedia, awaiting retrieval when needed.

This is undoubtedly how it happened for Holmes. He didn't always know the tread patterns of forty-two different bicycle tires, but once he realized that treads could be significant, he made it a point to learn them. Then, when he found a set of tracks in the field near the boarding school, he had enough data to draw from.

Inspector Gregory: "Is there any point to which you would wish to draw my attention?"
Holmes: "To the curious incident of the dog in the nighttime."
Gregory: "The dog did nothing in the nighttime."
Holmes: "That was the curious incident."[23]

That tantalizing bit of dialogue may be the most famous anecdote in all the Holmes literature. Even people who have never read even one story know about "the dog who did not bark."

Everywhere we turn when considering Holmes, we find situations like this one: Everyone else on the scene saw what he saw, but he was the only person who *understood* what he was seeing. Only he had the perception to take his observations and reason from them to a logical conclusion.

In this case, Holmes knew that if the guard dog did not bark, it must be because he knew and trusted the intruder. The person responsible for the disappearance of a valuable racehorse, and the brutal death of its trainer, was someone the dog did not consider threatening. So the investigation must focus on someone close and familiar. Once he explains his thinking, it's amazingly clear and simple, and all those standing on the sidelines wonder why they didn't see it too.

They didn't see it because only Holmes has Holmes's sharp and uncommonly quick mind. He thinks logically, and he thinks fast. He truly is, as Watson once remarked, "a reasoning machine."[24]

Holmes's method, you will recall, incorporates three separate mental activities: closely observing all the details, factoring in relevant information from his "brain attic," and reasoning his way to a logical deduction. In Holmes's mind, however, the elements are virtually inseparable, and when he is on the trail of the truth he runs through the mental process too fast for bystanders to discern individual steps; they can only watch in amazement. Since none of us is as smart as Holmes, we break the method down into steps in order to understand it—but we can also break those major steps down further, to see what investment lessons they hold.

First, he mentally circles back to the beginning: Are all the facts in place? If only partial information has been gathered, there is a danger of reaching the wrong conclusion. "It is a capital mistake," Holmes warns, "to theorize before you have all the evidence. It biases the judgment."[25]

That is why, if necessary, Holmes does not hesitate to cover the same ground twice. He returns to the room where the murder was committed, he talks again to the witness, he reexamines the spot where he collected evidence, he studies once more the findings from the inquest. "The temptation to form premature theories upon insufficient data is the bane of our profession,"[26] he says, referring to the detective business—but this wise statement could as well apply to the profession of investment adviser.

Of course, at the start of the process Holmes does not know (and neither do investors) which pieces of information will turn out to be relevant and which inconsequential. That is why he collects everything. But too much information can slow things down. As he says, "The principal difficulty lay in the fact of there being too much evidence. What was vital was overlaid and hidden by what was irrelevant."[27]

Thus the next phase of the process is one of sorting. "It is of the highest importance in the art of detection to be able to recognize, out of a number of facts, which are incidental and which vital. Otherwise your energy and attention must be dissipated instead of being con-centrated."[28]

Holmes's way of sorting is both methodical and intuitive. It depends largely on common sense. He takes one fact that he knows absolutely to be true, then lays another fact next to it and compares them. If the second does not invalidate the first, he retains both. He then runs through in his mind what the combination of the two facts might suggest, and if the answer is not illogical, he has one element of a theory.

> **HOLMES & INVESTING: MANAGING THE INFORMATION**
> **Apply to the question at hand all the information that is relevant to it—but no more.**

Each additional bit of information is examined the same way, and either added to the theory or, if it seems to have no particular signifi-cance one way or the other, set aside.

Incidental pieces of evidence are also set aside if they lead to an impossible conclusion. It is one of Holmes's most famous concepts: "When you have eliminated the impossible, whatever remains, how-ever improbable, must be the truth."[29]

The next task is to arrange the facts in sequence and analyze their significance. "Of all the facts presented to us we had to pick just those which we deemed to be essential, and then piece them together in their order, so as to reconstruct this very remarkable chain of events."[30]

Holmes is, of course, reconstructing how a crime was committed, in order to pinpoint the identity of the criminal. Investors have a dif-ferent goal: reconstructing the chain of events that led to a certain financial outcome (whether good or bad) so that they may be on the lookout for a future occurrence of that same set of circumstances.

When piecing together a possible theory, Holmes is careful to remember that there may be more than one explanation. What appears to be the most obvious answer may be completely wrong. "There is nothing more deceptive," he says, "than an obvious fact."[31]

And sometimes the correct answer depends on additional research. "I have devised seven separate explanations, each of which would cover the facts as we know them. But which of these is correct can only be determined by the fresh information which we shall no doubt find waiting for us."[32]

HOLMES & INVESTING:
FLEXIBILITY
Keep an open mind. What seems obvious may hide important subtleties.

Note that Holmes is *always* alert for new data, and maintains the mental flexibility to incorporate it, even if the new information leads in a different direction. In fact, he points out, having a new avenue of possibility is often a good thing. "When you follow two separate chains of thought you will find some point of intersection which should approximate to the truth."[33]

A sedative that went undetected in a highly spiced supper dish. A surgical knife, useless for self-defense, found in the victim's hand. A candle stub in his pocket. Three sheep that had gone lame. An invoice for an expensive dress. And most significant of all, the dog that did not bark.

These are some of the facts that Holmes had to work with in the mystery of the missing racehorse, facts that led him to a conclusion wholly different from the police theory. In describing his thinking, he gave us a very clear template for analyzing data: "The difficulty is to detach the frame of absolute undeniable fact from the embellishments of theorists. Then, having established ourselves upon this sound basis, it is our duty to see what inferences may be drawn and what are the special points upon which the whole mystery turns."

The chief undeniable fact was that the dog did not bark. After that, all the others fell into place, for "one true inference invariably suggests others."[34]

Watson opens an early-morning telegram:

Have you a couple of days to spare? Have just been wired for from the west of England in connection with Boscombe Valley tragedy. Shall be glad if you will come with me.[35]

And so they are off: Sherlock Holmes, at the request of Inspector Lestrade of Scotland Yard, and Watson, at the request of Sherlock Holmes. It was a frequent pattern for Holmes: In situations where standard police procedures failed, officials from Scotland Yard had often asked the assistance of the famous detective, generally with a mixture of reluctance and admiration.

As they travel to the area, "two middle-aged gentlemen flying westward at fifty miles an hour instead of quietly digesting their breakfasts at home," Holmes summarizes the situation. Charles McCarthy, a native of Australia who leases a farm in Boscombe Valley, has been found with his skull bashed in. A gun belonging to his son James was lying near the body. Father and son had been seen arguing violently just minutes before James, his clothes covered with blood, ran to a neighboring cottage for help. James has been arrested and charged with murder.

Alice Turner, the daughter of John Turner, the McCarthys' wealthy neighbor and landlord, has known James since childhood. She believes passionately in his innocence, and it is her pleas that have spurred Lestrade to call for Holmes.

This case interests Holmes greatly. The evidence against the accused is strong, and that is exactly the sort of situation that Holmes believes requires close study.

He begins with the report of James's own statement. James had been away from home for several days and had returned unexpectedly. He had gone for a walk and without knowing it happened to follow his father's path. When he heard his father make the distinctive "Cooee" call that was their signal, he hurried forward and found him standing by Boscombe Pool. Each man was surprised to see the other.

They argued heatedly, and James walked away. Suddenly, he heard his father cry out, and rushed back to find him seriously injured. As he cradled his father's head in his lap, James heard him mutter something about "a rat." James also testified that he had seen something like a gray coat on the ground, but that it had disappeared while he was kneeling next to his dying father.

On his first day in Boscombe Valley, Holmes learns vital information: That the fatal injury was to the left side of the skull. That the senior McCarthy had an appointment to meet someone by the pool where he was killed. That he did not know James had returned from his brief trip. That Charles McCarthy and John Turner had known each other in Australia. That McCarthy was urging a marriage between his son and Alice Turner, who stood to inherit a fortune.

The following day, Holmes continues his investigation. First he obtains careful shoe measurements for both McCarthys. Then, accompanied by Lestrade and Watson, he goes to the spot where the body was found. Watson recounts that traces of the fallen body and the footprints of those first on the scene were plain. But "to Holmes, as I could see by his eager face and peering eyes, very many other things were to be read upon the trampled grass. He ran round, like a dog who is picking up a scent."

The first thing he sees is a pattern of footprints, and he lays down in the mud to study them more clearly. He finds prints that belonged to James McCarthy and verified his story. He also finds another set, with an unusual shape and a very revealing pattern: "Tiptoes. They come, they go, they come again—of course that was for the cloak."

Following these unusual prints into the woods, he once again lies down on the ground and begins turning over bits of leaves. Here too he examines the bark of a tree with his lens, and picks up a jagged stone. It is the kind of painstaking search for details that is Holmes's hallmark.

A few minutes later, he calmly announces to Lestrade that the murderer is "a tall man, left-handed, limps with the right leg, wears thick-soled shooting boots and a gray cloak, smokes Indian cigars, uses a cigar holder, and carries a blunt penknife in his pocket."

Who is it? Holmes knows, but for his own reasons does not say. Instead, he runs through the case with Watson, explaining all he found at the scene and what it led him to deduced about the killer.

Two points in particular are critical to the case: When Charles McCarthy called out "Cooee," he was not signaling his son; he thought James was still out of town. He was, however, using a call that would be recognized by another Australian, for "Cooee" is distinctly Australian. Somewhere in his life, Holmes had come across that bit of trivia, and had filed it away for future use. And the dying man's mumbling about "a rat" also points to Australia, for he was trying to say the name of a town, Ballarat. This, together with all Holmes had uncovered, points to just one person: John Turner, the victim's friend.

So Holmes and Watson call on Turner, who is by now gravely ill. By his skillful and compassionate questioning, Holmes pulls out the full story. As a young man Turner had made his money in Australia through a string of robberies, and McCarthy had been a witness to one. Later, in England, Turner married, became a father, and led an exemplary life. Then a chance meeting with McCarthy turned everything upside down. McCarthy blackmailed Turner for years, and Turner always paid, trying desperately to keep his beloved daughter from learning about his past. But when McCarthy demanded callously that Alice be given in marriage to his son, with his eye on her inheritance, Turner refused. The two met by the pool to discuss it, and Turner snapped.

Holmes is moved by the old man's sincerity and his fierce dedication to his daughter. He obtains a written confession, but pledges not to use it unless it becomes necessary to clear the innocent James. In the end, James is acquitted because of the evidence Holmes presents in court, and John Turner's deadly secret remains secret.

In this case, then, we witness an unfurling of Holmes's full method.

First, he collects a complete portfolio of information—from the coroner's report, from his own interviews, and from his detailed search of the murder scene. He then pulls in bits of knowledge—about Australia, about footprints, about cigar ash—to help him make sense of what he found. Then he applies to all that the considerable power of his logical mind and reaches a sound conclusion.

And in Boscombe Valley we see one thing more, an aspect of Holmes's nature that is not always visible: a passion for justice. Holmes has found the true killer, but he has also found the truth about the victim, and one outweighs the other. When the law points one way and pure justice another, Holmes comes down on the side of justice, compassion, and morality. To the seriously ill Turner he promises, "You are yourself aware that you will soon have to answer for your deed at a higher court than the Assizes. I will keep your confession and if McCarthy is condemned I shall be forced to use it. If not, it shall never be seen by mortal eye."

It is exactly what Father Brown, our third Great Detective, would have done in the same situation. Like Holmes, the gentle cleric is uncommonly smart and able to uncover the truth when others miss it. He is also far more interested in redemption than vengeance, and uses his skills as a detective not to help police identify the criminal but to help the criminal do the right thing. You will meet him in Chapter 6.

Summaries cannot do justice to Arthur Conan Doyle's graceful writing; there really is no substitute for reading the stories for yourself, and few greater pleasures. As you do so, keep an eye out for Holmes's habits of mind that are worth emulating.

Holmes once remarked about a French policeman, "He possesses two out of the three qualities necessary for the ideal detective. He has the power of observation and that of deduction. He is only wanting in knowledge."[36] Of course, Holmes himself possessed all three—a combination that should be found in the ideal investor as well.

CHAPTER FIVE

Holmes on Wall Street

What would Sherlock Holmes do if he were thinking about investing in today's stock market? I submit he would approach the situation exactly as if the London police had asked him to untangle a puzzling mystery.

Here's what we know of his methods: He begins an examination with an objective mind, untainted by prejudice. He observes acutely and catalogues all the information, down to the tiniest detail, and draws on his broad knowledge to put those details into context. Then, armed with the facts, he walks logically, rationally, thoughtfully toward a conclusion, always on the lookout for new, sometimes contrary information that might alter the outcome.

And if, while visiting Wall Street, he chanced to meet an investment professional who operated the same way, what would such a person be like?

I believe that the type of professional who most closely embodies Holmes's abilities and intellectual approach is actually a synthesis of two investment professionals: a credit analyst and a security analyst.

Credit analysts. No doubt you have considered purchasing bonds at some point in your investing life, and so you are aware that bonds are given a rating that designates their quality, from AAA (the highest), to AA, to A, then BBB, and so on all the way down to C. When you buy a bond, you are essentially loaning your money to the company, which pledges to repay the loan incrementally, with interest, at regular intervals. Whether the bonds are issued by corporations, by countries, or by public agencies, the paramount question always is: How likely is it that the issuing organization will default and be unable to repay the bondholders? The ratings are a shorthand way of describing creditworthiness.

The ratings are set by specialists known as credit analysts, working for firms such as Standard & Poor's and Moody's. As they go about collecting the research that will ultimately produce the rating, they display several mental qualities of which Sherlock would approve—three in particular:

1. *Objectivity.* This is one of the most important, for our present purposes. It's fair to say, I think, that no one group of Wall Street professionals has less of a vested interest in their reports than rating companies. Researchers and analysts who work for large brokerage firms often have a great deal to gain or lose by recommending one stock over another, especially if their firm has an investment banking division. Fund managers and individual money managers are at risk of losing clients if their decisions produce unpleasant results. And even famous investors have

been known to make choices based on emotion rather than rationality. But credit analysts have nothing to gain by over- or understating their opinion of a certain company, by being anything less than purely objective in their ratings. Their job security is not tied to the market performance of any one company.

> **"Each fact is suggestive in itself. Together they have a cumulative force."**
>
> —SHERLOCK HOLMES, "THE ADVENTURE OF THE BRUCE-PARTINGTON PLANS"

2. *Thoroughness and attention to detail.* To reach their conclusion and establish a rating for the bonds of a certain company, credit analysts interview numerous executives, keep up on industry trends, study macroeconomic issues that might affect the company, visit the company's outlets, even sit in parking lots of retail locations and count the number of customers who walk through the door—all this in addition to exhaustively poring over every one of the company's financial documents.

3. *Willingness to factor in new information.* In the process of collecting information, credit analysts are keenly alert for new facts that might change a company's rating, either for better or worse. This means they must maintain a certain mindset: They must be willing to take in material that contradicts an earlier decision and must resist the all-too-human tendency to discount it.

Security analysts. Most investors who work through brokerage firms have their primary contact with the firm through a stockbroker, the person who starts the ball rolling when stocks or bonds are bought or sold. Often the conversation between investor and broker revolves around the firm's analysts, the research they have done into various stocks, and the reports that bear their recommendations.

It is the job of these analysts to evaluate the economic health of securities—stocks and bonds—and guide the firm's clients into making good decisions. The analysts study the individual company, the current state of the industry to which the company belongs, and the overall economy. They then analyze this information against the backdrop of what they know about the company's past and the historical trends in the industry, and develop an informed judgment about the security's future value. The brokers in turn

> "Let us get a firm grip of [what] we do know, so that when fresh facts arise we may be ready to fit them into their places."
>
> —SHERLOCK HOLMES, "THE DEVIL'S FOOT"

present the analysts' recommendations to their clients, who rely with confidence on the advice of these professionals, thereby relieving themselves of having to do the same research.

At least that's how it is supposed to work.

Sometimes the problem is one of conflict of interest between the investment banking side and the brokerage side (see the section about the "Chinese Wall" in Chapter 1). I do not mean to suggest that all firms that have both investment banking and brokerage divisions are acting inappropriately, but this is a growing concern and investors owe it to themselves to be vigilant.

Even when there is no question of conflict of interest, investors need to pay attention for another reason: Security analysts can get caught up in the excitement swirling around a certain stock, and lose some degree of objectivity about it. It may be that the company's charismatic CEO has captured everyone's imagination. Or analysts have fallen in love with the technology of the company's newest product line. Or an innovative marketing program is showing amazing results. Or the whole country is talking about the company's very cool television commercials. Whatever the specific cause, analysts get swept up in the dazzling "story," and forget to keep an eye on the big picture.[1] We in the investment business know a great deal about behavioral finance, and we are supposed to be immune to the pull of such psychological impulses, but we are not.

Still, even with these limitations, it is security analysts who best reflect two of Sherlock Holmes's critical traits: breadth of knowledge and reasoning ability.

Most analysts concentrate on just one industry, and follow the companies within that industry for years. When a new company appears on the scene, or an existing company announces a change, they know how that fits within the broader perspective of the entire industry. They keep tabs on government regulations that will affect the industry. They understand the ins and outs of the business, whether it involves a product or a service. They can rattle off the engineering specifications of the products, they can tell you the latest data on market share, and they know what the company has up its R&D sleeve.

All this gives them the intellectual background to generate a reasoned view of the company's future value. It isn't guesswork, but rather pure reasoning: We know this one thing, we see that, we can be fairly sure about this

> **"We balance probabilities and choose the most likely. It is the scientific use of the imagination."**
>
> —SHERLOCK HOLMES, "THE HOUND OF THE BASKERVILLES"

other, and taking all of it into account leads us to believe the stock will behave in a certain way in a certain time frame.

In a perfect world, all financial analysts would be a combination of the best qualities of credit analysts (objectivity, thoroughness and attention to detail, and willingness to factor in new information) and of security analysts (broad knowledge and ability to reach a sound conclusion through analysis). Until that day comes, smart investors will make it their business to learn those abilities for themselves, following the methods of the Great Detectives. If they do, they might be able to spot a young company poised to become a dramatic success story.

Michael Dell first fell in love with computers in his seventh-grade math class, when he was thirteen years old; three years later, he bought his first machine (an Apple II) and promptly took it apart to see how it worked. His high school yearbook photo shows a stereotypical computer geek with thick glasses, peering at a computer screen. But what was not apparent in the photo was Dell's entrepreneurial flair, which had already manifested itself every bit as strongly as his fascination with computers. At the tender age of twelve, he had held an auction for stamp collectors that provided him $1,000 in pocket money. During his senior year in high school, he used his Apple computer to create a well-conceived database of potential new subscribers to a Houston daily newspaper, and sold enough subscriptions to buy his first car— a BMW—for cash.

To please his parents, Dell enrolled in a pre-med course at the University of Texas in Austin, but he seemed already to realize that he was headed for some kind of future in the computer business. It didn't take long for the young entrepreneur to outdistance the young college student.

Dell began hanging around computer stores in Austin, and one of the first things he noticed was that people who really knew computers weren't happy shopping there, because the salespeople knew more about vacuum cleaners than they did about computers. He quickly perceived that there existed a large base of savvy computer users who knew just what they wanted and were prepared to pay for it, so he began assembling upgrade kits and selling them to people who already had a computer but wanted to increase its power. He knew instinctively that the only way to reach his target computer-literate customers was to sell to them directly: His first customers were other students, but he quickly branched out to local businesspeople and began going to trade shows and local computer fairs, and advertising in specialty computer publications. In January of his freshman year, he made $30,000; in April, $80,000.

Back home in Houston for spring break, Michael told his parents he wanted to quit school. They convinced him to finish out the first year, then agreed that he could devote the summer to his new business; for his part, Michael agreed that if things did not go well during the summer, he would scrap the business and return to school.

So, in May of 1984, he incorporated the Dell Computer Corporation, with the $1,000 capital that Texas law required as a minimum, and started selling computers full-time. The first month, sales were $180,000. By January 1985, the young company had 39 employees and $6 million in sales. Michael Dell was 19 years old. He never went back to school.

By then, he had already hit on three concepts that would ultimately make him a multimillionaire and his company number one. The first was the notion of selling directly to customers, eliminating the middleman. This core strategy, the one that drives the company to this date, was one of those flashes of insight that underpin so many success stories. Another key realization was that smart computer users know what they want—a machine loaded with the exact features they need—and they want it at a good price. They don't need to be "sold," and they don't need their hands held. From this understanding it was an easy step to the fundamental Dell business model: build each computer to order, with the exact components that each customer specifies.

Custom building automatically gave the fledgling company another key element of its strategy: minimal inventory. From observing retail stores, Michael Dell had already learned what happens when computers sit on shelves: They lose value with every tick of the clock. This was, in fact, the source of his earliest business. He would buy up these outdated machines on the cheap, upgrade them to order, and sell the customized machines to Austin businesses at a price they still considered a bargain, but that represented a nice profit for the young entrepreneur.

The lesson was simple: In an industry driven by innovation, where product becomes obsolete in a matter of days, you don't want to be caught with inventory sitting on the shelf. So Dell built a company that carries virtually no inventory at all.

In the early days, working from his college dorm room, he would take orders from local businesses, get half the money up front to pay for components, and deliver a custom machine in a fraction of the time the businesses were accustomed to. The company's first real production facility consisted of three guys with screwdrivers working at 6-foot tables. Today, trucks from suppliers deliver components daily at one end of the Dell production line, and at the other end, UPS trucks leave every day loaded with completed computers. The entire process, starting the moment an order is received via telephone or online, takes 36 hours.

From selling outdated computers upgraded to order, the next logical step for the young company was to build the product from scratch, using the same components as were in the brand-name boxes. They looked like IBMs and worked like IBMs, but, since they didn't carry IBM's heavy distribution and marketing costs, they sold for substantially less. One typical result: In 1992, Dell's marketing and administrative expenses represented 14 cents out of every $1 of revenue, compared to 24 cents at Apple and 30 cents at IBM.

Michael Dell once remarked, "Our model is all about the most effective way to get technologies from Intel [which makes the microchips that make the computers run] and Microsoft [which makes the software that makes the computers do their work] to the customer. We're going to shine the bright light of reality on the fact that the customer has been overcharged."[2] He was speaking in 1997, but he was articulating a model that had been understood within the company from the very beginning.

The new company was successful from day one. From $6 million the first year, sales climbed to $159 million four years later. By 1992, four years after that, revenue had risen to nearly $2 billion. One reason for the rapid growth was that competitors were caught by surprise: They thought it was all about price, and thought it would never last. Price *was* a factor, of course, but as every business owner knows, price will get you only so far, and it will get you there only once. After that, you have to prove yourself on quality and service.

One potentially huge problem with buying computers direct from the manufacturer is that if they ever need repair, they have to be shipped back to the manufacturer, usually at the customer's expense. Michael Dell knew he had the right idea with direct selling, but he also knew he had to offset this liability aggressively. His solution was superior customer service, and he wasn't kidding around.

The first benefit: a 30-day unconditional guarantee. The second: free, unlimited, lifetime telephone technical support. The Dell people working the phones were trained for six months before they were allowed to answer their first call. If the customer called back a second time, the same technical person helped them. Dell claims that more than 90 percent of problems can be solved with the phone consultation. For the rest, the company provided its third benefit: a year's worth of on-site service, usually by the next day.

Inside the company, managers and engineers held troubleshooting meetings every Friday; nagging customer problems were spread on the table, and the group would keep at it until every problem was solved.

Every Dell employee buys into this philosophy: The customer must be pleased—not just satisfied, but pleased.

The world noticed. In 1991, when J. D. Power & Associates decided it was time to give their renowned "customer satisfaction award" to a computer company, the first one went to Dell.

For a while it seemed the company could do no wrong. Dell had gone public in June 1988, and quarter after quarter, seemingly regular as clockwork, financial reports noted significant increases in revenues and profit. Some insiders, looking back, say that the company's three goals in those days were "growth, growth, and growth." Ironically, the few mistakes made were in the very strategic areas that had produced such success.

In 1989, at the very same time the price of microchips dropped through the floor, Dell found itself with a serious oversupply of component parts that were technically obsolete and seriously overpriced. For fiscal year 1990, earnings dropped to $5.1 million, down from $14.4 million the prior year. (Dell's fiscal year ends at the end of January. So "fiscal year 1990" runs from February 1989 to January 1990.) Important lesson relearned: In the computer industry, inventory control is critical.

The following year, Dell bounced back: For first-quarter 1991, sales were up 45 percent and profits up almost 50 percent. Total sales that year passed $800 million. By June of 1991, the company was the number six U.S. computer supplier, a stunning jump from the number twenty-two position it held only two years earlier.

The numbers just kept going up. In the first quarter of fiscal 1992, sales doubled and profits were up 96 percent. In the first quarter of fiscal 1993 (which occurred in calendar year 1992, remember), sales doubled again. By the end of that fiscal year, sales had hit $2 billion.

Then Dell hit its first major iceberg. During 1993, several "grow too fast" mistakes combined to attack the bottom line. A lack of coordination between marketing and production again left the company with overvalued inventory, and a new line of notebook computers had to be scrapped when serious engineering problems showed up. The company had also been trying to establish a beachhead in retail—again, going against its own proven strategy—but it wasn't working.

Perhaps most critical, senior managers had no system for keeping track of operating costs and profits in the different business lines, so no one really knew how the company as a whole was doing. By the time this structural flaw became fully apparent, the company had endured seven consecutive quarters of negative cash flow. That, plus write-downs and restructuring charges, added up to a loss of $35.8 million in fiscal 1994. The stock price dropped from $49 in January 1993 to $16 by July, and quite a few people on Wall Street muttered, "I told you so."

The advances at Dell had not gone unnoticed in the financial world, but in the first four or five years after the initial public offering in 1988, many analysts had serious doubts about the basic Dell business model. They simply could not believe that enough people would be willing to buy a computer through the mail, which is how they characterized the Dell process. Even though Michael Dell vehemently protested whenever anyone called Dell a "mail-order company," many analysts persisted in thinking of the company that way. After all, they argued, ordering a computer by calling an 800 phone number and having it shipped to your door by UPS was no different from calling the 800 number in any mail-order catalog.

And even though Dell had anticipated the points of consumer resistance and neutralized them with guarantees and free technical support, and even though the number of units sold continued to climb at a blistering pace, Wall Street couldn't seem to overcome its preconceptions. Sales for fiscal 1994 hit $2.9 billion, but many on Wall Street were still saying, in effect, "I don't know, I just don't think people are going to buy computers through the mail."

This skepticism was echoed in the financial press. An article in *Fortune* in September 1995 questioned whether Dell's decision to rely exclusively on direct selling, just as the home computer market was blasting off, represented a real impediment to growth. Some people, the article's authors noted, wondered whether Dell would ever be "anything more than a niche player in the industry."[3] And the previous December, a senior vice president at Dean Witter Reynolds had predicted that not being in retail would make it "highly unlikely they can move [up]."[4]

> "It is a capital mistake to theorize before one has data. Insensibly one begins to twist facts to suit theories, instead of theories to suit facts."
>
> —SHERLOCK HOLMES,
> "A SCANDAL IN BOHEMIA"

Dell—both the company and the man—kept moving forward, undeterred. Dell the man bolstered his effectiveness by bringing in smart, strong, seasoned executives to help him run the company. The differences showed up in Dell the company almost immediately.

After the rough experiences of 1992–93, the company nimbly regained its balance. Its limp experiment in retail selling was axed. Its focus on international sales was increased. And its new mantra, replacing "growth, growth, and growth" became "liquidity, profitability, and growth."

Cost-cutting strategies instituted in 1994 had a strong positive effect on profitability. The number of companies providing component parts was drastically reduced, which meant that much more favorable pricing deals could be negotiated. The company also worked out similar deals with freight carriers, giving all their business to just a few companies in exchange for better prices.

Some things, however, remained the same . . . only better. The primary customer focus was still high-end, sophisticated users in corporations, government agencies, and educational institutions. The bulk of Dell sales, sometimes as much as 75 percent, came from this group. And Dell provided serious services to these clients. A corporation could order any number of Dell computers, configured differently for different departments, preloaded with specialized software appropriate to that industry, and have them drop-shipped to as many different work sites as needed, with individual inventory tags already in place. If they needed technical support, they could just whistle for the on-site systems engineer Dell provided. And if they decided they really should have bought more computers, a Dell account executive was standing by, just down the hall, to help assemble the order.

The basic Dell ordering process remained essentially the same as well: A customer calls up the 800 number, talks options and add-ons with a representative who understands computers, and possibly ends up placing an order right then and there. The one aspect that changed was simply a matter of mechanics: Starting in 1996, customers could also use the company's Web site to browse through a range of component options. As customers clicked their way through various configurations, the purchase price adjusted; at the end, if they were ready to buy, a final click sent the order. By the end of 1997, one year later, Dell was selling computers via the Internet at the rate of more than $4 million a day.

Dell has always recognized that its strategy of direct selling provides more than one benefit. It cuts out the middleman, thereby allowing the company to offer better prices. It speeds up the process: manufacturer to customer in just one distribution step. And it gives the company a direct, immediate link to its customers: Every phone call, every Internet visit, translates into on-the-spot customer feedback, and becomes part of a very sophisticated database of customer preferences. Dell uses the customer input to tweak existing products, develop new product lines, and fine-tune their day-to-day operations—they even know which color on the front of the sales literature customers find most attractive. Many consumer companies have to rely on costly marketing research to learn what their customers want and don't want; Dell gets the same information essentially for free, as an integral part of how it does business.

All these strengths—superb customer service, reputation for reliability, competitive pricing, renewed profitability, and rapid inventory turnover—eventually persuaded the doubting Thomases on Wall Street, and in early 1996 Dell's stock price began to take off. It was a very wild ride.

In January 1996, few people saw what was coming. The conventional wisdom on Wall Street then held that the smart technology buy was software companies, because their products are protected by patents, rather than PC manufacturers, whose products quickly become commodities. Dell proved them wrong.

The stock price started to rise early in 1996; by the first quarter of 1997 it had tripled in value over the prior twelve months. Then, in the second quarter of 1997, it doubled again. On July 23, 1997, the share price was $167.25, up 211 percent from first-quarter 1997 and an astonishing 500 percent from the prior July. In August 1997, *Fortune* magazine called it "the hottest stock on Wall Street."[5]

A month later, *Fortune* declared Dell "the hottest stock of the 90s."[6] It was the single biggest gainer of the S&P 500 during the decade—up an unbelievable 20,000 percent since 1990. Now, you may protest that those years were the boom times for all technology stocks, and you would be right. Still, what happened at Dell was truly extraordinary. In the same time period when Dell shares increased by 20,000 percent, the stock of Microsoft, the poster child for high-tech magic, gained a measly 2,600 percent.

Let's look at this another way: At its IPO in June 1988, Dell sold 3.5 million shares at $8.50 each. By 1995, the shares (on a presplit basis) were worth $100 each; by 1997, $1,000 each. If you had invested $10,000 in Dell in June 1988, by September 1997—not even ten years later—you would be holding stock worth more than $1 million.

On the face of it, this seems your typical Cinderella story: Very smart young man has good ideas, builds a strong company, makes a few mistakes but recovers quickly, stock goes through the roof, and all those involved—smart young man, employees, suppliers, customers, and shareholders—live happily ever after.

Could it really be that simple?

What we are about in this book, remember, is learning to be good investment detectives. And often that means looking at the scenario in a slightly different way and seeing what others do not see, just as a Great Detective sees clues that police officers overlook.

Think of it this way: We can say that traditional Wall Street analysts are like the traditional police; they have limited vision. Great investment detectives are like the fictional Great Detectives; using different means than their traditional counterparts, they find their way to the truth. Sometimes that means uncovering the cankers on what appears to be a very healthy company (think back to the Sunbeam story in Chapter 3) and sometimes, as with Dell, it means spotting great potential while others

> **"Circumstantial evidence is a very tricky thing. It may seem to point very straight to one thing, but if you shift your own point of view a little, you may find it pointing in an equally uncompromising manner to something entirely different."**
>
> **—SHERLOCK HOLMES, "THE BOSCOMBE VALLEY MYSTERY"**

are hemming and hawing and hedging their bets. Most Wall Street observers, you will remember, were unimpressed with Dell's business model—but not all. In fact, some of them looked very much like Great Detectives.

Here and there in the financial press, investors could have found insightful descriptions of Dell's business model. As far as back as 1988, a *Forbes* reporter took note of the company's strategy of keeping inventories lean and "eliminating layers of marketing and distribution costs."[7] In 1991, another *Forbes* writer pointed out that "by cutting his marketing and distribution costs, Dell was able to undersell manufacturers like IBM and Compaq."[8]

The following year, in an article titled "Why Dell Is a Survivor," *Forbes* reporter Julia Pitta described the Dell model as "almost a job-shop approach to manufacturing. This both keeps capital costs low and permits greater flexibility." As the article pointed out, in 1992 Dell earned $2 billion in revenue with just $55 million in fixed assets (land, property, plant, and equipment). That translated into $33 of sales for every $1 of fixed assets, at a time when IBM was getting $2 of sales for every $1 of fixed assets. Furthermore, Pitta noted, it's "a capital base with very little debt, so Dell can deliver a high return on equity."[9]

So even in the early years, long before the rising stock price caught everyone's attention, the evidence was starting to mount that something was happening at Dell. These three journalists picked up on several key points of evidence: the cost savings from Dell's distribution apparatus, the competitive price advantage it created, the minimal inventory, and the low capital costs. But, as they made sure to point out in their articles, Wall Street analysts were doubtful. The evidence was available, but most people didn't see it. Or, perhaps more accurately, they didn't realize what they were seeing.

In 1992, Charles Wolf, then vice president of equity research at First Boston, noted that "Dell's strategy of pricing aggressively and driving operating costs down is working."

Vadim Slotnikov, the technical-industry analyst at Sanford C. Bernstein in New York, was asked about Dell in November 1995, a period when the company was experiencing difficulty obtaining the components it needed for certain models. Dell's problems, he said, were actually a reflection of its success in the high-end market, and the company would overcome the temporary problem the way it always had: with flexibility and nimbleness. "They've been able to get high-end PCs to market faster because they don't have the whole supply chain to worry about. They can buy complete boards directly from Intel and keep low internal inventory in the channel, since they don't participate in the retail channel. They can shift the inventory faster."[11]

While working on this book, I had a chance to ask Slotnikov about his analysis of Dell at the time. Looking back on those days with the benefit of hindsight, he acknowledges that he did not get the full story right. With a candor that is both refreshing and admirable, he admits today that he didn't see that the success of the business model was going to translate into higher stock prices to the degree that it eventually did.

"I could see that the process of commoditization in computer hardware, which had been happening for thirty, forty years, was just going to continue," he said. "Now with any commodity, the two foremost elements of competitive advantage are price and distribution. And we could see that the Dell model, which is the most efficient model for distribution, was going to be successful. It seemed to me that as time went by, more and more of the market was going to be commoditized and thus susceptible to a direct selling approach.

"And then about that time prices started to come down throughout the industry, and more people became more familiar with the product, [and] the whole process of commoditization just increased. We did a survey back then about brand loyalty and switching costs, and we found that individual users would switch to a different brand if it saved them $50. As we kept doing those surveys, that switching cost declined;

THE DETECTIVE AND THE INVESTOR

> "On the contrary, Watson,
> you can see everything.
> You fail, however, to reason
> from what you see. You
> are too timid in drawing
> your inferences."
>
> —SHERLOCK HOLMES,
> "THE ADVENTURE OF THE
> BLUE CARBUNCLE"

people were placing more and more emphasis on price."[12]

I greatly admire Vadim for what he said next: "To be perfectly honest, I didn't get the stock right. I wrote positive things but I emphasized value more than growth and that was my mistake." When I reminded him that he accurately understood the Dell business model when many did not, he responded, "Sure, I got the business model right but I got the stock wrong. There are certain things in my life that I have gotten very right, and some not."

He was by no means alone. Most of those on Wall Street, if they were noticing Dell at all, were seeing a smart business model, and nothing more.

The Dell business model can be summarized rather easily.

- Selling direct to customers, thus eliminating the middle layer, creates a significant competitive advantage in pricing. From the beginning, Dell computers cost anywhere from 10 to 20 percent less than comparable models from other manufacturers.

- Lower prices translate into higher sales volume, which in turn translates into better margins.

- Assembling each computer as it is ordered eliminates standing inventory, which reduces both capital outlay and the threat of obsolescence.

What ultimately sparked the spectacular rise in stock price was Dell's low capital costs, and almost no one made the connection. Even those who saw and understood the business model missed the under-lying significance of lower cost of capital. Carrying our earlier analo-gy one step further, we can say that they were like good police detectives: They diligently uncovered all the evidence. Where they fell short was in analyzing and interpreting that evidence. To grasp the full significance of what was happening at Dell, and therefore what was about to happen, Wall Street needed a Great Detective.

The key was to be found in correctly understanding and interpret-ing a new concept that was just beginning to be talked about at almost the same time as Dell was starting to break out. That concept is known as "economic value added," or EVA. And it is the second half of the story.

Economic value added is one way of measuring a business's financial success. Like some other familiar measures, it is a snapshot of how a company is doing at a specific frozen moment. But, as its proponents argue, EVA's snapshot is a truer picture because it shows the full story, whereas some of those other measures are based on formal rules of accounting that tend to obscure pieces of the picture.

In simple terms, economic value added is a company's operating profit, after taxes, less the total cost of capital. It rests on a profound piece of common sense: Unless a company can earn more on its capi-tal than the capital costs, it is not really profitable.

That seems obvious enough, but what trips up many companies is an incomplete understanding of what "capital" really consists of. The most common conception is that it represents operating cash: the money raised by selling stocks and bonds. But very few know how much it actually costs to obtain that capital. The cost of bond capital is easy to understand: It's the interest the company must pay out to bondholders. But the cost of equity capital is a ghost; many managers, knowing they did not write out a check for it, have difficulty conceiv-ing of it as a "cost" at all.

Further, most managers know that capital also includes the money tied up in buildings, land, manufacturing equipment, rolling stock, and so forth. But certain other costs, such as inventory, are not always thought of as capital costs because they are not so designated in standard accounting methods. In the same way, items such as research and development and staff training are considered expenses by standard accounting, rather than as capital costs.

All of which led to a troublesome reality: Pre-EVA, many business owners did not know how much capital they had, because they were defining it in limited terms, and furthermore they did not know what it cost them to acquire it.

What EVA did was turn the spotlight on cost of capital and force managers to take it into account in the day-to-day running of the business.[13] For example, where some companies had been in the habit of loading up their warehouses with product near the end of the quarter because it made the quarterly numbers look good, with EVA they understood for the first time that that inventory represented capital, and so did the warehousing cost. Once they saw capital this way, it was easy to understand that they could actually be losing money, even though the traditional accounting statements did not reflect it.

> "To let the brain work without sufficient material is like racing an engine. It racks itself to pieces."
>
> —SHERLOCK HOLMES, "THE DEVIL'S FOOT"

This, then, is the significance of EVA as a management tool: It helped companies understand how to manage their operations in a way that would add economic value to the company. The significance of EVA as an investment tool was a bit less obvious. To understand it fully, we have to do a little arithmetic.

Calculating EVA requires that we answer two questions: (1) how much capital does a company have tied up, and (2) how much did that capital cost? The first is relatively easy to answer: Total the cost of all hard assets, factor in the cost of long-term investments such as R&D and training (even though accounting rules say you can't count them, count them anyway), then add in the dollar amount of working capital.

That's how much capital you have. But how much did it cost you? Again, the cost of hard assets, R&D, training programs—all those are fairly easy to pin down. Where it gets tricky is in calculating the true cost of working capital.

If it's borrowed capital (either a bank loan or bonds), the cost is the interest paid out, adjusted for taxes. But equity capital is a different matter altogether. As we mentioned earlier, most business owners have no idea what it costs to acquire money from shareholders. Some of them think of it as free money, when in truth it is anything but.

The best way for business owners to think about the cost of equity capital is to equate it with a term that you as an investor probably already know: opportunity cost. Owners need to consider that when investors buy shares in their company, the investors have certain expectations; if those expectations are not met, they will sell their shares and move their money elsewhere, with the ultimate result that share price declines and new money dries up. To prevent this, the company must provide the shareholders with at least the minimum expectation in terms of both appreciation and dividends. Calculating the cost of equity capital is the process of putting a real number to that expectation.

It would be much easier if "cost of equity capital" appeared as a line item on the balance sheet. But it does not. So we turn to the stock market itself. Historically, averaged over the long term, stocks have produced returns that are 6 percent higher than long-term government bonds. So the opportunity cost, the expectation cost, at any moment is the current long-term government bond rate plus six. For any specific company it may be higher or lower, if the company is especially risky or especially stable, but it must always be seen in comparison to other similar companies with similar levels of riskiness.

If a company has both debt and equity capital, the total rate must be a weighted average. For example, if 40 percent of the capital is debt and it costs 6 percent, then the debt portion costs .40 times 6, or 2.4; if the remaining 60 percent is equity that costs 12 percent, the cost of the equity portion is 7.2; adding the two numbers together would give you the total cost of capital, in this case 9.6.

Now we're ready for the arithmetic. Multiply the company's total capital by the rate of capital cost; that gives the real dollar cost of capital. Subtract that number from after-tax operating profit, and the answer is your EVA. Or, in a simple formula:

$$(\text{operating earnings} - \text{taxes}) - (\text{total capital} \times \text{cost of capital})$$

What you have uncovered is the amount of value that the company created during the period in question. It is what the shareholders most care about: the net cash return on their invested capital.

As an investor, with EVA you now have your hands on a very powerful piece of information. What we have learned in recent years is that stock price follows EVA more closely than any other traditional measuring stick. If a company's economic value added increases steadily, it is almost axiomatic that its stock price will rise. So if you find a company whose EVA is on an upward track, you have found a company whose stock is likely to rise significantly, far more likely than most other comparable companies.

And that is precisely what happened at Dell.

The Dell story is a case of one plus one equals three.

On one hand, we have the fact that Dell operates with a very low capital base, and, because of its minimal inventory (which is a form of capital), has a very low total cost of capital. The company's entire economic model is built on maintaining low capital costs.

On the other hand, we have the notion that cost of capital is a key ingredient in economic value added, and that economic value added is the truest measure of profitability and therefore the best predictor of future stock prices.

Taken together, those two ideas translate into something huge: When a company is earning at a rate considerably higher than its cost of capital, as Dell was, its stock is set to explode.

Of course, this insight is most valuable to the visionary few who figure it out first; after the connection becomes common knowledge, the stock price will have already adjusted.

In those critical early years of 1992 through 1994, most investors and analysts who followed computer companies were still operating on old assumptions. Conventional wisdom at that time held that the time to buy stocks of PC manufacturers was when the price was six times earnings, and the time to sell was when it hit twelve times earnings. That was the historical trading pattern, and few people saw any reason to question it. The simplistic view of most on Wall Street was, *This rule of thumb has worked reasonably well in the past, so why change it?*

The concept of economic value added hit the mainstream financial press in 1993, with a cover story in *Fortune*.[14] Anyone reading the article carefully would come away with an important message: If a company's cash earnings represent a high return on capital, that should bode well for its future stock price.

At that point, thoughtful investors could have reasoned their way to a profitable conclusion: *I should be looking for companies with strong earnings and low cost of capital.* And if they were looking at computer companies, they would have hit on Dell.

Let me say this another way, since it's so important: If you recognized that a company with high return on its cost of capital was going to increase in value, and if you understood that Dell's economic model successfully emphasized low capital costs, then you could conclude that its future value was going to be much higher than twelve times earnings. And you would maintain your holdings, while everyone else was selling.

At the time that the concept of economic value added was first being articulated, Dell's stock price had not yet begun its spectacular climb. Even when people started talking about EVA, many were unwilling to incorporate it into their analysis. So the few who were able to see that one plus one was going to become three profited significantly.

> **"We have not yet grasped the results which the reason alone can attain to."**
>
> —SHERLOCK HOLMES, "THE FIVE ORANGE PIPS"

One of those was Legg Mason's Bill Miller. He is the only mutual fund manager to have beaten the Standard & Poor's 500 Index over the last eleven straight years (1991–2001). Bill was named Morningstar's Domestic Equity Manager of the Year in 1998. The following year, analysts chose Bill as Morningstar's Investment Portfolio Manager of the Decade. Over the eleven-year time span, Legg Mason's Value Trust has achieved an annual return of 18.6 percent, placing Miller far ahead of most value-managers. The reason is because Bill is able to uncover value where others overlook the important details.

Bill purchased shares of Dell Computer in 1996. Worries over the cyclical downturn in personal computer sales caused the stocks of computer manufacturers to sell-off. At the time, Bill purchased Dell at about five times projected earnings. This was in line with the historical trading patterns of computer manufacturers. These stocks typically sold at between six and twelve times earnings. When Dell reached twelve times earnings, most value investors sold their shares, but Bill held on.

Like Warren Buffett, Bill Miller analyzes stocks as businesses and does not rely on historical trading patterns for decision-making, so he quickly could see that Dell Computer going forward was much different than it had been, historically. On a split-adjusted basis, Bill started buying Dell at $2 per share, figuring it was worth closer to $8 per share. He made this calculation based on his analysis of the company's growing cash flow and high return on capital—about 35 percent, according to his reckoning. But when the personal computer business recovered and Dell's revenues and earnings began to grow rapidly, he watched in amazement as, in 18 months, its return on capital went from 35 percent to over 230 percent, the highest in American history.

By 1999, Dell's stock price had far outpaced the stock market and other personal computer manufacturing stocks. Some investors began switching out of Dell and into Gateway. At the time, Gateway was selling at twelve times earnings and Dell was selling for a lofty thirty-five times earnings. Some questioned the wisdom of holding on to shares of Dell. But Bill looked at the two companies and held on to Dell stock. He saw that Gateway was earning a respectable 40 percent return on capital while Dell was continually earning over 200 percent on capital—five times higher than Gateway, yet Dell was only trading at three times Gateway's price earnings. Bill's initial investment in Dell became a "ten-bagger" for Value Trust shareholders.

Along about now you may be wondering how individual investors like yourself could have seen what was going to happen at Dell when so many investment professionals missed it. My answer is simple: by thinking like Sherlock Holmes. The Great Detective exhibited several qualities that today's investors could put to good use.

- He was able to view the situation objectively, resisting the sometimes dangerous pull of emotion.

- He took the time to do a thorough investigation, and kept at it until he had uncovered the tiniest details.

- When new evidence presented itself that contradicted an earlier theory, he considered it carefully.

- He maintained an immense intellectual file cabinet, with a vast store of knowledge on many topics that he applied to the situation at hand.

- And, most significant for our present purpose, he had an unparalleled ability to apply the power of his mind, to analyze the evidence and reason his way to a conclusion.

It is that reasoning capacity that sets Holmes apart from so many other fictional detectives. Clear reasoning would have revealed the true value of Dell, and so it is the one quality we will focus on here. The others are fairly obvious, and need only the briefest comment.

Calm, objective observation. In the heady early days of the high-tech bonanza, many people who should have known better were swept up in the frenzy. Without bothering to do their homework, they bought any and every high-tech stock that caught their eye, hoping, I suppose, that a few of them would hit the top.

Attention to detail. It isn't often that a big investment win falls into your lap; most of the time, they are uncovered by people willing to work their way through all the financial evidence, even the parts that are boring. The people who got a glimpse of what was going to happen at Dell had done a thorough investigation of its business model and economic structure. They also had read widely enough in the financial press to spot the early discussions about economic value added.

Openness to new information. Collecting information does you no good if you reject part of it because it contradicts what you already believe. Those who relied on a widely accepted rule of thumb about PC stocks (sell at twelve times earnings) may have done so because using shortcuts is easier, or perhaps because they simply could not accommodate the notion that anything else might be true. In any case, looking at Dell with a mind already made up turned out to be a serious mistake.

Breadth of knowledge. Sherlock made himself an authority on many things, never knowing when a small bit of knowledge would prove relevant to a case. Investors, too, will find that there is value in knowing more than one field. Looking back, we can say today that those in the best position to get an early fix on Dell were those who understood not only computer hardware but also traditional and nontraditional distribution mechanisms, the psychology of price sensitivity, the historic pattern of industry consolidation, the process of commoditization, and the inevitable growth of computer usage.

All these attributes are important, but all are essentially wasted if not used appropriately. In the aggregate, they provide the raw material for insightful analysis, but that analysis doesn't happen automatically. It's not a case of discovering one piece of information, then another, and another, and at the end finding the answer, like an Easter egg hunt. You get to the answer only by *thinking through* all you have observed.

It is that deliberate, careful, follow-it-to-the-end reasoning process that Sherlock Holmes can teach us.

Our stereotypical image of Sherlock Holmes is that of a tall, thin man with a large magnifying lens, on his hands and knees, examining carpet fibers or blades of grass. We know, because he often tells us (via Watson), how critical it is to gather in the smallest details. Yet the real work of solving the case comes from applying his logical mind to the analysis of those details.

Time and time again in the stories, we see Holmes sitting quietly in his Baker Street room, where, long legs stretched out in front of a warm fire and pipe in hand, he turns the facts over in his mind. Of a particularly complex case, he once wryly noted, "It is quite a three-pipe problem."[15] But the man Watson admiringly describes as a "reasoning machine" never fails to arrive at the answer.

I believe that were he presented with the Dell scenario, Holmes would have reached the correct conclusion.

- He would have been able to look beyond the conventional wisdom then prevalent about computer stocks.

- He would have taken the time to dig up the facts about Dell's business model, and would have recognized a company that was operating with very little capital and potentially very high profit.

- He would have made it his business to read widely and so would have been aware of the concept of economic value added, and would have incorporated it into his thinking.

- Most significant of all, he would have been able to lay the two tracks side by side—the theory of economic value added, plus the facts of what was occurring at Dell—and realize the significance of their synthesis. One plus one equals three.

> "When you follow two separate chains of thought ... you will find some point of intersection which should approximate to the truth."
>
> —SHERLOCK HOLMES, "THE DISAPPEARANCE OF LADY FRANCES CARFAX"

The Dell price surge was remarkable in many respects, not the least of which is that it caught so many by surprise. The only ones not surprised were those few who had the reasoning power to follow two separate ideas and find truth at the intersection.

Just as Conan Doyle learned his method of investigation by studying under Dr. Bell, it is my hope that investors will learn better analytical skills by studying the methods of Sherlock Holmes. But it would be a large mistake for you to limit your reading to Conan Doyle alone. You would deprive yourself not only of the pleasure of reading other great mystery stories but of the opportunity to sharpen your analytical skills by observing the investigative methods of other detectives who share some of Holmes's traits. One of the key features in the Holmes investigations is the forensic use of scientific advances; it captivated Doyle's Victorian-era readers, and it continues to enthrall readers to this day.

When the twentieth century arrived, there was already a growing fascination with the study of science. After Charles Darwin's *The Origin of Species* took root in the public mind, anyone who could help explain the mysteries of the physical world was held in high regard. We could say that when Conan Doyle teamed the medically trained Dr. John Watson with the research scientist Sherlock Holmes, his literary timing was perfect. As such, Doyle has always been credited with launching the tradition of the scientific sleuth within the genre of mystery and detective fiction.

Among the writers who sought to benefit from Sherlock Holmes's popularity, none was more successful than R. Austin Freeman (1862–1943). Born in London, the son of a tailor, Freeman trained first as a pharmacist, then graduated as a surgeon from Middlesex Hospital Medical College, where he taught for a short time. Like Doyle, Freeman also supplemented his medical income by writing short stories. With the introduction of Dr. John Thorndyke in 1907's *The Red Thumb Mark,* Freeman took over domination of British detective fiction from Conan Doyle, who had by this point already produced all his best work.

The Oxford Companion to Crime and Mystery Writing calls

Dr. Thorndyke the "first and greatest medicolegal detective of all time." He was, like Holmes, a man of many talents: a lawyer and forensic scientist as well as an authority on Egyptology, archaeology, ophthalmology, botany, and criminal jurisprudence. But what lent Dr. Thorndyke his high degree of expertise was Freeman's own willingness to dedicate himself to the actual study of scientific detection. Freeman developed and tested many of the techniques and devices Dr. Thorndyke used to solve crimes. He was always a modest man, but many around him, including the police, credit Freeman with discoveries in dust analysis and footprint preservation, as well as the examination of blood, hair, and fiber using X rays. Freeman's own scientific discoveries were later emulated by enforcement agencies worldwide.

In the United States, the role of the scientist-detective was first found in the writings of Arthur B. Reeve, whose character, Professor Craig Kennedy, was known as the American Sherlock Holmes. Professor Kennedy was a teaching professor of chemistry at Columbia University. As we might imagine, a detective who was a chemistry professor would have expertise in blood sampling, but what also made Professor Kennedy popular with readers was his use of many new technological devices, including the Dictaphone, the typewriter, and the X-ray machine. Today, the mastery of these devices might not be enough to qualify a detective as having special talents, but in the first third of the twentieth century they were highly rated scientific instruments familiar to only a very few people.

What unites the work of Doyle, Freeman, and Reeve is that each of their characters embraced the scientific method. Holmes, Dr. Thorndyke, and Professor Kennedy were not classified as mere detectives but became known as scientific heroes. The scientific hero as detective has continued to capture readers' interest ever since.

Popular writers who later followed the Doyle-Freeman-Reeve framework include Lawrence G. Blochman, Patricia Cornwell, and Kathy Reichs. Blochman's detective, Dr. Daniel Webster Coffee, works as a pathologist at a Midwestern hospital; Cornwell's Dr. Kay Scarpetta is the chief medical examiner for the Commonwealth of Virginia. Kathy Reichs, herself a forensic anthropologist for North Carolina's office of the chief medical examiner and for the province of Quebec, has given a high level of authenticity to her detective-scientist, Temperance Brennan.

Despite the highest regard I have for these writers and their detectives, there is something extraordinary about the treasure-chest of detective stories that Conan Doyle gave to the world. When I think back on the adventures of Dr. Watson and Sherlock Holmes, I am struck most by *The Adventure of the Abbey Grange*—not because it was Doyle's best story, but because of what Holmes had promised to deliver. "At present I am, as you know, fairly busy," said Holmes, "but I propose to devote my declining years to the composition of a textbook which shall focus the whole part of detection into one volume."

Of course, Holmes never wrote that book. Instead, he wrote something quite different. In his later years Holmes retired to the countryside and took up a new hobby, beekeeping, eventually writing a how-to manual on the subject. As he proudly told Watson, "Here is the fruit of my leisured ease, the magnum opus of my latter years, *Practical Handbook of Bee Culture, with Some Observations upon the Segregation of the Queen*. Alone I did it. Behold the fruit of pensive nights and laborious days when I watched the little working gangs as once I watched the criminal world of London."[16] It was here, while watching his bees and contemplating his long career, that Sherlock Holmes crossed paths with a remarkable young woman who eventually became his wife.

Wife? The "real" Sherlock was a lifelong bachelor, and never married. True. But the character presented in a fascinating modern series by Edgar Award–winning author Laurie King moved in a different direction.

Laurie's Sherlock first appeared in 1994, in *The Beekeeeper's Apprentice: On the Segregation of the Queen*. It is not the detection textbook

Sherlock promised to write someday, but it captures perfectly the lessons that a student of the Great Detective might be privileged to learn.

The Beekeeper's Apprentice begins in 1915 with a retired Sherlock Holmes engaged in a reclusive study of honeybee behavior on the Sussex Downs. It's there that he stumbles over Miss Mary Russell, a confident fifteen-year-old girl whose mental acuity matches his own. As their friendship grows, Holmes engages Mary in a sort of informal tutorial in the art and science of detection. Each day brings a new lesson, and it isn't long before the pleasure of teaching stimulates Holmes to drop his self-imposed retirement and set off with Russell (as he always calls her) on a series of exciting adventures, portrayed in six books so far.

I asked Laurie why she decided to write a book about Sherlock Holmes; surely it must have been intimidating to recreate such a famous character. Her answer surprised me. "I think the reason I didn't feel intimidated," she explained, "is that in my mind I was not writing a book about Sherlock Holmes. Rather I was writing a book about Mary Russell. . . . I wanted to write about the interaction between the two of them. You know, Mary has the same type of brain as Holmes. Although there are essential differences between the two—he is a man and she is a woman—the pleasure I got from writing came from matching their basic mental similarities."[17]

The strength of Laurie's books, in my view, is that readers who have become comfortable with Doyle's treatment of Sherlock Holmes can step easily and comfortably into these new adventures. When Holmes and Russell set out to solve a case, we never once feel that someone unqualified has written the story. And, most important for our purposes, those who tag along with King's Holmes and Russell continually receive the same solid advice on investigative methods they would expect from Conan Doyle.

Although she says that her books are more about Russell than Holmes, still I believe that Laurie has an uncanny knack for capturing Holmes's essence. One quality that we have noted is Sherlock's ability to set aside his emotions and think analytically about a situation. "I think Holmes has the capability of making himself cold and reasoning," Laurie said, and she certainly presents him that way in *The Beekeeper's Apprentice*. At one point Holmes admonishes Russell, "A quick mind is worthless unless you can control the emotions with it as well."[18] Later, he is at it again: "Russell," he says, "I have already told you that a mind which cannot control its body's emotional reactions is no mind worth having."[19]

I asked Laurie about Holmes's investigative methods and reasoning process. Clearly, she explained, "Holmes has an attention for detail. That is definitely a part of Holmes in Conan Doyle's book and it is certainly in mine as well." He also emphasizes the essential requirement of gathering facts, she said. Holmes abhors guessing and is only satisfied by the accumulation of facts, facts, and more facts. She reminded me that in one of the first exchanges between Holmes and Russell, the detective turns to the young girl and says, "Incidentally, I hope you do not make a habit of guessing. Guessing is a weakness brought on by indolence and should never be confused with intuition."[20]

One of Holmes's mental traits that Laurie especially appreciates is his willingness to examine different hypotheses. "It is very difficult to work around a full-fledged hypothesis and completely discard it if it does not seem to fit," said Laurie. "Working from fact, you build a hypothesis, and if there is some major fact that does not fit, you discard the hypothesis and go for another. Most people, certainly ones who are involved in professional investigation, tend to form a hypothesis early on and then try to force the facts to it.

"We become very comfortable with our structures, and then we attach things to [them]," she said. "It takes a mind like Holmes—and I think Mary reflects this in the book—to have the ability to remove one element from the whole. Completely remove that one fact from your mental picture and look at it absolutely and objectively. It is something I don't think most people can do. Most of us depend very heavily on the surrounding structure. The ability to look at things as they are and not fit them into a preconceived notion of how they should be—that's rare."

Laurie King did not start out as a big Sherlock Holmes fan. She barely recalls reading the mystery stories in high school. It wasn't until she began thinking about the character of Mary Russell that she began reading her way through all of Doyle's short stories and novels. "Coming into the Holmes stories as an adult is quite an interesting experience," she said. "One thing I came to appreciate was the fact that Holmes runs on passion. These are not just adventure stories, but rather they are stories about a man who is passionate about justice and setting the world right. The attraction to Sherlock Holmes these past one hundred years is the amalgam of a brilliantly rational mind combined with a deep passion to ensure that justice prevails, which helps drive his investigative process."

Is it possible to condense the Holmes method into a solid guideline that will work for investors trying to make good decisions as well as it works for detectives solving mysteries? "It only works if you're willing to listen to every word and pay attention to every detail," says Laurie. "The Holmesian style of investigation first looks at the broad spectrum, then lists the details, and then takes note of minute changes in the crime scene. It is a forensic way of thinking about things, but if you are going to mimic [his] detective methods, it is very necessary."

For investors who wish to improve their financial results, we can now combine the lessons of Sherlock Holmes with the methods of Auguste Dupin and begin to see clearly how these two Great Detectives can aid our investment process. But our discovery is not concluded. There is still one more Great Detective to examine, one who will show us that the art of detection is more than just cigar ash and footprints.

CHAPTER SIX

G. K. Chesterton and Father Brown

On a passenger train making its way through the English country-side from a North coast seaport toward London, a Frenchman in earnest pursuit of one particular man watches all the passengers care-fully, but no one watches him, for he has mastered the trick of being inconspicuous.

This is Aristide Valentin, head of the Paris police, the most famous investigator in Europe. The man he seeks is none other than Hercule Flambeau, the French jewel thief whose international exploits have made him wealthy, famous, and in many circles admired for his brazen cleverness.

But on the train, unobtrusively watching for Flambeau, Valentin is distracted by the behavior of a very short Catholic priest with "a face as round and dull as a Norfolk dumpling."[1] The priest's clumsy actions attract everyone's attention. He has several brown paper parcels, which he is quite incapable of collecting. He has a large, shabby umbrella, which constantly falls on the floor. He doesn't seem to know which is the right end of his return ticket. And most distressing to the French policeman, he doesn't seem to know how to keep quiet, telling anyone who will listen that one of his brown paper parcels contains a very valuable piece of silver with blue stones.

When the train reaches London, however, Valentin quickly forgets the clumsy little priest, so intent is he on tracking the thief Flambeau. He has no real idea of Flambeau's destination in London, but has one thing in his favor: Flambeau is well over six feet, the one thing this master of disguise cannot hide.

Valentin's approach is simple and, in the end, brilliant. Since he has no notion which way Flambeau will move through the big city, he decides to search unconventionally. "Instead of going to the right places, he systematically went to the wrong places" on the off chance that "any oddity that caught the eye of the pursuer might be the same that had caught the eye of the pursued."

On that theory, Valentin stops, without quite knowing why, in front of a restaurant that has attracted his attention on account of its unusual entry steps. Seated inside, he orders a cup of coffee and spoons in some sugar. At that point, he encounters the first of what will turn out to be a chain of bizarre events.

The very ordinary sugar bowl contains salt, and the saltcellar contains sugar. Inquiring of the waiter and the manager, he learns this was not the first strange event of the day: Two clergymen had sat at this same table earlier, and one of them had thrown a half-empty cup of soup at the wall; the stain is still there.

Two clergymen? The city is full of clergymen, as a major religious conference is taking place. Still, any unusual behavior is worth following, and it *could* have been Flambeau. *So,* Valentin inquires, *which way did they go?* Around the corner into Carstairs Street.

In that street, the police chief passes a greengrocer's stand where the signs for oranges and nuts have been switched, and where the proprietor is still fuming over a recent incident in which a parson had knocked over his bin of apples, sending them rolling into the street. A parson? The coincidences are beginning to pile up.

Valentin grabs two local constables and sets off on the same track, urging them to be alert for the next unusual thing. He finds it hours later, in a restaurant with a broken window. From the waiter, he learns the full story. "Two of those foreign parsons that are running about" had had a quiet lunch, and had overpaid their bill. When he called this to their attention, two strange things happened: He himself looked again at the bill and saw it had been altered to a much higher amount, and the shorter of the two parsons commented, "Sorry to confuse your accounts, but it'll pay for the window." When the waiter asked which window, the priest said, "the one I'm going to break," at which point, as the waiter described it, he "smashed that blessed pane with his umbrella."

Valentin, his hopes building, continues to follow the path of the two clergymen. It leads him next to a candy shop, where the attendant tells him not to worry, she has already shipped off the brown paper parcel that the short priest had asked her about.

Finally, the trail ends in a public park, where Valentin spots two figures walking together in the distance: Two men, one short and one tall, both wearing clerical garb. One is undeniably Flambeau, and the other, to Valentin's astonishment, is the dumpy little priest from the train. The policemen follow at a distance, and then, when the two priests sit on a bench to continue their conversation, draw close enough to listen.

I've made a fool of myself in front of these British constables, Valentin thinks to himself. *These really are priests, talking about God, the church, and the incorruptible heavens.* But then suddenly the conversation takes an abrupt left turn, and the tall priest demands that his companion hand over the sapphire cross.

Valentin is astonished by what happens next. It turns out the short priest has suspected all along that the tall priest was not a priest at all but a criminal. He watched the impostor switch the parcel containing the cross for another containing unimportant items, switched them back again, cleverly arranged for the real cross to be shipped to safety by the candy store clerk, and left an unmissable trail for the police to follow. He even knew, without turning around, that the police were nearby, hiding behind a tree and listening to every word, ready to arrest the great Flambeau.

The story is "The Blue Cross," and in it a new Great Detective is introduced to the world: the endearing Father Brown, creation of the amazingly prolific English writer G. K. Chesterton.

In this first Father Brown story, Chesterton incorporates many of the features that later came to define his style of writing detective fiction, and the qualities that define his detective. Because it thus serves us as such a good template for understanding Father Brown, we will spend some time digging into the story.

Perhaps the single most significant quality about Father Brown is his deep and compassionate understanding of human nature. It is both the reason for and the result of his vocation, and it is also, not incidentally, the quality that leads him to find answers to puzzling mysteries while others are walking the wrong path.

This gift of understanding goes by many names. Today we might call it psychology, and indeed Father Brown himself sometimes uses that term. Some might call it intuition, and in fact they are related, although I believe intuition is not a synonym for empathy but its result. However, here in "The Blue Cross" we see this understanding in its purest form: Father Brown's work as a priest has brought him into intimate contact with people of all sorts, and from them he has learned a great deal about humanity.

He knew, for instance, that Flambeau was a criminal and not a priest because he noticed "that little bulge up the sleeve where you people have the spiked bracelet." Now I confess I don't know exactly what a spiked bracelet was—presumably some hidden weapon comparable to brass knuckles—but Father Brown surely knew. And he knew because in the course of his ministry he had crossed paths with thieves, from whom he had learned about this bracelet as well as several other professional secrets. All this knowledge astonished Flambeau when Father Brown revealed it. "Oh, one gets to know, you know. We can't help being priests. People come and tell us these things."

More important than this kind of esoteric knowledge, however, is that Father Brown's work has taught him much about the human soul. His vocation puts him smack in the midst of his parishioners' most desperate hours. He knows, from hearing confessions and ministering in times of trouble, how people act when they have done something wrong. From observing a person's behavior—facial expressions, way of walking and talking, general demeanor—he can tell much about that person. In a word, he can see inside someone's heart and mind, and form a clear impression about character. He is never wrong.

His feats of detection have their roots in this knowledge of human nature, which comes from two sources: his years in the confessional, and his own self-awareness. What makes Father Brown truly exceptional is that he acknowledges the capacity for evildoing in himself. In "The Hammer of God" he says, "I am a man and therefore have all devils in my heart."

Because of this compassionate understanding of human weakness, from both within and without, he can see into the darkest corners of the human heart. This ability to identify with the criminal, to feel what he is feeling, is what leads him to find the identity of the criminal—even, sometimes, to predict the crime, for he knows the point at which human emotions such as fear or jealousy tip over from acceptable expression into crime. Even then, he believes in the inherent goodness of mankind, and sets the redemption of the wrongdoer as his main goal.

Over and over in the stories, we see the gentle priest quietly observe someone involved in the mysterious situation and reach a conclusion about that person's role in a way that seems magical to others on the scene. To Father Brown it is not magical at all: It is plain as day.

He does not, however, as some other famous detectives might, bring the spotlight onto himself in announcing his conclusions. Quite the opposite: He is always quiet, soft-spoken, and humble. Indeed, his humility, while genuine, serves as his disguise. On the train he seems clumsy and befuddled, constantly dropping his packages and umbrella, but he is actually keenly aware of what is happening with Flambeau. This unobtrusive style serves him well in future cases: As a nondescript village priest, the sort of person easily overlooked, he can work in the background without attracting much attention.

> **Those who are able to understand human behavior are in the best position to predict future actions. This is also true in markets, which are, let us not forget, composed of human beings.**

In "The Blue Cross," Flambeau makes one grievous mistake, and it confirms for Father Brown that he is not a priest, despite his otherwise convincing disguise. In their conversation on the park bench, the jewel thief argues that reason has no place in religion. Quite the contrary, Father Brown counters, "God himself is bound by reason." And when Flambeau's true identity is revealed, we see that it was this specious argument that sealed his fate. "You attacked reason," said Father Brown. "It's bad theology."

This belief in the power of reason is a critical part of Father Brown's essence. It would be a mistake for us to think of him as a kind of religious mystic who happens upon the truth through divine intervention. Rather, he is a mortal human being with a keen mind and a well-developed sense of observation, both of which are brought to bear in the solution of future mysteries.

And yet we also see here the companion side of his unique method: He always allows for an alternative explanation. After observing all the concrete facts, and incorporating the less tangible aspects that come from his empathetic understanding of human nature, he is willing to keep open the possibility that the obvious conclusion is wrong, that something else is at work. It is a key to his ability to solve mysteries: knowing that things may not be what they seem, that often the truth is to be found in some other explanation.

In "The Blue Cross," this idea is presented in subtle ways. To catch the eye of the police, Father Brown constructs a trail of bizarre actions. He knows

In all areas of life, it useful to recall that things are not always what they seem.

instinctively that when things are surprising, they attract attention, and with keen attention, the truth is more likely to be uncovered. Soup thrown against a wall and a window deliberately broken might signal nothing more than a crazy person wandering the streets of London. But perhaps there is more to it, if those on the scene are willing to consider an alternative explanation.

In this story, it is Valentin who must keep an open mind, and he does so brilliantly. In the stories to come, it is usually Father Brown who is the first to see that things are not what they seem, that some other explanation should be considered.

"The Blue Cross" is important for Father Brown's future in another way, too, as it introduces two men who will play a significant role in the priest's life and in future stories. The thief Flambeau, after several other daring escapades, is persuaded by the little priest to give up the life of crime; in later life he becomes a private investigator who works with police agencies and frequently teams up with his old friend the priest. And Valentin, the famous detective, turns to crime and nearly gets away with murder.

That kind of twist—the policeman becomes a murderer, the thief becomes a law-abiding citizen—is pure Chesterton. We can't know if he planned it that way from the beginning, but a writer who so relished paradox and irony must have quickly seen the possibilities of flipping his characters. For one thing, it gave Father Brown a rich opportunity to do what he does best and cares about most: saving souls.

This first Father Brown story is also of interest because of what it reveals about its author. G. K. Chesterton had a remarkable career as a writer, as we will see shortly. But it is specifically as a writer of detective stories that his contributions are really important, and we begin to see them in "The Blue Cross."

Before Chesterton, most detective fiction was purely about the elements of the puzzle. The crime occurs, the police are baffled, the detective solves the mystery. We are told little about the detective's personal life, and certainly few earlier authors would waste time describing the landscape.

With Chesterton, all that changed. As much as we admire the intricacy of his plots, and the cleverness of his priest/detective, we are also struck by the liveliness of Chesterton's writing style. We watch with delight as the police follow the trail of weird happenings; not only is it clever, as the resolution of the mystery reveals, it is also highly entertaining to read. We can see, because Chesterton describes it so vividly, the exasperation of the greengrocer chasing his apples down the street, the dismay of the restaurateur with soup splashed on his wall, and the puzzlement of an honest waiter who finds himself with too much money. And we grin with joy when the priest says, *This will pay for the window I'm about to break.* I can see that scene as clearly as if I were watching a movie, so graphically is it told.

Chesterton seduces us with his beautiful writing into accepting a highly unlikely coincidence. We might resist believing that Valentin somehow just happened upon the restaurant that was the start of the priests' trail, if Chesterton had not first told us: "The most incredible thing about miracles is that they happen. A few clouds in heaven do come together into the staring shape of one human eye . . . and a man named Williams does quite accidentally murder a man named Williamson. In short, there is in life an element of elfin coincidence which people reckoning on the prosaic may perpetually miss."

With the eye of a poet (which he was), Chesterton enriches his stories with lyrical portraits of the environment. Here is the opening of "The Blue Cross": "Between the silver ribbon of morning and the green glittering ribbon of sea, the boat touched Harwich and let loose a swarm of folk like flies."

These bits of poetry are sprinkled throughout the stories, never overdone but always memorable for their beauty. In "The Secret of Father Brown," for instance, he writes: "It was dusk turning to dark, and as all that mountain air sharpens suddenly after sunset, a small stove stood on the flagstones, glowing with red eyes like a goblin." I'm relatively certain that if Sherlock Holmes were sitting on an outdoor patio in the early evening, there would be no stove with eyes like a goblin.

Nor would Edgar Allan Poe, the poet of the macabre, describe a coach trip in Italian hill country this way: "The white road climbed like a white cat; it was flung round far-off headlands like a lasso. And yet however high they went, the desert still blossomed. . . . It was like a Dutch tulip garden, blown to the stars with dynamite."[2]

One other point worth noting here: Chesterton is not afraid of small loose ends. We never are told how Flambeau managed to escape Valentin's notice on the ship or the train. We never know for sure how he and Father Brown first made a connection. But we are still satisfied with the story, for Chesterton treats his readers with respect. All the important information is presented. There are no unreasonable explanations, no preposterous last-minute surprises. He does not gather all the principals in the drawing room for a long summary by the detective, as so many other mystery authors have done. He simply tells his story, and in the process permits us the pleasure of watching his remarkable detective moving through the world in his unique way, solving mysteries and saving souls.

Gilbert Keith Chesterton was born in London in 1874 and died in 1936, which makes him an approximate contemporary of Arthur Conan Doyle (1859–1930). It is one of the few ways the two are alike.

It was apparent early on that Chesterton possessed a gifted mind. When his mother visited his schoolmaster to ask about her seventeen-year-old son's progress and solicit advice for his future, he told her, "Six feet of genius. Cherish him, Mrs. Chesterton, cherish him."[3] At a time when his friends moved on to Oxford or Cambridge, the six-foot genius went instead to art school and attended lectures in English literature at University College. When writing about this period in his life in his *Autobiography*, Chesterton called the chapter "How to Be a Lunatic."[4]

He did indeed have a gift for drawing, but he never became a professional artist. Instead, while still in school, he found what would ultimately become his calling. As is so often the case, it was essentially an accident.

An art-school friend, the son of a publisher, arranged for Chesterton to write reviews of books on art for a monthly magazine called *The Bookman*. As Chesterton himself later recounted, "Having entirely failed to learn how to draw or paint, I tossed off easily enough some criticisms of the weaker points of Rubens or the misdirected talents of Tintoretto. I had discovered the easiest of professions, which I have pursued ever since."[5] He meant writing literary criticism, and indeed Chesterton later gave us some of the most insightful and best-written critiques of literature in the English language. But that is only one side of this very prolific writer.

For the next forty years, he produced an amazing number of works in an astonishingly wide array of fields. A bibliography listing all his works goes on for many pages. Perhaps the best way to appreciate Chesterton's enormous output is to note the description of him in the Literature Resource Center, an electronic database created by librarians. In this database, each author listing starts with a very brief sketch, and one of the items in that sketch is genre. Here's what is listed under "genre" for Chesterton: "short stories, autobiography, biography, historical works, novels, plays, fantasy fiction, epics, journalism, literary criticism, essays." They forgot one: He also wrote poetry. The man known in his lifetime and ever since as simply GKC packed a great deal of brilliant writing into his sixty-two years.

It is interesting to note that Chesterton, unlike many writers now considered geniuses, was recognized even in his own lifetime for his many literary successes. His contemporaries in British literary circles called him a "reincarnation of Samuel Johnson," and George Bernard Shaw, the only other literary figure then recognized by his initials, said Chesterton was "a man of colossal genius."

He was well known about town for his wit. Someone once asked him that old question: If he were stranded on a desert island and could have only one book, which would it be? Without hesitation, he answered, *"Robertson's Guide to Practical Shipbuilding."* The American writer Christopher Morley, a contemporary of Chesterton, noted that "One of Chesterton's best pleasantries was his remark on the so-called Emancipation of Women. 'Twenty million young woman rose to their feet with the cry, We will not be dictated to: and proceeded to become stenographers.' "[6]

The famous Chesterton wit sprung from the exuberance and high spirits that characterized his entire life. Reading about him, I found myself captivated by this letter he wrote to a friend, deliriously announcing that the young woman with whom he had fallen in love at first sight had agreed to marry him:[7]

THE DETECTIVE AND THE INVESTOR

Dear Mildred,

On rising this morning, I carefully washed my boots in hot water and blacked my face. Then assuming my coat with graceful ease and with the tails in front, I descended to breakfast, where I gaily poured the coffee on the sardines and put my hat on the fire to boil. These activities will give you some idea of my frame of mind. My family, observing me leave the house by way of the chimney, and take the fender with me under one arm, thought I must have something on my mind. So I had.

My friend, I am engaged.

He was, of course, poking fun at himself, but in fact Chesterton was famously absentminded. He often traveled about England giving lectures, and just as often forgot where he was or where he was going. So his wife was not at all surprised to receive this telegram from him one day: "Am in Market Harborough. Where ought I to be?" Her response: "Home." She later told Chesterton's biographer that it was "easier to get him home and start him off again."[8]

His flamboyant personality was matched in his later years by his physical proportions. He reportedly weighed over three hundred pounds, and was fond of wearing large capes and greatcoats that made him seem even more monumental in size. One oft-told story is that once he and his pal G. B. Shaw met on the street and Chesterton remarked to his thin friend, "I see there's been a famine in the land." To which Shaw calmly replied, "Yes, and now I see what caused it."[9]

One of the most engaging portraits of Chesterton comes from Patrick Braybrooke, who was a relative of GKC and a frequent guest in his home. In his small biography, *Gilbert Keith Chesterton*, Braybrooke mostly addresses Chesterton's literary reputation, but includes near the end a chapter entitled "Mr. Chesterton at Home."[10] Here we find charming and genuine glimpses of the famous writer, from one who knew him well.

When I first knew Chesterton he was living in a flat in Battersea. Here . . . the inhabitants of that part of London began to realize they had a great man in their midst, and grew accustomed to seeing a romantic figure in a cloak and slouch hat hail a hansom and drive off to Fleet Street.

He was headed for Fleet Street, where most of Britain's newspapers have their offices, because he was working primarily as a journalist, in the days, as Braybrooke says, "when he was becoming famous." Later, after their marriage, Chesterton and Frances made their home in Beaconsfield, in the English countryside. Braybrooke visited them often.

If there is one thing that is characteristic of Chesterton, it is that he always seems genuinely pleased to see you. Many people say they are pleased to see you, yet at the same time there is the uncomfortable feeling that they would be much more pleased to see you leaving. This is not the case with Chesterton; he has the happy advantage of making you feel that he really is glad that you have come to his home. . . .

I have often and often sat at his table. He talks incessantly. There is no subject upon which he has not something worthwhile to say. His memory is remarkable; he can quote poet after poet, or compose a poem on anything that crops up at the table.

Mr. Braybrooke is particularly eloquent about Chesterton's affinity for art; the interest that had drawn the young man to art school instead of a more traditional university apparently never left him.

Chesterton is a remarkably clever artist. I would solemnly warn anyone who does not like his books defaced not to lend them to Chesterton. He will not cut them, he will not leave them out in the sun, he will not scorch them in front of the fire, but he will draw

143

pictures on them. I have looked through many books at his home, and nearly all of them have sketches in them.

Knowing that readers are always interested in how authors go about their work, Mr. Braybrooke gives us a little look inside Chesterton's routine.

Chesterton does nearly all his work in his little study, a sanctum littered with innumerable manuscripts. . . . It is remarkable the amount of work that he gets through. He has masses of correspondence, he has articles to write, books to get ready for press, and yet he finds time to help in local theatricals and to give lectures in places as wide apart as Oxford and America, and what is wider in every way than those two places?

At the end of this short chapter, Mr. Braybrooke gives us a summary view of what a visitor to Chesterton's home would find.

What are the general impressions that a stranger visiting Chesterton would get? He would, I think, be impressed by his genial kindliness; he would be amazed by his extraordinary powers of memory and the depths of his reading; he would be gratified by the interest that Chesterton displays in him.

How splendid it must have been to visit a man who could make up a poem on any topic that came up at dinner, a man who never hesitated to sit down on the floor with children and draw pictures for them, a man who laughed easily and often and whose laugh was, according to his kinsman, "like a clap of thunder that suddenly startles the echoes in the valley."

Such zest for life is certainly wonderful to behold. Yet there was much more to G. K. Chesterton than quick repartee, amusing draw-ings, and spur-of-the-moment poetry. He was also a person of great depth and compassion, with a highly developed sense of social justice. Much of his work reflected his religious and political beliefs and his efforts to bring about social changes that embodied them. Even the Father Brown stories, entertaining puzzles though they are, turn on questions of justice and morality.

In "The Blue Cross," Flambeau, amazed that he has been found out by a clergyman rather than a policeman, makes a sneering reference to a "celibate simpleton." Few of Chesterton's readers at the time knew the story behind that remark.

Some six years before writing the first Father Brown story, Chester-ton had been invited to give a lecture (a common form of pre-televi-sion entertainment) in Yorkshire and was guest of honor at a dinner afterward at the home of a friend. At this dinner, in what he later described as a "very accidental meeting," he first made the acquain-tance of Father John O'Connor, a local Catholic priest. The following morning, the two men went for a walk, and, in Chesterton's words, "after a few hours talk on the moors, it was a new friend whom I intro-duced to my old friends at journey's end."[11]

Not long after this, the two friends were again engaged in their favorite activity—walking together and discussing many things—when Chesterton happened to mention a new writing project that involved "rather sordid social questions of vice and crime." Father O'Connor, to Chesterton's great surprise, pointed out that his descrip-tions of these "perverted practices" were inaccurate. "It was a curious experience," Chesterton later recalled, "to find that this quiet and pleas-ant celibate had plumbed those abysses far deeper than I. I had not imagined that the world could hold such horrors."[12]

When they returned to the home at which both men were guests, they found there two young students from Cambridge and fell into conversation with them. The talk ranged from music to landscape, and then "deepened into a discussion on matters more philosophical and moral." After a time Father O'Connor left the room and one of the two students made a remark about people who are "all shut up in a sort of cloister and don't know anything about the real evil in the world."[13]

Chesterton tells what happened next.

> To me, still almost shivering with the appallingly practical facts of which the priest had warned me, this comment came with such a colossal and crushing irony that I nearly burst into a loud harsh laugh in the drawing room. For I knew perfectly well that . . . these two Cambridge gentlemen (luckily for them) knew about as much of real evil as two babies in the same perambulator.
>
> And there sprung up in my mind the vague idea of making some artistic use of these comic yet tragic cross purposes; and constructing a comedy in which a priest should appear to know nothing and in fact know more about crime than the criminals.[14]

And that, Chesterton tells us, is "how the first notion of this detective comedy came into my mind."[15]

In his writings, Chesterton often used the concept of paradox to make his point—a statement that seemed to contradict common sense and yet was both true and significant, often because of the very contradictory nature. Today's literary critics and historians often call him a "master of paradox." His own description of Father Brown is a fine example:

> In Father Brown, it was the chief feature to be featureless. The point of him was to appear pointless; and one might say that his conspicuous quality was not being conspicuous. His commonplace

exterior was meant to contrast with his unsuspected vigilance and intelligence; and that being so, of course I made his appearance shabby and shapeless, his face round and expressionless, his manners clumsy, and so on.[16]

In defense of his friend, however, Chesterton is quick to point out that Father Brown resembled Father O'Connor only in their "inner intellectual qualities"; the real man was "not shabby but rather neat; not clumsy but very delicate and dexterous."[17]

"I permitted myself the grave liberty of taking my friend and knocking him about," Chesterton added; "beating his hat and umbrella shapeless, untidying his clothes, punching his intelligent countenance into a condition of pudding-faced fatuity, and generally disguising Father O'Connor as Father Brown. The disguise, as I have said, was a deliberate piece of fiction, meant to bring out or accentuate the contrast that was the point of the comedy."[18]

It's rather interesting to speculate on why Chesterton called his mysteries "comedies." It may have been an instance of his own self-deprecating way of referring to himself and his work; he once described the Father Brown stories as "the interminable series of tales with which I have afflicted the world."[19] I conclude that he used the term in the Shakespearean or Greek sense, to mean that which is not a tragedy. But let us not get sidetracked. The more important point for us to take away is the contrast between outward appearance and inner strengths, a deliberate choice by the author to strengthen his notion that a "celibate simpleton" understood more of the world and its inhabitants than those who professed to.

It was perhaps inevitable that Chesterton, who was himself a huge fan of detective stories and usually had one or two stuffed in the pockets of his coat, would turn to writing them. As a matter of fact, he had written some detective stories earlier, even before he knew Father O'Connor. Most of those have, however, been lost in the tide of affection for the Father Brown stories.

Although he always incorporated in the stories his own strong ideas on morality and social justice, Chesterton never hid the fact that he wrote them mostly for the money. Like Conan Doyle before him, he dashed the stories off hurriedly to satisfy magazine publishers' pleas, using the fees to finance his own political newspaper, *G. K.'s Weekly.* It is a great testament to Chesterton's enormous talent as a writer that even when churning out what today we would call potboilers, the work he produced was of such lasting quality.

GKC's Father Brown stories appeared over the course of three decades, from 1910 to 1935, coming out one by one in popular magazines of the day. Eventually, they were collected into five books: *The Innocence of Father Brown* (1911), *The Wisdom of Father Brown* (1914), *The Incredulity of Father Brown* (1926), *The Secret of Father Brown* (1927), and *The Scandal of Father Brown* (1935). During that period, the detective story as we know it today had taken permanent shape, a distinct genre with established conventions, and much of the credit for this belongs to G. K. Chesterton.

Even during his lifetime, Chesterton's influence on British mystery fiction was huge and widely acknowledged. When Anthony Berkeley founded the Detection Club in 1928, it was Chesterton, not Conan Doyle, who became its first president, a position he held until his death.

Chesterton, you will remember, had a fine reputation as a literary critic, and so it is not surprising that he held strong views on what constituted good mystery writing. It was he who insisted resolutely that mystery authors should be fair with readers rather than try to trick them, and that obfuscation is a poor substitute for a good plot. In a 1925 essay called "How to Write a Detective Story,"[20] he insisted:

The first and fundamental principle is that the aim of a mystery story is not darkness but light. The story is written for the moment when the reader does understand, not merely for the many preliminary moments when he does not understand. Most bad detective stories are bad because they fail on this point. The writers have a strange notion that it is their business to baffle the reader; and that so long as they baffle him it does not matter if they disappoint him.

The second great principle is that the soul of detective fiction is not complexity but simplicity. The secret may appear complex, but it must be simple; and in this also it is a symbol of higher mysteries. The writer is there to explain the mystery; but he ought not be needed to explain the explanation. The explanation should explain itself.

As early as 1901, long before the first Father Brown stories, Chesterton defended detective fiction vigorously against his literary contemporaries who considered it inconsequential. In an essay called "A Defence of Detective Stories," he eloquently makes two important points about the value of this type of popular fiction.[21] First, that mysteries make poetry out of ordinary events. A fan of detective stories who was also a poet, Chesterton wrote that detective fiction was "a satisfying medium of expression, where the most mundane item may become a vital clue to a crime or the most casual phrase an insight into the mind of a murderer." Second, he argued that the hero of detective fiction, who engages in a solitary search for truth on behalf of all, symbolizes the "ideals of respectability and goodness." The detective is thus "the agent of social justice . . . the original and poetic figure." Detective fiction, Chesterton summarized, presents both "the poetry of the everyday and the splendid loneliness of the guardian of the law."

Although Father Brown is vastly different in almost every possible way from Sherlock Holmes, Chesterton admired Conan Doyle and took many opportunities to say so publicly, both in his essays and in his own detective stories. One telling example: The collection of

Chesterton essays published in book form as *A Handful of Authors* features his thoughts on many important writers, from Shakespeare, Shelley, and Ibsen, to Oscar Wilde and Mark Twain. Included among them are two brief essays on Sherlock Holmes—a fictional character.

Sometimes he pokes gentle fun at Conan Doyle. In an early, pre–Father Brown story, Chesterton's detective muses, "How facts obscure the truth. I may be silly—in fact, I'm off my head—but I never could believe in that man—what's his name, in those capital stories?—Sherlock Holmes. Every detail points to something, certainly but generally to the wrong thing. Facts point in all directions, it seems to me, like the thousands of twigs on a tree."[22]

At the same time, he quite freely expresses his admiration. In "The Shadow of the Shark" (another pre–Father Brown story), he refers to "the late Mr. Sherlock Holmes, in the course of those inspiring investigations for which we can never be sufficiently grateful to their ingenious author."

Playful but fond references to Sherlock crop up in several Father Brown stories. Among the most intriguing is this conversation between a retired police detective and an "amateur" interested in detection.[23]

> Ours is the only trade [the police detective says] in which the professional is always supposed to be wrong. . . Let's take any imaginary case of Sherlock Holmes and Lestrade, the official detective. Sherlock Holmes, let us say, can guess that a total stranger crossing the street is a foreigner, merely because he seems to look for the traffic to go to the right instead of the left. I'm quite ready to admit Holmes might guess that. I'm quite sure Lestrade wouldn't guess anything of the kind. But what they leave out is the fact that the policeman, who couldn't guess, might very probably know . . . merely because his department has to keep an eye on all foreigners.

• • •

In all, Chesterton wrote fifty-three stories about Father Brown. They are, like most good literature, enjoyable and also enlightening; they teach us new ideas at the same time as they give us pleasure. Part of me wishes I could tell you all of them, but of course that is not possible. I will, however, tell you about a few more, those that especially reveal one or another of Father Brown's unique skills. To begin, let's pause for a moment and summarize some of the qualities that the little priest displays throughout the stories.

Father Brown's primary interest is spiritual but that does not mean that he is blind to things temporal. In story after story, he finds tangible evidence that escapes the notice of the police. He does not hesitate to get down on hands and knees to inspect blades of grass or carpet fibers; he quickly spots evidence that a body found by a river was killed elsewhere; and he can deduce a time line from an unbroken cigar ash.[24] Indeed, he is no less skilled at making a close, detailed observation of the scene of the crime than is Sherlock Holmes; he is merely quieter about it.

To this close study of the physical apparatus of the crime, Father Brown adds the insights into human behavior he has gained over years in the confessional. This compassionate understanding of human nature, the sense of shared humanity, permits him to, in effect, put himself into the mind and heart of the criminal and, in so doing, to identify him. "As one knows the crooked track of a snail," he says, "I know the crooked track of a man."[25]

This skill allows him not only to identify the guilty but to absolve the innocent. He can predict what a person will do from observing that person's basic character; likewise, he can deduce character from observing the physical elements of the scene. He knows, therefore, when the facts at hand do not match the character of the person first accused of the crime.

To these two types of observations—the physical evidence, plus insights into the heart and mind of the criminal—Father Brown adds a third dimension. For lack of a better word, let us call it intuition, that instinctive sense of rightness that sometimes defies common sense. It springs from his accumulated knowledge of the world and the deeds of man, from his inner wisdom, and from his deeply felt sense of good and evil.

Working in solitude in a small private room of an exclusive dinner club, Father Brown hears two sets of footsteps in the hallway, "and for an instant he smelt evil as a dog smells rat." Something strange is happening, but what? When a member of the club, leaving in haste, mistakes Father Brown for the coat clerk, the answer comes in a flash of intuition. "In that instant he had lost his head. His head was always most valuable when he had lost it. In such moments he put two and two together and made four million."[26]

Intuition is not a bad word. Trust your instincts.

A ghostly face is seen in the window of a house that has been robbed; a body is discovered in the garden, wearing a false beard. Two different people, or one? Father Brown suddenly sees the answer. "The more I thought of it the more I felt there was something funny about his having a completely new outfit. And then the truth began to dawn on me, by reason, which I knew already by instinct."[27]

Taking together all these threads—observing the physical evidence, plus insights into the heart and mind of the criminal, plus his own intuition—Father Brown unerringly finds the truth, and often it hinges on an alternative explanation, something not obvious on the surface. As he himself once wryly commented, a straight stick might seem to point to the truth but "the other end always points the opposite way. It depends whether you get hold of the stick by the right end."[28]

He sees these alternative explanations because he is willing to, because he approaches the mystery with eyes *and mind* wide open. The police investigating the disappearance of a Scottish aristocrat are completely baffled because the evidence is a strange tangle of facts that add up to nothing. "We have the truth," Father Brown observes calmly, "and the truth makes no sense." Yet looking at the collection of bizarre facts from a different perspective, he is able to find a connecting thread.[29]

Visiting an exotic household with his friend Flambeau, Father Brown has the uneasy sense that things are not what they seem. "We are on the wrong side of the tapestry. The things that happen here do not seem to mean anything; they mean something somewhere else. Somewhere else retribution will come on the real offender. Here it often seems to fall on the wrong person."[30]

We have met official police investigators who excel at collecting evidence but frequently falter at interpreting it; we have met legendary amateur detectives such as Dupin and Holmes, who meticulously gather facts and analyze them with brilliant logic. Father Brown adds one more element: He solves mysteries by "moral reasoning"—clear thinking plus compassion. As one modern admirer of Chesterton put it, "Sherlock Holmes fights criminals; Father Brown fights the devil."[31]

His goal is not to send a criminal to jail, but to bring him to redemption. In some of Chesterton's stories (for example, "The Wrong Shape" and "The Hammer of God") the murderer is persuaded to turn himself in. With a stunning piece of insight, Father Brown figures out who is stealing the valuable silver from a dinner club but, rather than turn the thief over to the authorities, he convinces him to renounce his life of crime.[32]

Sometimes the priest, mindful of larger questions of justice, simply lets the murderer escape; he puts his faith in the man's conscience and God's mercy. This attitude is apparent in the story called "The Eye of Apollo." As the criminal seems about to escape, Flambeau, now working on the side of the law, asks, "Shall I stop him?" "No," says Father Brown, with a strange deep sigh that seems to come from the center of the universe. "Let him pass. . . . Let Cain pass by, for he belongs to God."

We would not be wrong, I think, to wrap these powerful qualities of Father Brown together and call them by one name: wisdom.

I'll mention one final trait, not because it qualifies as a detection method worth emulating but simply because I cannot resist: Chesterton, through Father Brown, reveals an enchanting sense of humor. Two examples, from many: An investigator arrests a man, convinced he is an escaped criminal who has stolen a guard's bullets and is suspected of plotting against the life of a local millionaire. "A brilliant piece of rapid deduction," said Father Brown, "but had he got a gun? I've been told a bullet is not half so useful without it."[33] A man is found dead in his garden, and the mystery of how he was killed is solved by the one man among the crowd of investigators who entered the house in the normal fashion. "I came in by the front door," Father Brown explained; "I often come into houses that way."[34]

One more example, in the story whose joke hides in the title: "The Absence of Mr. Glass." A young woman is in love with her mother's lodger but fears for his safety. She has overheard a violent quarrel with a dangerous visitor named Mr. Glass, heard her sweetheart shouting, "That's right, Mr. Glass," and "No, Mr. Glass." Unable to open the door, she finally manages to look into the room through a window and sees her sweetheart huddled in a corner. Father Brown's assistance is urgently needed. The door is forced open, revealing signs of a frightful struggle, a deadly sword, and a dismayed young man tied up in ropes.

The joke is this: the young man was teaching himself magic tricks, including swallowing a sword and escaping from ropes. And what of the mysterious, threatening Mr. Glass? He never existed. The young man was practicing juggling, using drinking glasses, and often exclaimed in frustration, "Oh no, missed a glass!"[35]

INVESTMENT GUIDELINES FROM FATHER BROWN

As a man of the cloth, we can assume that Father Brown had little interest in accumulating wealth. However, as you will see in more detail in the chapter that follows, it is possible to convert many of Father Brown's particular skills into guidelines for intelligent investing.

1. Look carefully at the circumstances; do whatever it takes to gather all the clues.

2. Cultivate the understanding of intangibles.

3. Using both tangible and intangible evidence, develop such a full knowledge of potential investments that you can honestly say you know them inside out.

4. Trust your instincts. Intuition is invaluable.

5. Remain open to the possibility that something else may be happening, something different from that which first appears; remember that the full truth may be hidden beneath the surface.

As you will see in Chapter 7, Father Brown's rather remarkable way of looking at a mystery offers several important lessons for investors. The most significant elements of his methods have already been described in this chapter, in the paragraphs above and in the more detailed retelling of "The Blue Cross" at the beginning of the chapter. Now I would like to delve a bit deeper into Father Brown's methods by telling you the highlights of three stories. It is, need I say, not nearly as good as reading the original stories for yourself, but perhaps it will inspire you to do so.

• • •

One aspect of Father Brown's thinking that is especially relevant to investors is the notion that "things are not always what they seem." Somehow, Father Brown is always able to uncover the true explanation of what happened, even when it is contradicts that which appears first or even seems to be the most obvious. To get a stronger sense of how he manages to find the alternative explanation when others are stuck on the wrong course, I am going to tell you about the flying fish.[36]

A very rich man named Peregrine Smart (Chesterton loved to give his characters fanciful names) brags to anyone who will listen about his goldfish—which are actually fish-shaped trinkets made of solid gold, kept in a beautiful bowl of Venetian glass. Everyone in Mr. Smart's circle of friends and employees has urged him to be more circumspect about their value and to keep them in a safer spot, but he's always dismissed both suggestions. Each evening, he moves the goldfish bowl to a small back room next to his bedroom, and sleeps with a gun under his pillow.

When business calls Mr. Smart away from home, he asked his private secretary and the head clerk from his office to sleep in his bedroom, to guard his treasures. Sometime during the night, the secretary is awakened by the sound of music and finds the clerk already awake, standing on the balcony and shouting something about a prowler in the street below. The clerk then rushes downstairs, leaving the secretary watching from the balcony, and on the ground below finds a barefoot stranger dressed in a head-to-toe garment like a desert Bedouin and playing an unusual stringed instrument. "I have a right to the goldfish," the stranger says, "and they will come to me." At that, he shouts a command and strikes a very sharp note on his instrument. Hearing unusual noises coming from the room where the goldfish are kept, the secretary looks in and sees the bowl smashed on the floor, and the fish gone.

The police are called and begin their work. After having a thorough look around, the inspector realizes that he had "examined everything, measured everything, taken down everybody's deposition, taken every-body's fingerprints, put everybody's back up, and found himself at the end left facing a fact which he could not believe. An Arab from the desert had walked up the public road and stopped in front of the house, where a bowl of artificial goldfish was kept in an inner room; he had then sung or recited a little poem, and the bowl had exploded like a bomb and the fishes vanished into thin air."

A neighbor, a man of science, quickly realizes that the bowl was shattered by the loud and piercing note from the strange violin. But what happened to the fish? Enter Father Brown.

At the inspector's request, Father Brown looks carefully all around the house. He quickly sees that there are no footprints in the soft red dirt between Smart's home and the neighboring houses, which means the neighbors must be eliminated as suspects—in modern terms, he determines that it had to have been an inside job. He also determines that the bars locking the front door make noise only when they are shut, not when they are opened. It is a measure of Father Brown's genius that he grasps the significance of this small detail.

He then invites the young secretary to "come outside the house again for a moment. I want to show you how it looks from another standpoint." He means this both literally and figuratively: looking upward at the balcony from the street below, and also looking at the situation from a fresh perspective.

I won't give away the secret of how the stranger called the fish to fly through the air with his bizarre song. But Father Brown knew what happened, and helped his young friend to understand by encouraging him to look at the matter from a different direction. Obviously, gold-fish don't fly (and gold ones even less than real ones), so the answer must lie elsewhere, visible only from a different standpoint and only to those willing to look from a new perspective. This is a useful approach for investors as well as detectives.

• • •

Earlier in this chapter we took note of Father Brown's remarkable ability to enter into the mind of a criminal, and from there to identify the guilty party. But exactly how did he do that? In "The Secret of Father Brown," he explains after a stereotypically insensitive American presses him to reveal how he manages to solve famous crimes when the police cannot. Father Brown tries to avoid the question, but, when his interrogator suggests the priest must have occult powers, he groans and says in a dull voice, "Very well. I must tell the secret."

> You see, I had murdered them all myself. So of course I knew how it was done....
>
> I had planned out each of the crimes very carefully. I had thought out exactly how a thing like that could be done, and in what style or state of mind a man could really do it. And when I was quite sure that I felt exactly like the murderer myself, of course I knew who he was.

The argumentative American blithely assumes Father Brown is using a figure of speech, and Father Brown reacts angrily. "This is what comes of trying to talk about deep things.... I mean that I really did see myself, and my real self, committing the murder."

Undeterred, the American then tries to bring in the science of detection. Again Father Brown interrupts. It is one of his most eloquent moments.

> Science is a grand thing when you can get it. But what do these men mean, nine times out of ten, ... when they say detection is a science? ... They mean getting *outside* a man and studying him as if he were a giant insect.... Well, what you call "the secret" is exactly the opposite. I don't try to get outside the man. I try to get inside the murderer.
>
> Indeed it's much more than that, don't you see? I *am* inside a

man. I am always inside a man, moving his arms and legs; but I wait till I know I am inside a murderer, thinking his thoughts, wrestling with his passions; till I have bent myself into the posture of his hunched and peering hatred; till I see the world with his bloodshot and squirming eyes, looking between the blinkers of his half-witted concentration; looking up the short and sharp perspective of a straight road to a pool of blood. Till I am really a murderer.

That kind of intimate knowledge of the other party helps Father Brown know that he is looking at a criminal. In the same way, in-depth knowledge of a company will help investors determine whether they are looking at a good investment or a questionable one—more on this in the next chapter.

One final story, and then I send you off to your own reading. "The Three Tools of Death" seems a fitting close to this chapter because it contains several of the traits we have been following: good detection skills, understanding of human nature, intuition, and the appreciation that things are not always what they seem.

A popular public figure has been murdered. His broken body was found near a railway embankment, a scrap of rope entangling one leg; his skull had been crushed, but no murder weapon has been found. Father Brown, called to the scene, believes the victim was thrown from a high window, from which another piece of the same rope still dangles. The same servant who first discovered the body also found the victim's daughter hiding in an attic room, clutching a knife.

In the attic room, the police immediately see signs of a struggle, and on the floor lies a revolver, recently fired. The victim's secretary, who uses the attic room as his office, and who owned both the gun and the rope, turns himself over to the officials, claiming he killed the man in a drunken fury and offering a spilt whisky bottle as proof.

Father Brown, meanwhile, is "on his hands and knees on the carpet in the doorway, as if engaged in some kind of undignified prayers." He quietly points out to the police that whereas at first there seemed to be no weapon, now there are three: "the knife to stab, and the rope to strangle, and the pistol to shoot; and after all he broke his neck by falling out of a window!"

From his position on the floor, with clear logic that Sherlock Holmes would surely approve, Father Brown continues:

> And now three quite impossible things. First, these holes in the carpet, where the six bullets have gone in. Why on earth should anybody fire at the carpet? A drunken man lets fly at his enemy's head, the thing that's grinning at him. He doesn't pick a quarrel with his feet, or lay siege to his slippers. And then there's the rope. . . . In what conceivable intoxication would anybody try to put a rope around a man's neck and finally put it around his leg? And plainest of all, the whisky bottle. . . . I'm awfully sorry, sir, but your tale is really rubbish.

Through that intuitive sense that seems magical to others, Father Brown grasps the true meaning of the whisky bottle. The dead man, known for his cheerfulness and vitality, was actually in despair and had turned to drinking. Father Brown considers this possibility because he knows human nature, and he knows that cheerfulness is often false. "Cheerfulness without humor," Father Brown points out, "is a very trying thing."

As Father Brown reminds the young policeman that the rest of the household was the opposite of cheerful, he watches "a window in [the policeman's] mind let in that strange light of surprise in which we see for the first the things we have known all along." Thus the policeman, under Father Brown's guidance, begins to develop his own intuitive understanding of human nature.

Father Brown can draw the truth from people. Away from the police, he talks with both the secretary and the daughter; only then do all the conflicting pieces of evidence make sense. The murder victim was not murdered at all, but committed suicide. The secretary tried to prevent his using the revolver by shooting all its bullets into the floor, and then lassoed his employer to keep him from jumping out the window. At that moment the daughter, drawn by the shouting, burst into the room; thinking that the secretary was trying to strangle her father, she snatched up a knife and cut the rope, which sent her father plunging to the ground below, to meet the death he had sought.

Father Brown is not as well known to modern readers as is Sherlock Holmes, and Chesterton does not enjoy the same popularity today as does Edgar Allan Poe. In my view, this is a great shame, for the stories are wonderfully written, with clever plots, memorable dialogue, and beautiful descriptive passages. They also provide, not incidentally, insights that are of tremendous value to today's investors.

If there were sufficient space, I would be tempted to tell you the story of all fifty-three Father Brown tales, for all are charming and worthy of our attention. Instead, I urge you to dip into them for yourself, enjoying both the life lessons of Father Brown and the skillful writing of his talented creator.

CHAPTER SEVEN

Father Brown on Wall Street

My first case," said Father Brown, "was just a small private affair about a man's head being cut off."[1] The case is described in the story called "The Secret Garden," and it is one of my favorite mysteries, beginning shortly before dinnertime at the home of Aristide Valentin, chief of the Paris police. Valentin is hosting a dinner party, and his guests include Lord and Lady Galloway and their daughter Margaret; the Duchess of Mont St. Michel and her two daughters; Dr. Simon, a French scientist; Commandant O'Brien, of the French Foreign Legion; Julius Brayne, an American multimillionaire; and Father Brown.

Valentin's residence, architecturally speaking, is unusual. Nestled on the banks of the river Seine, it is an older home with high walls, tall poplar trees, and a large elaborate garden. Although there are several exits from the house into the garden, there is no exit from the garden to the outside world. The only way someone could leave the garden would be to reenter the house, and the only way to exit the house is through the front door, always guarded by Valentin's servant, Ivan. The garden walls were tall, smooth, and unscalable. Even if someone managed to reach the top of the garden wall, he would be met with an encircling row of sharp iron spikes. So, there is little chance someone could hop over the wall into the garden.

After dinner, all the guests retire to the drawing room except Commandant O'Brien and Margaret Galloway, who move toward the garden. Sensing that the commandant is making a play for his daughter, Lord Galloway excuses himself and goes into the garden to look for them. Instead of his daughter, however, he finds a blood-soaked corpse lying face down in the grass. His loud scream immediately brings Valentin, Dr. Simon, and Father Brown out into the garden. As the doctor bends down to check the body, its head falls completely away.

The puzzle is immediately apparent to all those present: How did the murdered man get into the garden? He could not have gotten by Ivan at the front door, nor could he have scaled the garden wall. Who killed and decapitated the stranger? And how did the murderer escape from the garden?

"The Secret Garden" is such a good story that I don't want to spoil it for you by revealing the secret. Without giving too much away, let's just say the murdered man found in the garden . . . was never in the garden.

In "The Secret Garden" we find light echoes of both Edgar Allan Poe and Arthur Conan Doyle. When Dr. Simon lifted the dead man's body and the head separated, I was immediately reminded of poor Mme. L'Espanaye in "The Murders in the Rue Morgue." When Valentin got down on his hands and knees to scrutinize the dented grass blades and scattered twigs, I could not help but think of our friend Sherlock

Holmes. But what I most enjoy about "The Secret Garden," and why I believe studying Father Brown is so important, is what it shows about his way of thinking. In his quiet, unassuming way, Father Brown found the clever twist that explained this apparently inexplicable mystery.

"The Secret Garden" first appeared in *The Saturday Evening Post* in the summer of 1910 and was later included in a collection of twelve stories published in book form as *The Innocence of Father Brown*. Ellery Queen called it "the miracle book of 1911," and it gave fans of detective fiction a new Great Detective to admire.

Without question, Sherlock Holmes dominated detective fiction in the first decade of the twentieth century, but when Conan Doyle stopped writing about his Great Detective, those writers next in line thought the way to build a good mystery was to come up with more baffling and convoluted situations that could be solved only by uncovering the tiniest of details. In short, the detectives who followed Holmes were still wandering around the same detective cul-de-sac invented by Conan Doyle. That is, until Chesterton's Father Brown set detective fiction in a new direction.

In the preceding chapter, we learned about Chesterton's brilliant career. His writings covered topics as diverse as religion, economics, history, travel, and social justice, as well as literature. In fact, Chesterton was the first respected literary critic who turned his talents toward writing mystery stories.[2]

In all his work, Chesterton enjoyed using paradox, wherein he would present a seemingly contradictory statement that in the end becomes the ultimate expression of truth. In some Father Brown stories, Chesterton described an ordinary set of events that later were revealed to be quite extraordinary. At other times, he would take the opposite tack and begin to solve a mystery with the most extraordinary explanation, only to reveal later a solution that was completely ordinary. Without getting tangled up in the multiple literary devices, it is enough for our purposes to recognize that Chesterton's Father Brown

165

was quite adept at understanding that "things are not always what they seem."

A fundamental requirement for becoming a successful investor is the ability to recognize when the stock market's price for a company is an accurate reflection of the company's underlying value and when it is not. If you believe the market's price is an accurate reflection of underlying value, then we might say, "Things are what they seem." Stock price and value are one and the same.

But if your analysis leads you to believe the real value of the company is either higher or lower than the market's price, then we can say, "Things are not what they seem." And if your goal is to generate an investment return that is in excess of the stock market's return, a minimal requirement is being able to recognize when things are, or are not, what they seem.

When Benjamin Graham and David Dodd wrote their seminal book *Security Analysis* in 1934, they gave investors a reference point to determine whether a stock was undervalued or overvalued relative to its price. The basic guideline presented in *Security Analysis* is this: An investor's task is to calculate a company's hard book value and then to pay a price for the company that is below that book value. Because the Great Depression had wiped out the earnings of most companies, the only sure way to determine value, said Graham, was to add up the hard assets of a company and assign a reasonable market value to them. Any investor trying to decide between Stock A for $1 per share or Stock B for $1 per share should first look at each company's book value. If Stock A's book value is $2 per share and Stock B's is 50 cents, then the smart investor would choose Stock A.

As years passed and the economic penalties of the Great Depression diminished, companies once again began to generate profits and some began paying dividends to their shareholders; at that point, dividend yield became another factor for making decisions. Because the interest rates on government bonds at the time was low (1 percent or sometimes less), a company with a common stock dividend yield of 8 percent was considered attractive. Now if Stock A and Stock B both sold for $1 per share and both companies had a book value of $2 but Stock A also paid an 8 percent dividend while Stock B paid no dividend, the choice was clear: Stock A was the better investment.

Granted, today determining book values and dividend yields is not high-level financial detective work, but in the 1930s this analysis was central to determining value. But more important for our purposes, the brief historical summary above helps us appreciate the differences that sometimes occur in markets and how the talents of a financial detective can be brought forth to profit. Consider Stock A and Stock B. If both stocks have the same book value but different dividend payouts, but the market prices them the same, we can argue "things are not what they seem." Although the market views the stocks the same, our analysis reveals something different.

Let's keep moving forward. It did not take analysts long to realize that if a stock's value was largely determined by its dividend yield, then it would become increasingly important to figure out what a company would earn in the future, because future earnings would determine dividend payouts. So, if Stock A and Stock B are both priced the same and both stocks have the same book value, the same dividend yield, and the same earnings per share, but Stock A is growing its earnings faster than Stock B, an investor would be wise to choose Stock A.

The focus on calculating future earnings was lent credence by the work John Burr Williams did in 1938. His book, *The Theory of Investment Value,* gave investors a mathematical roadmap to determine a stock's value. After more than sixty years, the dividend discount model remains the best and most widely taught method for calculating value.

But whereas Williams's formula focused on dividends because dividends were the cash return shareholders received, investors quickly grasped that the most important variable for a company's value was that company's *future* earnings. This lesson was hammered into investors' thinking by Warren Buffett, who is considered by many to be the twentieth century's most accomplished investor. Buffett reminded investors that it was not just a company's dividend that determined a stock's value but also the company's retained earnings.[3]

Buffett also helped investors understand the value of cash earnings as opposed to GAAP (generally accepted accounting practices) earnings. Buffett has often claimed that his success as an investor has been aided by his simultaneous experience of being a business owner—a situation that gave him a business owner's perspective on earnings. The business owner, he says, is only interested in the cash the business earns over time. Calculating earnings per share using GAAP does not always produce an accurate reflection of a company's true cash earnings, because GAAP does not adjust for capital expenditures or for noncash charges that are deducted from earnings.

Because GAAP requires that amortization and depreciation expenses (both noncash charges) be deducted from earnings, sometimes earnings per share underestimate true cash earnings. However, because GAAP calculation of earnings does not take into account the amount of money the company is required to reinvest in capital expenditures in order to maintain the same level of sales and earnings, GAAP earnings have the tendency to overstate exactly how much cash a business actually earns. The only way an investor can get a true sense of a company's value, Buffett feels, is to adjust the GAAP earnings for capital expenditures and other noncash charges and then, using Williams's dividend discount model, estimate the discounted present value of the company's future cash earnings.

If Stock A and Stock B have the same book value and the same dividend yield, if both report the same earnings per share, if both are determined to have the same future earnings per share growth rate, and if the stock market prices both stocks at $10 per share, can we say they have the same value? According to Buffett, we cannot answer the question until we calculate each company's true cash earnings. If Stock A's cash earnings are $1 and Stock B's cash earnings are 50 cents, then they do not have the same value even though the market prices them the same. So once again, things are not always what they seem.

Buffett's purchase of The Coca-Cola Company is a perfect example of how a good analytical investor can determine when the stock market has mispriced a security. In 1988, when he invested $1 billion in Coca-Cola, Buffett paid five times book value for a company with a below-average market dividend yield and an above-average price-to-earnings ratio. With this purchase he violated what at the time appeared to be the very basic tenets of value investing. Value investors followed the methods taught by Ben Graham and always sought to purchase companies with high dividend yields, low prices to book value, and low prices to earnings. In every aspect, it appeared Buffett had violated those precepts. Some argued that when Buffett purchased Coca-Cola, he turned his back on his teacher, Ben Graham.

Buffett calculated the company's cash earnings and quickly determined they were significantly higher than reported earnings per share. When he applied Williams's dividend discount model, plugged in with conservative growth expectations, he realized that Coca-Cola was selling in the market at a significant discount to what he believed the company was worth. In fact, assuming a cash earnings growth rate of 10 percent for the first ten years, and a 5 percent growth rate into perpetuity after that, he determined Coca-Cola was selling at *half* of what it was worth. At a slightly more optimistic growth rate of 12 percent, the company was undervalued by as much as 70 percent.

How well did Buffett do with his Coca-Cola purchase? Twelve years later, his $1 billion investment was worth $10 billion. Over the same period, a $1 billion investment in the overall stock market would be worth $5 billion. Things are not always what they seem.

In Chapter 5 we analyzed the story of Dell Computer and discovered one more important financial variable that investors need to appreciate: return on capital. A company's return on capital has a direct impact on its value. By way of comparison, let us assume both Stock A and Stock B report $1 in cash earnings and both are expected to maintain identical growth rates into the future. The stock market has priced both stocks identically. Your analysis reveals the cost of capital for both companies is 10 percent. Stock A has $5 in total capital employed while Stock B has $20 in total capital employed. Which stock is more attractive? A quick bit of math shows that Stock A earns 20 percent on capital, way above its cost of capital, while Stock B earns 2 percent, way below its cost of capital. Yet the market has priced both securities the same. You have discovered another case where things are not what they seem.

This brief historical review of the evolution of financial analysis was meant to help you appreciate how a good analytical detective could spot the periods when the market has accurately priced a stock and those times it has evidently mispriced a stock. But if we are going to apply Father Brown's "alternative" method of explanation to financial investigation, we need to dig deeper.

When a good analytical investor recognizes the differences between book value, dividends, earnings per share, cash earning per share, and return on capital, we can say the investor has mastered basic financial detective work. But we are still operating in a discipline that focuses largely on the physical evidence. That is to say, we have not expanded our analytical effort past what Sherlock Holmes would have discovered. What we have learned about Father Brown is that his detective methods go beyond the physical evidence and take into consideration evidence that might be called intangible value.

The idea of intangible value has always mystified Wall Street. Investing is thought to be an exercise that adds, subtracts, multiplies, and divides. It is a world full of spreadsheets and decimal points. It is

a profession that prides itself on numbers, and therefore many investment professionals have a tendency to discount items that are not
described in numbers. Intangi-
ble values are not easy to measure, and to use the familiar
expression, many people believe
"that which cannot be easily
measured can sometimes be badly
measured." It is for this reason
that many investors shy away
from studying intangible values,

> **"Every crime depends on
> somebody not waking up too
> soon, and in every sense most
> of us wake up too late."**
>
> —FATHER BROWN,
> "THE SONG
> OF THE FLYING FISH"

preferring instead to focus only on that which can be measured mathematically.

One easy way to appreciate the challenge of measuring intangible
values is to ask the question, *What is the value of a company's management?* Some in the financial community believe that it is impossible to
measure accurately the value of management, and thus any attempts to
alter a company's value based on who is running the company should
be avoided. Others believe the value of management is already reflected in the financial results of the company, and so any attempt to
include a value for management is the equivalent of double accounting. But Warren Buffett believes differently.

In determining what price to pay for a company, Buffett considers
the value of management central to his calculation. He says he seeks
managers who are honest, candid, and rational. He also wants managers who are able to resist the institutional imperative—the mindless,
lemminglike tendency to imitate whatever is currently popular. Granted, trying to place a numerical value on honesty, candor, and rationality is problematic, but just because the calculation is not convenient
does not mean we should ignore these attributes when we are trying to
determine the value of a company.

As an example, let's say Stock A and Stock B are priced the same and possess similar financial results, including book value, dividends, cash earnings, and return on capital. However, after studying the annual and quarterly reports of the two companies and carefully reading interviews with senior executives in financial magazines and newspapers, you can plainly see that the managers of Company A are being honest about the successes and failures of the business. They candidly and publicly confess their previous managerial mistakes while articulating a straightforward rationale for building shareholder value. By comparison, the management of Company B has nothing but good news to report. There are no problems with the company and there have been no managerial missteps.

Given that both Stock A and Stock B have identical financials and are priced the same, which company has more value? According to Warren Buffett, Stock A does; he places more value in a management team that is honest and confesses its mistakes. No company, explains Buffett, is managed perfectly. There are always mistakes made and the management team that publicly confesses its mistakes is less likely to make that same mistake twice. If you don't admit your mistakes and shortcomings, says Buffett, there is always the tendency to sweep the problems under the rug—no one will be the wiser, which sets up the possibility of making the same managerial mistake all over again.

This brief discussion of the value of management is meant to serve as a reminder that just because something does not lend itself to easy measurement doesn't mean it is without value. The reason we want to study Father Brown is that he places value on the intangible— whereas Sherlock Holmes is only interested in the physical facts, Father Brown adds to this a deep appreciation of psychology and human behavior. A man who has spent more than half his life listening to confessions has learned a bit about human nature. These insights, we can say, aid Father Brown in his detective pursuits.

Just as Father Brown made use of psychology in solving mysteries, so too can investors rely on the study of human behavior to ascertain when stocks have been mispriced. Although Ben Graham is largely credited with giving investors a mathematical approach to determining the value of stocks, he also devoted a significant amount of his time to the study of stock market behavior. In both *Security Analysis* and *The Intelligent Investor*, Graham makes a point of reminding us that there are two parts to becoming a successful investor: determining the financial value of a stock, and becoming aware of the missteps that can occur when investors are distracted by psychological forces in the market. Graham's most famous lesson centers around the story of "Mr. Market."

Think of Mr. Market as your business partner, said Graham. You and Mr. Market own shares in the same company. Every business day Mr. Market shows up with an offer to buy your shares or sell you his. What investors learn, explained Graham, is that Mr. Market's prices are all over the place. On some days he offers you a very high price for your shares. On other days, his price is way below what you think the business is worth. The key lesson for investors, said Graham, is to recognize that Mr. Market is not the boss. He does not tell you what to do. Investors are free to ignore Mr. Market's prices or take advantage of them. But it will be a disaster, warned Graham, if investors fall under Mr. Market's influence.

The study of crowd behavior in markets dates back one hundred years before Graham wrote his first book. In 1841, Charles MacKay wrote *Extraordinary Popular Delusions and the Madness of Crowds*. In it, he warned that speculative bubbles such as Tulipmania in 1636 were caused by periodic outbreaks of mass hysteria. Gustave Le Bon, a French sociologist, took MacKay's work one step further. In his book *The Crowd* (1895), Le Bon argued that individuals, who may be very different from one another in every respect, are transformed psychologically when they form groups. In a group, explained Le Bon, individuals form a collective mind that causes the members to behave differently than they would if they were operating individually. The power of the crowd is so powerful and so contagious that it forces individuals to sacrifice their personal interests to the collective interest.

For a more contemporary treatment of crowd behavior in the stock market, you might want to examine Robert Shiller's *Irrational Exuberance*. This book was published in 2000, shortly before the mass hysteria surrounding the Internet boom blew apart, causing investors to suffer dramatic losses in their portfolios.

Today, the study of psychology in investing is called *behavioral finance*. This discipline was officially launched in 1985 when the *Journal of Finance* published two landmark papers. The first, by Werner De Bondt and Richard Thaler, was titled "Does the Stock Market Overreact?" In it, De Bondt and Thaler argued that investors have a tendency to overreact to new information, no matter whether the news is good or bad. Because of this overreaction, investors have a tendency to move stock prices far above or far below what the company's economic fundamentals would dictate.

The second paper was titled "The Disposition to Sell Winners Too Early and Ride Losers Too Long: Theory and Evidence." In it, authors Hersh Shefrin and Meir Statman describe what they called a disposition effect: the tendency of investors to sell their winners quickly while hanging on to their losers far longer than they should.

Thinking like Father Brown, it is easy to see how an additional study of psychology would lend important insights to the understanding of a stock's price and value. Without an appreciation and understanding of human psychology, what would the investor make of a seemingly unexplainable and extraordinary drop in a stock price that on the surface appears inconsistent with the company's fundamentals? Would an investor who had no training in behavioral finance erroneously conclude that there is something dramatically wrong with the company? Would it lead the investor to reanalyze the physical (financial) evidence in such a way that it supports the change in the stock price? Would a different investor, one who understands psychology, be able to recognize when a stock is repriced justifiably or unjustifiably, and profit accordingly?

Since 1985, psychologists and finance professors have devoted considerable time and effort to the relationship between psychology and investing. Many research reports, journal articles, and books have been written on behavioral finance, and collectively they represent a rich literature that is available for all investors to read and study. I believe that any investor who took the time to absorb the numerous studies on the psychology of investing might achieve something equivalent to what Father Brown accumulated after listening to hundreds and hundreds of confessions—a deeper understanding of human psychology and its possible effects. Just as Father Brown's skill as an analytical detective was greatly improved by incorporating the study of psychology with the method of observation, so too can individuals improve their investment performance by combining the study of psychology with the physical evidence of financial statement analysis.

Today, most financial analysts do attempt to include some of what we are calling "intangible" evidence in their analyses. Certainly most of them assess management capabilities when determining the value of a company. Likewise, portfolio managers often take into account the effect that market psychology has on stock prices. Even though judgments about a company's management and the impact of behavioral finance lack the mathematical rigor one gets from calculating a company's earnings per share, both of these intangible financial variables are useful inputs for investors.

But it would be shortsighted of us to assume that the study of intangible values stops with corporate management and behavioral finance. For investors, the list of intangible values is considerably larger. I believe that exploring other disciplines gives us additional insights and a broader sweep of intangible values that, in the long run, makes

THE DETECTIVE AND THE INVESTOR

us better investors. One person who powerfully embodies this theory is Michael Mauboussin.

Michael is managing director of Credit Suisse First Boston and is also its chief U.S. investment strategist. He has accumulated numerous awards, including being named to the prestigious Institutional Investor's All-American research team, and in addition is adjunct professor of finance at Columbia Graduate School of Business and coauthor, with Alfred Rappaport, of an important investment book entitled *Expectations Investing*. In short, Michael is a research analyst, a teacher, a writer, and, most important, a thinker.

Michael's associates, clients, and friends knew early on that he was destined to explore new issues and ideas. While working as First Boston's food industry analyst, Michael began writing a clever research report titled *Frontiers of Finance*, a ten- to twenty-page essay on ideas he deemed important to the investment process. His first was called "Competitive Advantage Period (CAP)—The Neglected Value Driver."

CAP, explained Michael, "is the time during which a company is expected to generate returns on incremental investment in excess of its cost of capital." Michael then compared the competitive advantage period of several major food companies in the 1980s to determine which one had the highest CAP number. On average, the competitive advantage period for the group in 1982 was about 8.6 years. By 1989, that CAP number for the food group had risen to 17.4 years, with Campbell Soup and Kellogg's heading the list. How long a company was expected to extend its competitive advantage period became an additional yardstick in Michael's research.

Michael's second report was titled "What Have You Learned in the Past 2 Seconds?" It was a smart piece that wove together Darwin's theory of evolution, Daniel Goleman's best-selling book *Emotional Intelligence*, and Max Bazerman's book *Judgment in Managerial Decision Making*, and then linked the ideas to contemporary work in behavioral finance. What did Michael discover? The process of investing money successfully in capital markets, he wrote, is not something that most humans are designed to do—at least yet. From an evolutionary perspective, explained Michael, investors are much better wired to run from danger (a long-term evolutionary trait) than they are capable of estimating the expected returns on assets. The best antidote to this dichotomy was to be mindful of humans' inherent emotional limitations while simultaneously broadening one's understanding of the new environment one operates in. After all, the biggest challenge investors face is not how to outrun a lion, but how to navigate the financial pitfalls caused by bulls and bears.

In his first two written reports, Michael established a process that allowed him to explore new ideas down two separate pathways. With his CAP paper, Michael demonstrated what I would call his "tangible financial detective skills." That is, Michael was sharpening his insights into discovering which "tangible" financial results might have a future impact on a company's stock price. By tangible, I mean the easily measurable financial results that could be distilled from an income statement, balance sheet, and cash flow statement.

But with "What Have You Learned in the Past 2 Seconds?" Michael widened his search for investment understanding by examining other disciplines (biology and psychology). In the process, he brought attention to the value of using "intangible financial detective skills." This ability to combine the tangible with the intangible is a rare analytical trait.

Michael's research has navigated continually between these two worlds, with the contents of *Frontiers of Finance* divided into three intellectual buckets: The New Corporate Finance, The New Economy, and The New Capital Markets Theory. In the New Corporate Finance arena, Michael's writings are expanding beyond his work on the CAP and now include research on the financial impact of share repurchases and mergers and acquisitions. Over the past several years, share repurchases have increasingly replaced dividends as a way to return excess cash to shareholders. Companies have also used share repurchases to offset the dilution that comes from granting employees stock options. Michael's research outlines a framework whereby investors can determine whether a company's share repurchase program will actually increase or diminish shareholder value.

Investors have also witnessed a sharp rise in mergers and acquisitions. Typically, when a merger or acquisition is announced, management defends the strategy by claiming that combining the two companies will produce cost savings and improved earnings growth rates. But with academic research suggesting that two thirds of all mergers and acquisitions fail to deliver increased shareholder value for the acquiring company, one has to ask where the management assumptions are going wrong. According to Michael, "Mergers and acquisition analysis often starts and stops with earnings accretion analysis. This is one of the greatest investment errors that can be made, as accrual accounting earnings do not necessarily reflect the economic reality of cash-on-cash returns."[4] To help investors better understand the benefits (if any) that a merger or acquisition will provide, Michael has introduced a useful economic measuring stick called "Shareholder Value at Risk."

Many of the puzzles investors face today come from distinguishing the financial analysis of "brick-and-mortar" companies from "new economy" companies. New-economy companies typically have relatively few hard assets but are able to generate revenues and profits from people, ideas, and networks. In his new-economy research, Michael is trying to help investors better understand the economic differences that can occur between old-economy companies and their new-economy competitors.

In "Cash Flow.com: Cash Economics in the New Economy" (March 2, 1999), Michael provides a practical framework for analyzing the cash economics of different business models. It is clear that when new-economy companies become firmly established in the marketplace, they have superior cash economics when compared to their old-economy counterparts. For example, writes Michael, Barnes and Noble generated $150 million in cash earnings in 1988 but it also had to invest $240 million during the same period, translating into free cash flow of negative $95 million. During the same year, Amazon.com generated a $54 million cash inflow offset by a $59 million cash outflow, coming very close to generating positive cash flow. Of course, Wall Street's fixation on GAAP earnings per share, devised to explain the economics of old-economy companies, sometimes overlooks companies that on a reported GAAP basis show little earnings per share but have very large cash earnings.

To help investors better appreciate the cash flow dynamic of new-economy companies, Michael wrote an insightful financial report on Microsoft in fall 2001. Titled "Microsoft Corporation: Fun with Financial Statements" (September 24, 2001), the report was a reconciliation of Microsoft's earnings and cash flow. From the company's 10K for 2001, Michael noted that Microsoft's operating net income was $7.7 billion. But as he rightly pointed out, this number did not take into account other sources of cash flow, including changes in deferred revenue, capital expenditures, depreciation, amortization, noncash write-offs, and changes in working capital. After making these financial adjustments, Michael discovered that Microsoft's actual cash flow was $12.3 billion, 60 percent higher than reported earnings. It is important to realize that cash flow is what drives value, and the difference between Microsoft's reported earnings per share of $1.45 and its cash flow per share of $2.30 was a significant $.85 per share.

In addition, Michael's report revealed that Microsoft's return on invested capital was an incredible 200 percent. To calculate this number, Michael stripped out Microsoft's $30 billion in cash and marketable securities as well as $19 billion in equity investments in other

THE DETECTIVE AND THE INVESTOR

companies. His conclusion: Microsoft needs very little in physical infrastructure to operate its business, and current GAAP accounting treatments do not accurately reflect the true value of this new-economy company.

This line of thinking is not widely different from Buffett's explanation of why he bought The Coca-Cola Company. As you remember, Buffett was focusing on Coke's cash earnings. Michael's research also focuses on understanding cash flow economics, but he adds a new element: the dynamic explosion of free cash flow that can occur when a new-economy company becomes successful. The acceleration of cash flow growth far outstrips the cash flow growth realized from the economics of older, mature companies like Coca-Cola. Whereas old-economy companies can reach free cash flow (cash earnings in excess of required capital expenditures), new-economy companies have the potential to reach what Michael calls "super cash flow."

A byproduct of the new economy is the popular use of employee stock options to compensate and retain employees. Because most new-economy companies, like venture capital companies, were just getting started in the marketplace, they did not have the ability to attract and keep valuable employees by offering large cash salaries, so instead they offered generous employee stock options as part of the total compensation package. In "A Piece of the Action: Employee Stock Options in the New Economy" (November 2, 1998), Michael analyzed the economic cash impact of employee stock options. Of course, today employee stock options have become a lightning rod for debate in the financial community and almost all investors have taken it upon themselves to calculate their economic impact. But in 1998, when the stock market was sailing, few were taking the time to understand the value implications of these new compensation structures.

In the second half of Michael's Microsoft report, he walks investors through a careful examination of the economic impact of the company's employee stock options. According to Michael's research,

Microsoft's employee stock options represented a substantial economic liability: about $25 billion. To arrive at this estimate, Michael valued each group of options disclosed in the company's FASB 123 footnote. The figure was adjusted for anticipated employee departures (employees who leave the company forfeit their stock options), warrant conversions, and taxes. What Michael discovered was that the value of the company's employee stock options represented about 6 percent of the company's total market capitalization.

The new-economy framework and rapid technological innovations have introduced another financial puzzle for analysts. In trying to understand how technological innovation might alter the value of companies, Michael began to explore the concept of "real options" ("Get Real: Using Real Options in Security Analysis," June 22, 1999). Calculating the discounted present value of a company's future free cash flows is the proper way to value businesses, he argued, but it might not capture all of a company's net worth. To get an accurate sense of a company's complete value, you need to take into consideration a company's "real options."

A real option works something like a call option that is embedded in the value of the business. Like a call option, a real option gives the owner the right, but not the obligation, to buy something in the future at a set price. Take Viacom, for example. A traditional discounted present value of the company's future cash flows based on the company's 2002 business combinations might reveal the stock is worth $50 per share. But what additional value would you place on the company when you consider that fiber-optic cable will eventually allow customers to access the company's vast film library and purchase viewings on demand? Should you consider only the cash value of the films sold through television, cable, and the DVD/videocassette rental market, or should you place an option value on the eventuality of fiber-optic pay-on-demand viewings?

Are real options an exact mathematical exercise? No. But just because the value of real options cannot be measured with any precision, it would be a mistake, explains Michael, to ignore them altogether.

It strikes me that Michael is following the same path in his work that Benjamin Graham was in the 1930s. Granted, real-options theory might seem far removed from Graham's insistence on buying only companies with hard assets, but an epistemological examination of Michael's work clearly reveals he is working hard to better understand the tangible and intangible financial values of companies. These investigations have begun to take him into new disciplines which, at first, appear far removed from the study of investing.

Economics and capital markets theory rest largely on the concept of equilibrium, defined as a state of balance between two forces, powers, or influences. The idea can be traced back to Isaac Newton's *Principia Mathematica* (1687). So embedded is the idea of market equilibrium, it is difficult to imagine any other description of stock markets and economies. Alfred Marshall's celebrated *The Principles of Economics*, considered one of the most important economic textbooks ever written, devotes three separate chapters to economic equilibrium. Marshall's textbook taught economics to students for over fifty years until Paul Samuelson's *Economics* was introduced in 1948. But like Marshall, Samuelson also agreed the economy and the stock market were general equilibrium systems.

Financial theorists took their cues from the economists and they too embraced the idea of equilibrium. Eugene Fama, credited with launching modern portfolio theory, argued that the efficient market hypothesis was made possible by equilibrium. Likewise, Nobel prize winner William Sharpe, in his 1964 paper entitled "Capital Asset Prices: A Theory of Market Equilibrium under Conditions of Risk," argued that in market equilibrium there is a simple linear relationship between the expected return and the standard deviation of return.

When you sign up for the equilibrium view of economics and stock markets, you become a proponent of stock market efficiency, the rational behavior of market participants, and the normal distribution of stock market returns. But theory is one thing and reality is another. Everyday experience has led many to question whether stock prices do accurately reflect all available information. We also know from studying behavioral finance that the idea that investors are perfectly rational is highly unlikely. Also, we know that wide swings in market returns do occur, and they do not reflect the physics of an equilibrium system. In an equilibrium system, five-sigma events are so statistically unlikely they are thought mathematically to occur only once in 10,000 years. But the stock market's periodic five-sigma events suggest that a physics-based equilibrium system is not at work here. There must be a better description of market behavior.

> "Perhaps you had never seen it the right way up, I told you that artists turn a picture the wrong way up when they want to see it the right way up."
>
> —FATHER BROWN, "THE VANISHING OF VAUDREY"

Michael Mauboussin has long been troubled by the inconsistencies between classical theory and his own observations of the stock market. Although it has always been safe and convenient to promote the equilibrium view of markets, he found it increasingly difficult to defend such a view in light of experience. This intellectual tug of war led him to discover the work being done at the Santa Fe Institute.

High in the hills of Santa Fe, New Mexico, there is a research institute where scientists from various disciplines have joined together to study complex adaptive systems. Complex adaptive systems are systems with many interacting parts that are continually changing their behavior in response to changes in the environment. Examples include central nervous systems, ecologies, ant colonies, political systems, social structures, and, yes, economies and stock markets.

Remember that the standard equilibrium theory is rational, mechanistic, and efficient. The counterview at the Santa Fe Institute suggests that the market is not rational, is organic rather than mechanistic, and is imperfectly efficient.

The benefit Michael receives from the institute is twofold. First, he is able to work in a research setting that is operating with the correct descriptions of market behavior. Second, he gets a chance to rub shoulders with other scientists from other disciplines—biology, computer science, sociology, and research medicine—who are exploring the same phenomena. Each exchange between group members opens a whole new world of ideas and possible descriptions. Just imagine what it must have been like the first time an investor shared a conversation with a psychologist.

In the "New Capital Markets Theory" section of *Frontiers of Finance,* Michael enters into a deep exploration of the concept of complex adaptive systems. In "Shift Happens: On a New Paradigm of the Markets as a Complex Adaptive System" (October 24, 1997), he compares and contrasts the classical view of capital markets theory with the newer complex adaptive systems view of markets. In Michael's words, he believes a paradigm shift between the two models is now underway. He may be right. Five years after "Shift Happens," *The Journal of Applied Corporate Finance* published Michael's paper titled "Revisiting Market Efficiency: The Stock Market as a Complex Adaptive System," a deeper treatment of the subject.

But the greatest benefit to Michael's association with the Santa Fe Institute may be just beginning. Over the past five years, Michael has been a regular attendee at the institute's meetings and seminars. In 2001, he was named to the institute's board of trustees, and over the past several years, Michael and Credit Suisse First Boston have hosted a fall conference in Santa Fe where attendees have listened to presentations made by the researchers who work at the institute.

What does this all mean for investing? Simply this: By drawing on the research ideas of scientists who work in many different disciplines, Michael is accumulating new ideas and descriptions, some of which appear relevant for investors.

Studying complex adaptive systems moves us away from physics and mechanical systems and moves us toward biology and living systems. Biology, the scientific study of life and all its forms and processes, is a rich discipline for investors to examine. It is not hard to see how important Darwin's theory of evolution and the concept of adaptation are to the business world. The need for companies to change with the environment and adapt to their customers' needs is an often-used mantra in management textbooks. But the relationship between biology and business goes much deeper than the story of Charles Darwin.

Scientists at the Santa Fe Institute are deeply involved in the examination and meaning of power laws—those laws (quite common in both physical and social systems), in which one quantity is expressed as some power of another. The Gutenberg-Richter Law, for example, is used to describe the frequency of earthquakes of different magnitudes. Pareto's Law identifies a power law distribution of income among individuals. Zipf's Law describes the rank-frequency distribution of words in natural languages, as well as city sizes. (For example, the largest city is often twice as large as the second largest city, three times as large as the third largest city, four times as large as the fourth largest city, and so on.)

It also appears that power laws are evident in the marketplace. Researchers at Xerox Parc discovered that Internet Web sites, examined on the basis of distribution of visitors per site, followed a power law. Simply put, some Internet sites had very few users while a very few Internet sites had many users. Although this observation might at first appear rather simple and obvious, a powerful statistical fact underlies the phenomenon. This distribution of visitors per Web site indicated that Internet businesses were developing into a winner-take-all market in which a select few sites were destined to garner a majority of Internet users. What is even more important, it indicated the market was very likely to stay that way, since the power law phenomenon also suggests that once an entity is firmly established on the power curve, rotation between entities rarely occurs. In other words, if you are positioned number one on the power law, it is very unlikely that your position will change to number two, three, or four.

How are power laws relevant to investing? The best example lies with the study of America Online (AOL). The brainchild of Steve Case and Bob Pittman, AOL burst on the scene at the start of the consumer Internet revolution. In 1996, the company's market capitalization was $4 billion, but from the financial evidence (earnings per share) it was far from obvious the company was going to succeed.

The field of potential competitors was enormous, for there were no barriers to entry in setting up an Internet service provider (ISP) business—all it took was some venture capital money and you could begin searching for new viewers. AOL, like so many newly formed ISPs, was not profitable even though it was one of the few ISPs to charge a subscription fee. It was also plagued with sloppy service and constant busy signals, about which AOL customers would complain periodically—and loudly. But despite the poor visible economics and customer dissatisfaction, though, a valuable insight was waiting below the surface for those investors willing to look beyond the tangible evidence.

ISP distribution followed what became a predictable power law, and AOL quickly established itself as number one. An investor who understood the phenomenon of power laws could have looked at two similarly priced Internet companies with similar financial reports, charted their position on a power law curve, and would have seen that one of the companies was substantially mispriced. In other words,

AOL's number-one position on the power law was more significant than the difficulties the company faced. Things are not always what they seem.

Since Xerox's original research on Web sites, Michael Mauboussin has thrown himself into the study of power laws. On July 7, 2000, he published a paper titled "Still Powerful: The Internet's Hidden Order." What he discovered was that even after the drop in technology stocks and the decline in the major markets, the relationship between rank and market value of online companies continued to exhibit power laws. He then examined forty-six sectors from eighteen different industries for possible power law trends, and found that nine of them displayed strong power law characteristics: biotech, savings and loan institutions, telecom equipment, specialty chemicals, semiconductors, restaurants, software, apparel, and of course the Internet.

Have investors exhausted the knowledge basket from biology? Hardly. Michael and other scientists at the Santa Fe Institute have taken a keen interest in the work of Geoffrey West, a physicist and theoretical biologist at Los Alamos National Laboratory.

West, along with his colleagues James Brown of the University of New Mexico and Brian Enquist of the Santa Fe Institute, recently made an important presentation to the American Association for the Advancement of Science Annual Meeting. West has put together a set of principles that form a theory that explains the universal power laws found in biology, from the smallest living cells to the largest mammals. As such, West's theory, if proven, has the potential to place life on earth in a mathematical context. According to West, "life is the most complex system in the universe. Beyond natural selection, genetic codes and the like there are hardly any general principles or laws that we know it obeys. Power laws are the exception. These are quantitative laws, and remarkably they are absurdly simple given you are dealing with the most complex systems."[5]

Of course what is simple to Geoff West may not necessarily be simple to the rest of us. But I'll make a stab at attempting to explain the theory as simply as possible. West has discovered that "the metabolic rate, defined as the power to sustain life, appears to scale as the 3/4 power of mass over 27 orders of magnitude ranging from molecular, to the smallest unicellular organisms, and then to the largest plants and animals". In addition, "time-scales, including heart rate, life span, and size, such as the radius of a tree trunk or the density of mitochondria, change with size with exponents which are typically simple powers of 1 over 4."[6]

Is it possible there could be a unified theory that can explain these power laws? If there is, explains West, "it will be found in a common mechanism that transports materials through linear networks that supply all parts of the organism." Examples of these networks include cardiovascular, respiratory, and plant vascular systems. These systems are based on three unifying principles. "First, in order for the network to supply the entire volume of the organism the network system needs to have a space-filling, fractal-like branching pattern," said West. "Second, the final branch of the network, such as a capillary in the circulatory system, must be size invariant, which means it is the same size in every organism. For example, the capillary in a mouse is the same size as one in a lion." Third, West argues, "the energy required to distribute resources is minimized. In other words, the distribution networks that have evolved in living systems must use the minimal amount of energy required to keep [them] alive."[7]

According to West, these three principles taken together might explain the nature of the universal power laws of biology. But how can we use them in investing? What is exciting to discover is that power laws appear to work at many different levels. West and his colleagues are now investigating whether these power laws might also apply to river systems, which have similar branchlike circulatory systems, and to corporations. Corporations! It is possible these biological discoveries might help us understand the optimal organizational structure for large multinational corporations. One day, an intuitive investor might observe two similarly priced companies with similar financial returns but with disparate organizational structures and recognize that one company is organized for optimal performance while the other is not.

Whereas the *Frontiers of Finance* research papers focus attention on issues largely related to finance, Michael Mauboussin's work at the Santa Fe Institute is also opening his eyes to the possibilities of discovering new ideas in other areas. To explore these new disciplines, Michael has launched a new research series titled "The Consilient Observer: Applying Cross-Discipline Frameworks to Investing." According to Michael, "The Consilient Observer" seeks to link market-based facts to new mental models from various disciplines in order to help individuals make better investment decisions.

Michael takes his title from a wonderful book written by the esteemed biologist Edward O. Wilson, *Consilience: The Unity of Knowledge.* Consilience, Wilson explains, means the "jumping together" of knowledge. *The Consilient Observer,* Michael says, "is going to be a group of shorter research papers but draws in information and knowledge from all over the place."[8]

The concept of thinking in multidisciplinary terms is not new. Even before the United States existed as a country, Benjamin Franklin was an ardent early advocate for a "liberal arts" education. In *Proposals Relating to the Education of Youth in Pennsylvania* in 1749, Franklin recommended strongly that students take a wide variety of courses. "As to their studies," he wrote, "it would be well if they could be taught everything that is useful and ornamental." In the 250 years since Franklin's proposal, proponents of liberal arts study have been in a tug-of-war with those who argue the need for specialization, and mostly they have been losing.

Today, the business of investing is highly specialized. Students who aspire to be professional investors often begin with an undergraduate degree in business. Most of them go on to obtain a Masters of Business Administration degree, and then usually they layer on a Chartered Financial Analyst (CFA) designation to fill out the credentials. This specialized education in matters of business, finance, economics, and accounting qualifies an individual to analyze stocks and bonds and even perhaps to manage portfolios. Then why bother studying other disciplines? Because, according to Michael, "thoughtful investing requires an understanding of both immutable principles [finance specialization] and changing contexts [liberal arts background]. Changing economies, companies, and markets often render rules-of-thumb ineffective and yesterday's investment wisdom stale."[9]

The best way to approach investing is to build a latticework of mental models drawn from various disciplines.[10] First articulated by Charlie Munger, vice chairman of Berkshire Hathaway, a latticework of mental models can help to improve an investor's ability to identify key patterns and processes. These key patterns and processes are visible to someone who studies other disciplines but remain hidden from the person who harbors a narrow view of how the world works.

Just as Father Brown improved his analytical abilities by adding an understanding of human psychology to his detective methods, so too have investors improved their results by adding the study of psychology (behavioral finance) to their study of finance and accounting. In addition, we have seen how the study of biology has also enabled some investors to gain a competitive advantage. What Charlie Munger, Edward Wilson, and Michael Mauboussin are advocating is the idea that thinking across disciplines deepens our understanding of how the world works.

When, late in his life, Father Brown visits his old friend Flambeau at his Spanish estate, he finds himself in a situation that provides us a further opportunity to learn about the priest's methods. It is early evening. Father Brown, Flambeau, and an American traveler named Grandison

Chace, who is leasing the adjoining estate, are enjoying a glass of wine. Chace is aware of Father Brown's celebrity and urges the priest to reveal his secrets. Father Brown demurs, but Chace persists. He attempts a challenge: comparing Father Brown to Auguste Dupin and Sherlock Holmes.

"Edgar Poe throws off several little essays in a conversational form, explaining Dupin's method, with its fine links of logic," said Chace. "Dr. Watson had to listen to some pretty exact expositions of Holmes's method, with its observation of material detail. But nobody seems to have got on to any full account of your method, Father Brown. . . . I may say that some of our people are saying your science can't be expounded because it's something more than just natural science. They say your secret's not to be divulged, as being occult in its character." Father Brown frowns but says little; the insistent American plunges on. He recounts several famous cases, adding "And there were you, on the spot every time, slap in the middle of it; telling everybody how it was done and never telling anybody how you knew. So some people got to think you knew without looking."[11]

Of course, we know something of Father Brown's analytical method, and we know it is not based on the occult, and it is certainly not done without keen observation. We know Father Brown's years of listening to confessions have given him a deep understanding of human nature. We also know Father Brown's tactic of putting himself inside the murderer's mind gives him an analytical advantage that helps him solve the crime.

But what I find particularly interesting is Chace's reference to the general belief that what Father Brown does in solving a case is paranormal, occult in character, that his methods are hidden from view and are available only to the initiated few.

Very often, when a detective solves a crime before we readers reach the solution, our first reaction is that the detective has supernatural power. After all, we have taken the same path as the detective but somehow he got there first—so it must be some type of divine revelation. But what we can now say about Father Brown is that he is able to solve the crime before anyone else not because he is mystical, but because he is multidisciplinary.

> "All these things, which may be seen later from other angles begin to form themselves into antecedents and arguments."
>
> —FATHER BROWN,
> "THE SECRET OF
> FATHER BROWN"

What do we call it when someone reaches a speedy conclusion that is far less obvious to others? We call it intuition. Carl Jung described intuition as "listening to the inner voice" or "heeding the promptings within." Jung said when we have intuition we are paying attention to what is going on inside ourselves, and that these promptings come as thoughts or feelings.

When we speak of "inner voices" or "gut instincts," it often sounds more like fantasy than science. But there are a few well-respected academicians who are examining the process of intuition, and what they have discovered might surprise you.

According to the Nobel laureate Herbert Simon, a professor of psychology and computer science at Carnegie Mellon University, when we rely on gut instinct we are drawing on established rules and patterns, but they're rules and patterns that we can't easily articulate. "All the time," he says, "we are reaching conclusions on the basis of things that go on in our perceptual system, we are aware of the result of the perception but we're not aware of the steps." It is Simon's belief that "intuition and judgment are simply analyses frozen into habit."[12] However, he believes we can break down the insight of intuition into an identifiable process.

Research suggests that the intuitive process depends greatly on the use of additive experiences, which in turn enable us to recognize key patterns.[13] What we are learning is that intuition is made possible by a relatively simple mechanism called "cross-indexing."

When Father Brown examines the physical evidence at the crime scene, the process of cross-indexing it against what he knows about human behavior allows him to achieve greater insight into the crime. Likewise, when an investor examines a balance sheet and income statement and then combines this with knowledge of behavioral finance and the new laws of biology, he or she begins to see a pattern that would not have been clear from studying the financials alone.

The ability to see patterns in different fields of study and then connect those patterns back to the area of examination is what elevates a person's intuitive skills. Obviously, intuitive powers—defined as the power of cross-indexing—increase with the amount of different material and experiences that can be recalled. We might say the ability to see patterns and processes where others see nothing is a talent given to those who study widely and reflect deeply.

When Father Brown speaks of entering the murderer's body, thinking his thoughts and "moving his arms and legs," we get the image of a person who has the complete view of the situation. He has accumulated the necessary physical evidence, and to that he adds the increasingly important intangible evidence that helps him solve the crime. The other characters in the story are working with an incomplete picture. They possess only part of the evidence, so they are slow to reach the same conclusion.

Chesterton is credited widely with elevating the mystery story to a new mental level. This does not mean that the techniques of Sherlock Holmes and Auguste Dupin are unimportant. On the contrary, the chief responsibility of a good detective is to conduct a thorough and detailed examination. But what Chesterton's Father

> "Then I thought for minute and a half more, and I believe I saw the manner of the crime."
>
> —FATHER BROWN, "THE QUEER FEET"

Brown brings to the mystery story is a requirement that all thoughtful analysis must include a willingness to think in alternative ways. As when trying to solve a Rubik's Cube, the detective must learn to twist and turn the mystery into every possible combination so as to leave no question unanswered, no possibility unexamined, leading to the single correct answer.

We can safely say that G. K. Chesterton invented the clerical detective. There are no examples before Father Brown, and none for fifteen years after him.[14] But since then, many have followed in his path. Ellis Peters's Brother Cadfael, a twelfth-century monk and herbalist whose sharp mind has solved many mysteries, is beloved by many thousands of readers. Umberto Eco gave us Brother William in *The Name of the Rose* (1983). Peter Tremayne has created Sister Fidelma, a seventh-century Celtic nun who also functions as a lawyer. Sister Carol Anne O'Marie introduced her sleuth, Sister Mary Helen, in *A Nun in the Closet* and *A Nun in the Cupboard*. D. M. Greenwood invented Theodora Braithwaite, a curate of London's St. Sylvester's, and Isabella Holland gave us Reverend Claire Aldington, an American woman Episcopalian minister.

Perhaps the most popular clerical sleuth is Ralph McInery's Father Roger Dowling. The Dowling stories began with *Her Death of Cold* and *The Seventh Station,* both written in 1977. Like Father Brown, Father Dowling has a distinct advantage over other investigators. He is allowed to roam where he chooses, speaking to everyone and asking whatever questions come to his mind. No one challenges his questions or his movements, perhaps because his immediate supervisor is a "higher power." No other investigator seems able to navigate the entire socioeconomic spectrum with such ease as does the clerical detective.

Despite all the examples above, not all clerical detectives are Christian. In *The Power of Nothingness,* Alexandra David-Neel demonstrates how a Tibetan Buddhist monk, Lama Yongden, solves a mystery. And then there's Harry Kemelman's Rabbi David Small, though he's not so much a spiritual leader as a man of intellect. He has intensely studied the Talmud, the Hebrew book of law, and relies on the art of *pilpul,* defined as "tracing of fine distinctions." According to *The Oxford Companion to Crime and Mystery Writing,* Rabbi Small's "detection is promoted also by the intellectual openness asserted for Judaism, its 'questioning of everything.' "[15]

No matter what your faith, your preference for male or female detectives, or for stories set in the seventh century or the twentieth, there are plenty of clerical mystery stories from which to choose. Another that has captured my attention recently is *Night Watch: A Long-Lost Adventure in Which Sherlock Holmes Meets Father Brown,* by Stephen Kendrick, who is himself a minister.

Night Watch begins on Christmas Day, 1902. An Anglican priest who is playing host to a conference of leaders from the world's major religions is found brutally murdered in his church. Because the church is closed for this secret high-level meeting, it is apparent that the killer must be one of the invited clerics. It is an extremely delicate situation, involving potentially explosive questions of international diplomatic relations. The prime minister has called for help on Sherlock's brother Mycroft Holmes, who holds a secret position in the government's intelligence department; Mycroft brings in Holmes and Dr. Watson to investigate the murder as quickly as possible. Within twenty-four hours, Holmes has solved the case.

Or so it seems. Two weeks later, a young Father Brown, who had worked as a translator at the conference, pays a visit to Baker Street and calmly points out that the Great Detective had overlooked a "few loose ends." As the two men converse, we learn again the fundamental difference between the two Great Detectives. "I do not work the way you do, Mr. Holmes," said Father Brown. "You look for facts, and I look for symbols."[16]

Night Watch is an entertaining book, and since it returns to life two of the Great Detectives we are studying, I found it especially gratifying to get a chance to talk with Stephen Kendrick about his view of Father Brown and Sherlock Holmes.

"I loved writing *Night Watch*," Kendrick told me, "but I didn't want to use just the work from Conan Doyle. I wanted to bring Father Brown into the story because Holmes is the sort of quintessential detective of reason and Father Brown is the quintessential detective of symbolism and acute psychological extensity."[17]

"What Holmes does," Kendrick continued, "is clear his mind so he can observe what others are missing because they project a solution too quickly. Holmes is deliberately keeping his mind blank so that he can perceive what is in front of him, and resists making theories until he truly understands what he sees. Father Brown does it the opposite way. He is purely intuition. [He uses] induction rather than deduction. So I thought it would be fascinating to take these two detectives who think so differently, who approach human nature differently, and put them in the same mystery together.

"Holmes is interested in the small things people overlook," said Kendrick. "I often use the phrase 'eternity is littleness piled high.' I think Father Brown isn't naturally interested in those physical things, although he is able to observe them. He is more interested in the paradoxical things people can't understand. Chesterton delights in turning the world upside down, and every Father Brown story generally turns on some measure of paradox."

Kendrick has made a detailed study of all Chesterton's mystery stories. "What Chesterton states over and over," explained Kendrick, "is the idea that religious sensibility lets someone understand the nature of an individual who commits sin. It is a wonderful twist on the notion of original sin. You don't discover the murderer by separating yourself from the murderer or just following clues. What Father Brown does is delve deep enough into human nature and then puts himself into the psychological state where he can most easily identify the murderer.

"The reason other characters in Chesterton's mysteries don't figure out who the murderer is is that they are not willing to lower themselves into the world of the criminal," Kendrick said. "But a person of holiness can. Theologically speaking, the most holy person and the most sinful person are both imperfect and are still held in God's grasp. As a priest, Father Brown has a sense of solidarity with the murderer. He has the sense that it is not so much about justice as it is about trying to save a soul—and no soul is beyond reach. A sin in theological terms is not doing something wrong, it is missing the mark. That is the actual Greek translation of sin—missing the mark; we all miss the mark, we are all imperfect."

In *Night Watch*, Kendrick writes that Sherlock Holmes sees Father Brown as a "soft Christmas pudding," but that he is also quick to see the priest's potential, remarking, "He might be the slyest one of them all." Why, I asked Kendrick, would Holmes make such a comment?

"Well, again, it embodies the sense of paradox Chesterton loved to utilize," explained Kendrick. "The person who has the blank stare, the meekest demeanor, the person who seems to be pleasantly above and out of interest with what is going around them is often the person who has the shrewdest analysis. Very often, the slyest person of all is the person we have most underestimated; and occasionally, if we are lucky, that person gets to be us."

One theme we see often in Father Brown's mysteries is the idea that things are not always what they seem. In almost every story, there are those who rush to a conclusion based on the obvious, only to watch in awe as Father Brown proposes an alternative explanation. Investing appears to follow a similar pathway. An investor who focuses all his or her energy on a company's earnings per share—the physical evidence—is always a step behind the more intuitive investor who gains an advantage from cross-indexing experience. There are always some investors who rush to judgment based on the accumulation of well-understood physical evidence, only to watch with awe or despair as someone else, with an alternative approach, picks off the profits.

The history of successful investing is a progressive development of alternative explanations. It began with Ben Graham's first analytical observation that book value matters, and then progressed to a greater appreciation of common stock dividends, then to the value of earnings per share, and then to the importance on a company's cash flow and return on invested capital. Each step along the way, investors were able to profit by looking past the consensus view, past the obvious physical evidence, until they reached a higher level of understanding.

How do investors succeed today? By taking the lessons learned from Dupin, adding the methods used by Holmes, and then embracing the intuitive process demonstrated by Father Brown. To become more intuitive, they must enlarge their cross-indexing file. To the study of business, finance, and accounting, they should add baskets of knowledge gained by studying psychology and biology. They should not be so shortsighted as to believe that one point on the financial statement is the only evidence they need to make a profitable investment. A company's financial statements are the starting line for investors, not the end to their investigation.

CHAPTER EIGHT

How to Become a Great Financial Detective

Human beings are unfailingly hopeful; it is one of our best qualities. We joyously celebrate the start of a new year because we believe that with a new beginning, things will be better. How much more welcome is the opening of a new century, with its promise of one hundred years of new beginnings—and how much more crushing when the promise turns sour.

For those of us whose professional lives are centered in the financial arena, and for the millions more who have their savings invested in the stock market, the twenty-first century opened with a bang and then quickly slid into one of the most distressing financial scenarios in modern times.

Starting in the spring of 2000, professional money managers and individual investors alike watched in horror as stock values crashed and wave after wave of financial scandals hit the news. Although people who lived through the days of the Great Depression will have a legitimate counterclaim, in my own lifetime I cannot remember a period when the financial environment was bleaker.

Throughout history, stock market booms have been followed by market busts. And in virtually every case, there was serious malfeasance by one or more players. Looking back, we can discern the pattern: senseless buying prompts an irrational rise in prices (the boom); at the height of the market it is discovered that certain parties engaged in fraudulent activities; stock prices collapse (the bust) before readjusting to fair value. Boom . . . scandal . . . bust. It has happened more times that we care to admit.

The boom of the 1920s led to the 1929 crash; massive financial fraud caused hundreds of corporate bankruptcies. As new federal regulations were put in place, the markets gradually stabilized. Then, by the 1960s, investors were once again mindlessly paying outrageous prices for a group of companies called the "Nifty-Fifty," companies believed to be invulnerable to economic cycles. When the 1973–1974 market crash rinsed away the last of the speculators, Peat Marwick Mitchell, a top-tier accounting firm, was charged by the SEC with failure to follow proper audit procedures for several companies, five of which declared bankruptcy.

Twelve short years later, in 1987, the market collapsed again as insider-trading scandals were uncovered, the junk bond market led by Drexel Burnham Lambert imploded, and hundreds of savings and loans declared insolvency. There were plenty of headlines when Michael R. Milken, the junk bond king at Drexel, and Charles H. Keating, Jr., the head of Lincoln Savings and Loan, stood before the court.

And now, straddling the turn of the century, the latest disaster period. It only seems worse than the others because the wounds are so fresh. Let's look at what happened.

Years from now, economists will look back on the last decade of the twentieth century and marvel at the amount of money that was made. Fueled by a massive boom in corporate spending on technology, investing shot up and whipped the stock market into a full gallop. On the first day of 1990, the Dow Jones Industrial Average closed at 2,810 and the NASDAQ Composite closed at 459. By March 1999, the Dow had reached 10,000. A year later, the NASDAQ crossed 5,000.

Individual investors were ecstatic. Already armed with stocks and mutual funds, many had also been given control over their 401(k) retirement accounts. The combined effect was that they had even more money under their control than ever. And, because investing in stocks had been so easy and so profitable, most thought the best idea was to plow their life savings back into the stock market.

The most dramatic increases were happening in technology stocks, and so that's where much of the investment money went, and for a while it seemed a no-fail proposition. Stock prices, especially technology stocks, just kept going up and up. Like a surfer who found the perfect wave, investors dreamily rode their portfolios to greater and greater wealth—until a few short feet from shore a giant wave came crashing down on top of them.

By March 2000, the tech boom turned into the tech bust. Stock prices that had spent the better part of the 1990s going up suddenly started going down. Pretty soon it was clear that what was unfolding was not a short-term market correction. The great technology bubble had finally burst. People who had invested primarily in technology, telecommunication, and Internet stocks suffered horrendous losses. What happened to them was the equivalent to a surfer's wipeout. When it was over, all they could do was watch as their portfolios, now broken in half, slowly drifted back out to sea.

As I write this, in mid-2002, the situation has deteriorated. It is no longer simply a question of stock prices falling. Prices are still bouncing all over the board, more down than up. Most experienced investors understand that in time prices will self-correct. What is far worse is the devastating effect of the scandals that have torn through the markets in recent months and the effect it has had on investor psychology.

Enron is currently the most notorious because its losses are so massive, but it is certainly not the only major corporation facing bankruptcy, shareholder lawsuits, and federal investigations because of accounting and securities fraud. Every day's headlines, or so it seems, bring a new story of fraud involving once-respected companies and their leaders. Adelphia. Global Crossing. ImClone Systems. Rite-Aid. WorldCom. By the time you read this, perhaps a dozen other names will have become familiar through negative headlines in the business pages.

What makes matters so much worse, from investors' perspective, is that the system of checks and balances that was meant to safeguard them has broken down too. Outside accounting firms, supposedly independent and objective, that carry the mandate to monitor companies' financial documents for just the kind of illegalities that are now coming to light, are themselves under investigation for illegal practices. At best they failed to uncover fraud; at worst they were a party to it. Arthur Andersen is the most infamous instance as of this writing.

And the investors' other safeguard—theoretically objective advice from their brokers—has also blown up in their faces. Well-known brokerage houses are being sued right and left, as it is becoming clear that analysts were pressured to produce positive stock recommendations on companies that, privately, the analysts admitted were a very poor investment.

Just a few—a very few—recent events:

- *June 25, 2002.* In what many suspect may turn into an even greater scandal than Enron, the telecom giant WorldCom admits that over a period of fifteen months, five accounting quarters, it hid nearly $4 billion in costs by improperly booking them as capital assets. The following day, the SEC files federal fraud charges, calling it a fraud of "unprecedented magnitude."

- *June 21, 2002.* The former CEO of Rite-Aid and two senior aides are charged with fraud, conspiracy, and lying to shareholders by posting $2.3 billion in phony profits.

- *May 22, 2002.* Merrill Lynch, perhaps the best known brokerage firm in the country, pays $100 million to settle charges that its brokers artificially promoted weak stocks to gain investment banking business.

- *April 2002.* Xerox is fined $10 million by the SEC for overstating revenues by $3 billion, in what an SEC official calls "a pattern of pervasive fraud." On June 28, Xerox discloses that the amount was actually $6.4 billion.

- *March 2002.* The television cable company Adelphia acknowledges $3.1 billion in debt from off-the-books loans to members of the founder's family; three months later the company is headed inexorably toward bankruptcy.

The cumulative effect of all this is a deepening attitude of cynicism. The public, I fear, sees the entire market environment as covered with an ugly coating of corruption. Even long-time investors, who have weathered other storms, now worry that the financial world has gone completely haywire and that nothing and no one can be trusted. It's easy to see how the average person, trying to do a responsible job of investing for college education or for retirement, might decide the whole system is crooked and opt out of the market completely.

The numbers reflect this widespread pessimism. On June 26, 2002, NBC News reported that the percentage of people saying they have confidence in the financial markets had dropped to 38 percent, the second lowest in history.

Yes, investors should have heeded the lessons of history. They should have known better than to let themselves be seduced by the wildly unrealistic prices of 1998 and 1999. Investors should have known what can happen when uncontrolled enthusiasm overtakes rationality. They should have been smarter than to put so much of our investment money into one asset class and then into just one industry sector because it was flying high.

But what about the rest of it? Could investors have spotted the deceptive accounting practices, the out-and-out fraud that came to light in 2001 and 2002? The perpetrators used such sophisticated methods to hide their misdeeds that it was many months, in some cases years, before these scandals were uncovered by trained professionals like SEC investigators. How could average investors, without benefit of that special training and experience, have seen the danger signs?

The answer is, they couldn't.

Should we have realized that so-called objective auditing by outside accounting firms might also be part of the conspiracy of fraud?

No.

Could we have known that analysts at brokerage houses were putting out deliberately inflated recommendations for questionable stocks?

No.

Considering all that, is there any way out for investors?

Yes. And it is this: Remember the lessons we have learned from the Great Detectives, these two lessons in particular:

- **Don't let yourself be stampeded by conventional wisdom.** At the moment, conventional wisdom seems to be that all American corporations are corrupt and all the participants in the stock market are guilty of criminal activity, some already charged and others just waiting to be found out. This isn't true.

  I can think of perhaps a dozen companies that are truly guilty—a dozen out of some 10,000 public companies. That leaves 9,988 worthy of your careful investigation.

  Would a good detective agree with the conventional wisdom that everybody is guilty, or would he try to separate those companies that might be guilty from the rest that are actually not?

- **Be alert to market psychology.** Don't forget what you know about behavioral finance; don't allow yourself to get swept up in fear and panic. Instead, realize that the sort of mass hysteria that paints all 10,000 companies with the same brush in fact creates wonderful opportunities for investors who can remain calm and objective.

  Good detectives will quickly see that in a climate of fear, many good companies will be sold off unfairly, and represent good bargains for rational investors.

  If you take away only one new idea from this book, let it be this: if your research turns up a good company that is for whatever reason underpriced, you should immediately see that as an opportunity to profit from other people's mistaken thinking.

This brings us to the next question. If we are actually in a good position for investing, what next? What's our best course of action? My answer would be, The same as it always has been—or should be. You must be ready to take responsibility for your own investment decisions.

Deliberately step into the shoes of our Great Detectives, and conduct your investment research just as thoroughly as they would investigate a crime. Whether in times of market turmoil, as now, or in "normal" investing environments, it is a fundamental approach that will serve you well.

When the traditional sources of advice prove untrustworthy, it's even more important that we be able to make good decisions ourselves. It's also more difficult. We have a lot of bad habits to overcome. That is why the lessons we have learned from the Great Detectives are so valuable: they provide us new habits of mind to replace the old ones we need to shed.

THE HABITS OF MIND OF THE GREAT DETECTIVES

AUGUSTE DUPIN
- Develop a skeptic's mindset; don't automatically accept conventional wisdom.
- Conduct a thorough investigation.

SHERLOCK HOLMES
- Begin an investigation with an objective and unemotional viewpoint.
- Pay attention to the tiniest details.
- Remain open minded to new, even contrary, information.
- Apply a process of logical reasoning to all you learn.

FATHER BROWN
- Become a student of psychology.
- Have faith in your intuition.
- Seek alternative explanations and re-descriptions.

• • •

If you do all this, if you consciously take on the mental habits of the Great Detectives and apply their investigative methods to the puzzle of selecting stocks, will you be guaranteed success?

I'm afraid not. Sometimes, even armed with a large magnifying glass and a detective's mindset, you will still overlook an important clue. At other times, the company you are investigating may not have disclosed all the essential facts. In cases of extremely sophisticated fraud like those we have seen in 2002, no amount of detective work would have uncovered the full truth.

However, I can assure you that if you apply the lessons you have learned here you will be far ahead of most other investors. In spite of the very real losses caused by periodic scandals, many more mistakes are made in investing because people continually rely on short-cut methods to reach a hasty decision. Like the bungling police detective who wants to make an arrest as quickly as possible, investors also have the tendency to race to a conclusion—often the wrong conclusion.

The proper financial analysis of a company and its stock price is much more complex than can be captured by lazily gathering superficial information and impatiently cutting corners. I believe that investors who diligently and consistently apply the methods taught by the Great Detectives will, over time, substantially improve their investment results.

As I think back over all the mystery stories I have read, I realize there were many detectives but only one hero. That hero is reason. No matter who the detective was—Dupin, Holmes, Father Brown, Nero Wolfe, or any number of modern counterparts—it was reason that solved the crime and captured the criminal. For the Great Detectives, reason is everything. It controls their thinking, illuminates their investigation, and helps them solve the mystery.

Now think of yourself as an investor. Do you want greater insight about a perplexing market? Reason will clarify your investment approach.

Do you want to escape the trap of irrational, emotion-based action and instead make decisions with calm deliberation? Reason will steady your thinking.

Do want to be in possession of all the relevant investment facts before making a purchase? Reason will help you uncover the truth.

Do you want to improve your investment results by purchasing profitable stocks? Reason will help you capture the market's mispricing.

The young, naive college student who was captivated by Nero Wolfe on the night shift twenty-five years ago still delights in detective fiction. Today I turn eagerly to a new mystery novel whenever possible, both for the delicious thrill of solving an intricate puzzle and for the balm of escaping, however temporarily, the pressures of a hectic world.

My only difficulty, if we could call it such, is deciding what to read. Each year the rich reservoir of terrific mystery novels gets wider and deeper, and those of us who love reading them suffer sometimes from the happy problem of having too many wonderful choices. I relish the new works of authors I already enjoy, and look forward to discovering talented new writers as well. But sometimes, nothing serves quite as well as an old favorite.

Not long ago, relaxing at home after a difficult day, I found myself reaching for a Nero Wolfe mystery. Something of the same impulse that makes children demand the same bedtime story over and over, till they know it by heart, made me want to step into the comfort of familiar territory, to spend the evening with an old friend.

For a while, it was an unabashed pleasure to listen in as Wolfe and his energetic assistant, Archie, go at it, to vicariously enjoy one of Fritz's amazing meals, to watch Wolfe fuss over some of his 10,000 prized orchids in the plant room. But my exhaustion caught up with me, and soon my eyelids became quite heavy. The words blurred on the page, and several times I lost my place. Within seconds I was asleep.

The next thing I knew, I was waking up in Nero Wolfe's office.

"Mr. Hagstrom. Mr. Hagstrom. Your attention, sir. As you are here, tell me what it is I can help you with." That commanding voice could only be Wolfe himself.

I looked down and saw that I was sitting in the famous red leather chair. The chair was positioned to face a large desk made of cherry wood, behind which was another leather chair whose proportions accommodated the enormous size of its occupant. My god, it really was him.

"Well," I stammered, "I . . . I'm not sure. Probably it has to do with this book I've been reading. I mean writing."

"Probably?" Wolfe arched one eyebrow, giving me a look of controlled disdain, and glanced over my shoulder at Archie Goodwin. I turned around in time to see Archie shrug at his boss, a shrug that eloquently said, "I have no idea either."

"Would you like a refreshment?" Wolfe suddenly asked. It seemed a fine idea. "I'll have what you're having," I said. Wolfe rang for Fritz. When he entered, Wolfe asked for two beers, his glass on the table was empty. While we waited I used the time to collect my thoughts. I would have to be on my toes here. Wolfe had little patience for fuzzy thinking and he despised clumsy syntax; in fact I read once that he charged clients more money when they used bad grammar in his presence.

I began again. "You know better than anyone how much I enjoy reading mystery stories; you started it for me. And I was very excited when I realized that the techniques of the Great Detectives could help individuals become better investors. But it's very difficult now. So many people have lost money, and I'm afraid they've lost faith in the stock market, too. They don't know what to think. I really want to help them find some answers, or at least try to help. But I'm just not sure what else I should be saying. So I think I'm here to see if you can shed some light on the matter."

"Very well." Wolfe laced his fingers together over his enormous midsection, tilted his head back, and closed his eyes. His lips pursed in and out until he spoke. "What are you most concerned about?"

That's a good start right there, I thought. Begin with the number-one problem. And so I laid it out.

"The biggest mistake, I think, is that people make investment decisions too quickly, on the basis of very little information. Maybe they're too busy, or think they are, or they don't really know how to go about it, but for whatever reason, they're reluctant to do the necessary work. And make no mistake about it, Mr. Wolfe, being a successful investor takes work."

Wolfe opened his eyes slightly. "Do you know of anything worthwhile in life that doesn't?" One corner of his mouth twitched; was he smiling?

No disagreement, so I continued. "Everyone seems to be looking for a shortcut. Some special tip or gimmick that will magically produce outstanding results in the shortest period of time. But there aren't any shortcuts. You just have to do the research."

"And, of course," Wolfe said, "you have to know where to look." For a moment he sat in silence, then abruptly asked, "Do you enjoy the game of bridge, Mr. Hagstrom?"

"A little," I answered, puzzled. What was he getting at?

"Do you remember who said this? 'He makes, in silence, a host of observations and inferences. So, perhaps, do his companions; and the difference in the extent of the information obtained, lies not so much in the validity of the inference as in the quality of the observation. The necessary knowledge is that of what to observe.'"

"Of course," I answered. "It was Dupin, in 'The Murders in the Rue Morgue.' He was talking about the analytical process used by a whist player. When I first read the passage, I didn't know the game whist.

"It is a card game," said Wolfe. "The precursor to bridge."

"That makes sense. In the story Poe described all the many variables that a good whist player needed to pay attention to, not just the play of the cards but the body language, changes in facial expression, mannerisms of the other players, things like that." I thought for a moment. "But of course it could apply to investors. To succeed, you have to do some homework, but you also need to know what to study—the tangibles as well as the intangibles."

Wolfe grunted, then glanced to my left, toward one of the empty yellow chairs. Only now it wasn't empty. It was occupied by a tall, well-dressed man with the unmistakable air of a European aristocrat.

"Monsieur Dupin," Wolfe asked, "what have you to add?"

"There is no method in their proceedings," Dupin said, "beyond the method of the moment. They make a vast parade of measures; but, not infrequently, these are so ill adapted to the objects proposed."[1]

Wolfe, looking rather pleased with himself, said, "So, let us summarize. Most investors must come to terms with the unpleasant truth that they need to do research—observations, as M. Dupin calls it—and they must know what to observe. Furthermore, they should proceed methodically, so that the observations fit the situation under study and nothing relevant is overlooked. Do you agree?"

Before I could respond, another voice broke in.

"They say that genius is an infinite capacity for taking pains. It's a very bad definition, but it does apply to detective work."[2]

"Ah, Mr. Holmes," Wolfe said. "Welcome, sir."

I quickly looked again to the side, and there, calmly sitting in a second yellow chair, was Sherlock himself. In his hand he held one of his favorite pipes, but in deference to Wolfe he was not smoking.

"It is, I submit, not such a bad definition after all," Wolfe said, "and certainly it applies to detective work in this house. Yes, Archie?"

Archie Goodwin had been quiet for so long I had almost forgotten he was in the room. At the word "genius" he made a small snorting noise, but not so small as to escape Wolfe's notice. Now, with one hand pressed against his mouth, he merely waved the other hand in that way that says, "Nothing; carry on."

With a glare at his assistant, Wolfe turned back to me. "Mr. Hagstrom, what say you?"

"I say that it is also a perfect definition of careful investors. Very often the critical facts about a company are buried deeply, and only someone who will take pains, as Sherlock Holmes puts it, to look at all the details will uncover the important information."

"The smallest point may be the most essential," Holmes said. "It has long been an axiom of mine that the little things are infinitely the most important."[3]

Dupin nodded in agreement. "Experience has shown that a vast, perhaps the larger, portion of truth arises from the seemingly irrelevant."[4]

Wolfe tapped his fingertips together. "So, can we then say that investors must take pains to look everywhere and collect all the data?" I nodded, but Wolfe was already continuing with his train of thought. "But surely there is more to it. You cannot know the answer until you have all the pieces—all detectives know this—but the pieces don't give up the answer until one applies one's mind to the problem."

At that, everyone tried to speak at once. Everyone except me. In the same room with three of the finest analytical minds I have ever come across, I knew enough to keep quiet. But something Sherlock once said to Watson about the importance of analysis flashed through my mind and I blurted out: "You can see everything. You fail, however, to reason from what you see. You are too timid in drawing your inferences."[5] Holmes smiled recognizing the quote.

"Let us consider the problem in the light of pure reason," Sherlock Holmes was saying. "There should be no combination of events for which the wit of man cannot conceive an explanation."[6]

The room fell completely quiet. It was one of those rather awkward moments when no one seemed to know what to say next. Wolfe turned to me. "You seem less than satisfied. Have we failed to conceive an explanation?"

"Not at all. Everything you say is exactly right. And I'd be willing to guess that, deep down, most investors already know it. But something keeps them from acting on it. It must be something to do with human nature."

"Ah," said Wolfe. "I expect you are correct. Let us ask someone who knows a great deal about human nature. Archie, if you please."

Archie rose from his desk chair and opened the door connecting to the front room. In came a very short, very round man wearing a rumpled brown coat and carrying a battered umbrella. Whereas the other two famous detectives had simply materialized in their chairs, Father Brown walked into the room in the normal fashion, using his umbrella like a cane.

"Good evening, Father Brown; welcome to my home," Wolfe said. "May I offer you some refreshment?"

Father Brown asked for a beer, and Wolfe rang for Fritz. Father Brown took the yellow chair that Archie pulled forward for him, and greeted each of us with his warm-eyed smile.

"Well, Mr. Hagstrom?" Wolfe finally asked curtly.

I wasn't sure how to begin, but the priest's expression was kind, and so I plunged in. "Father, I believe that you have a real understanding of how people act and think, because of your work. Now, in my work, I have seen people act and think, about investing I mean, in ways that don't always make sense. There are some things I think I understand, and more that I don't fully understand, and I'm not sure what to do about any of them."

Father Brown, listening closely, smiled and nodded in encouragement. It was very easy to talk to him.

"I know you know more about psychology than I do," I continued, "but it seems to me that some people have faulty psychological wiring where the stock market is concerned. They find it extremely difficult to take what we call a contrarian position. Most investors are only comfortable buying stocks after they go up in price and they will often want sell a stock that has gone down. Of course buying high and selling low is not the recipe for success"

Wolfe snorted, as if he wanted to say something, but Father Brown was listening carefully, giving me his full attention. Everything about his manner said, "Please go on."

So I continued. "People who have the intellectual ability to reason logically let emotions overtake their rationality. They tend to get very emotional when money is involved, Father, and forget to think clearly about what they are doing and what is really happening."

Sherlock Holmes spoke up. "It is of the first importance not to allow your judgment to be biased by personal qualities. The emotional qualities are antagonistic to clear reasoning."[7]

"And if that's not bad enough," I said, "I think that a lot of investors take that emotion to a very dangerous level. They suffer from what I call a gambler's itch. They see the stock market like a giant casino. Inside the casino are gaming tables where someone is always winning. In the market there is always one industry or one group of stocks that is doing well so investors flock to whichever gaming table has the best action and lay down their money. It all looks so easy, they just jump in. But winning streaks have a way of coming to an end, and in a snap all their winnings disappear. Now I know Auguste Dupin would never be tempted into a gambling frenzy just because everyone else is; and Sherlock Holmes would never place a bet without thinking. They would never let themselves be caught up in such destructive emotions and forget about logic."

Hearing their names, both men looked up quickly, then both nodded at me.

"In fact, sometimes I wonder if emotion isn't the biggest trap of all," I said. "It seems to explain a number of things."

Father Brown looked pleased, as if I had said something smart.

"For instance," I continued, "stubbornness. I've seen some people conclude, after quick research, that they have figured everything out, so there is no need to look any further. Partly it's overconfidence, I suppose. Or maybe it's just linear thinking. If things are going well, they expect that everything is going to be fine in the future. If things are bad, they expect that the future will remain dismal. They never stop to analyze exactly what is happening and consider how things might change, so they are caught unprepared when things do change. The world doesn't stand still, especially the financial world."

Wolfe shifted slightly in his chair and glanced in the direction of his safe, where I knew he kept a large amount of working cash. Father Brown's eyes never left my face. He leaned forward, encouraging me to go on.

"At first I thought it was a matter of people not wanting to take the trouble to update their worldview. But now I'm wondering if it's that they can only *see* one view."

Sherlock Holmes broke in. "Breadth of view is one of the essentials of our profession. The interplay of ideas and the oblique uses of knowledge are often of extraordinary interest."[8]

"It's one of the essentials of good investing, too," I said, "and I'm not sure investors are particularly good at it. Most investors latch onto one description of what is occurring with a particular company and they cannot see that something else might be happening. It's as though the facts are spread over all six sides of a cube, but they can only see one side."

"Aha," Wolfe cried, slapping his hands down on the arms of his big leather chair. "I have it! The truth in geometric shapes. Archie, fetch me down the copy of *Philosophical Investigations* from the shelf behind you. Wittgenstein says something about triangles that would elucidate the matter."

Wolfe took the book from Archie and began flipping through the pages until he found his place, then he spoke.

"Ludwig Wittgenstein," Wolfe said with a small sniff, "an Austrian born British philosopher considered by many the leading analytical philosopher of the twentieth century. Here's what he wrote. 'This triangle can be seen as a hole, as a solid, as a geometrical drawing; as standing on its base, as hanging from its apex, as a mountain, as a wedge, as an arrow or a pointer, as an overturned object which is meant to stand on the shorter side of the right angle, as a half parallelogram, and as various other things.'"9

"To this point," I said, "a company, like Wittgenstein's triangle, can have several different explanations and anyone whose mind can formulate multiple descriptions is going to be a better investor."

Father Brown, who had heard his share of confessions about human struggles, sat back in his chair and smiled softly.

Wolfe cleared his throat to collect everyone's attention. "Mr. Hagstrom, it appears that we have identified three overriding problems here. Most investors resist doing the hard work of investment research, they fail to resist the pull of emotion, and lastly they are unable to formulate a series of possible explanations. Everything we have talked about is a manifestation of one or the other."

Wolfe paused, probably for dramatic effect, but I interrupted him before he could continue his lecture.

"Actually, I think there is one situation that reflects all these mistakes. I've been seeing it a lot lately. It is the tendency of investors to go along with whatever they read, what everyone else is saying. Today we call it conventional wisdom."

"That's what I call it too," Wolfe murmured wryly.

"But the question is why," I went on. "And I think I understand it now. It's partly because being a part of the crowd is easy. If they accept that something is true because everybody believes it to be so, then they don't have to do any more work on the subject. Being a part of the crowd eases their fear of being wrong. Investors are afraid to trust their own judgment, they're confused and anxious about making a mistake.

Going along with what everyone else is doing or saying gives them a sense of comfort and safety, even if it might be a false sense."

Father Brown raised his finger to catch my eye. "I've noticed more and more in the modern world, appearing in all sorts of newspaper rumors and conversational catchwords . . . People readily swallow the untested claims of this, that, or the other. It's drowning all your old rationalism and skepticism, it's coming in like the sea."[10]

Now it was my turn to smile at him. "What everybody knows is short and plain enough," the priest continued. "It is also entirely wrong."[11]

I looked closely at Father Brown. Without the bombastic pronouncements of Nero Wolfe, or the cold logic of Dupin and Holmes, he had captured the essence of the dilemma, and yet managed to make me feel as I were the one who had figured it out. I found it extraordinarily comforting to talk to him; he invited confidence. Only later did I realize that throughout the gathering in Wolfe's office, he had hardly said anything. I had done most of the talking.

"The real question is, though," I asked, "how can I help people break those bad habits, if what we're talking about is basic human nature?"

"Human nature," Sherlock Holmes muttered, "is a strange mixture."[12]

"Amazing understatement, my friend," Wolfe said. "But true. I myself have seen little evidence that people change, although I suspect Father Brown would argue the point stoutly." He glanced over at the priest, who smiled beatifically. "However, Mr. Hagstrom, perhaps you will find that the mere act of putting these concerns forward, with the eloquent assistance of our guests, will have a salutary effect. Perhaps most investors will recognize their flawed thinking and decide to do something about it. This may the best we can offer you, or them. Of one thing I am certain: people have an infinite capacity for continued learning. The more you put in a brain, the more it will hold—if you have one."[13]

Wolfe wanted very much to have the last word on the matter, but he was upstaged by Sherlock Holmes, who added, "It is better to learn wisdom late than never to learn it at all."[14]

Yes, I thought to myself, it's better to learn wisdom late than never to learn it at all. Better late than never. Better late . . . late . . . My eyes felt heavy again.

Suddenly I heard a loud *thunk*. At first I thought it might be Wolfe slapping his hand on the desk, then I realized I was in my own chair in my own study, and the book I was reading had fallen to the floor. Someone was shaking me. "Robert," my wife was saying, "it's late. Very late. It's time for bed."

APPENDIX 1

WHERE TO GO FOR INFORMATION

In your search for information about companies, industries, and broad financial issues, I think you will find it useful to think like a reporter.

Take a moment to review the section in Chapter 3 that describes the three concentric circles of information: secondary, primary, and human sources. As an investor, you will focus your search on items that relate to your investment plans, so your three source levels will all deal with financial information.

It is in your best interest to cast your net widely. Of course you want to learn all you can about a specific company or industry you are considering investing in, but you also need to be aware of larger financial and economic issues.

In the same way, I strongly recommend that you not limit yourself to just one source in each category: one newspaper, magazine, or television program, for instance. It is easy to fall into the habit of turning to the same publications, because you have become familiar with their format and know where to find what you are looking for. But if you do that, you are shortchanging yourself—not because what you read is inaccurate (although that is always a possibility to keep in mind) but because it reflects just one viewpoint. Make a conscious effort to broaden your reading horizons. Develop the habit of reading publications with different points of view, so you are exposed to all perspectives.

Secondary Sources

Secondary information is that which is written *about* a person, a company, or an industry by an "outsider," someone who has no official connection and is presumably objective. The information has already appeared in some medium, and is available for your review. This includes daily and weekly newspapers, television and radio programs, magazines, newsletters, dissertations, theses, and books.

Reporters usually start with secondary information because it is the best source for background knowledge. I suggest you do the same. It is easier to evaluate primary information (that which comes directly from the person or company) once you have built a solid foundation of understanding from a wide range of secondary information.

Newspapers. A good first step is the local newspaper in the city where the company's headquarters or its major manufacturing facilities are located—or, if you are focusing your research on a person, the daily paper of his or her hometown. Read back issues for at least one full year. From there, move out to national newspapers like *The Wall Street Journal, The New York Times, The Washington Post,* and the *Financial Times,* and weekly financial newspapers such as *Barron's.*

Most newspapers, including local papers, make available a histori-cal index of story titles, and many offer access to the complete story via the Internet. There may be a small charge to access and print a story, but these charges are comparatively small considering the amount of money you might be investing.

If you find an especially thorough or revealing piece (a profile of the CEO, for example, or an investigative round-up of a company's legal problems), make special note of the publication and the reporter. Then search forward in time for any follow-ups the reporter might have done for that publication or some other. Also be on the lookout for corrections to the story or dissenting letters written to the editor.

Working reporters sometimes contact the person who wrote the original story, asking whether anything has changed since the story appeared. You may not be able to gain access to national reporters, but the person who wrote the story in your local newspaper may be will-ing to talk with you informally.

Magazines and newsletters. There are several financial magazines investors should read. The two most prominent monthlies are *Fortune* and *Forbes*, both of which employ impressive stables of investigative journalists and pride themselves on their ability to cast light on wide-ly misunderstood financial phenomena, whether company-specific or industry related. In addition, there are two weekly magazines that are also worthwhile reading. *Business Week* gives investors a quick snap-shot of a week on Wall Street, plus additional exposés on companies and their CEOs. I would highly recommend investors study *The Econ-omist* as well. First published in 1863, *The Economist* covers news events worldwide and continues to be one of the most in-depth and thought-provoking magazines available to readers. In addition to cov-ering the United States, the magazine also reports from elsewhere in the Americas, Asia, the Middle East, Africa, and Europe. The maga-zine's periodic survey reports alone are worth a year's subscription.

Investors should also take the time to read *Harvard Business Review*, which remains the high water mark for academic business and management research.

You can find other possibilities in magazine indexes such as the Business Periodicals Index, published by H. W. Wilson. Check the reference section of your library, or access the index via the Internet at www.hwwilsom.com. (Incidentally, your first stop for all research should be the reference librarian at your local library; he or she can point you to all the directories and indexes mentioned here, and many more besides.)

Try to at least scan the major financial magazines on a regular basis. Some people drop in at their local library every couple of weeks and spend an hour or so in the periodicals room. That's enough to give you a broad sweep of current events. Soon you will find that material on your area of interest jumps off the page, and you will want to slow down and read it more carefully. Like major newspapers, many magazines make their content available on the Internet, so you can do your scanning from home if you prefer.

In addition to general consumer magazines, you might want to explore the trade magazines, specialty publications that focus on a particular industry. The articles are written for people connected with that industry, and some may be more technical than you need, but you are sure to get an insider's perspective not always available in the more broadly targeted publications. One word of caution, however: Many trade magazines have small staffs, and depend on information they receive from the industry they cover. Articles may be derived largely from press releases provided by a company or the industry trade association, with only minor editorial follow-up. For a balanced picture, be sure to look into other information sources.

To find the trade publications for the industry you are interested in, start with one of these periodicals indexes (in your local library): Ulrich's International Periodicals Directory, Standard Periodical Direc-

tory, and the aforementioned Business Periodicals Index. Also, check in
your local library for the *Encyclopedia of Associations.* That may lead
you to an industry or professional association, and you can write to
them for information on any publications they sponsor.

Another source is specialty newsletters, which are often overlooked
but are sometimes packed with interesting information. To find out if
there is one relevant to the area you're interested in, contact the News-
letter and Electronic Publishers Association, 1501 Wilson Blvd., Suite
509, Arlington, VA 22209 (tel. 800-356-9302; www.newsletters.org).

Broadcast media. You should also be attuned to television news programs for national and regional events that affect your investments
plans. The major network news departments have Web sites, so you
can check on news developments if you miss their broadcasts; you can
also search the sites for past stories. Vanderbilt University Television
News Archive produces the *Television News Index and Abstracts,* which
covers the major evening news programs (TV News Archive, Vanderbilt
University, 110 21st Ave S., Suite 704, Nashville, TN 37203; tel. 615-322-
2927; www.tvnews. vanderbilt.edu). Burrelle's Information Services in
Livingston, New Jersey (www.burrelles.com), supplies the full text of
some news programs online. This is a fee-based service, but you may
find that your public library subscribes, and you can access it at no cost
via the library's computers.

Dissertations and theses. Graduate students doing academic research
for a master's thesis or doctoral dissertation are often received far more
cordially by a company than an investigative reporter would be, and
sometimes they turn up interesting insights that you won't find elsewhere. If there exists a dissertation or thesis related to the company or
industry you are interested in, it's worth your time to check it out.

To find them, start with the closest university library. Hard-copy or
online versions are available through Dissertation Abstracts Interna-

tional, available in most university libraries or via the Internet from www.proquest.com, for a fee.

Books. No investigation of secondary sources would be complete without examining any related published books on the topic. Libraries and bookstores (and their Web sites) can provide a list of relevant books to study.

Internet. If you are technologically wired (and I mean that both literally and figuratively), you can probably skip right over the foregoing and simply run an Internet search, using your favorite search engine. It's a good bet that it will turn up citations in most of the newspapers, magazines, newsletters, and other sources described above. In the same way, many public libraries are accessible from your home computer; using their extensive online reference sources and indexes, you can jump quickly to specific documents and publications. Of course if you have already done a detailed search using the sources outlined above, you might be covering the same ground. But you could also find a brand-new document source that would otherwise have been overlooked. Using the Internet remains a good and inexpensive way to gather valuable secondary information.

A separate step involves searching through commercial online databases. Hundreds of vendors comb the world for all possible information about a subject, a company, or an industry. Some of the larger database vendors include LexisNexis (www.lexis-nexis.com), Dialog (www.dialog.com), DataStar (www.datastarweb.com), and NewsNet (www.newsnet.com). These databases are subscription-based, and some of the fees are steep. Many large public libraries subscribe, so you can access the information from their linked computers. If you want immediate access from your home computer, you will have to decide for yourself whether you have already covered the bases, or whether you prefer to pay for the confidence of knowing there is little about a company or its industry that has not become part of your document file.

Primary Sources

Primary material originates directly with the person, the company, or the industry—it's produced *by* them, not written *about* them. It may be a speech by the CFO, an interview with a company spokesperson, a press release from the industry association, or official documents prepared and filed by the company. But whatever form it takes, primary information comes straight from the horse's mouth.

Many of the same sources that you investigated for secondary information (especially the Internet searches) will also turn up primary material, and it warrants your serious study. To supplement those, you definitely should become familiar with the documents that public companies are required to file, and other sources of government information. And you owe it to yourself to learn how to read an annual report and a 10K.

SEC-mandated financial documents. All publicly traded companies (those listed on a national exchange: New York Stock Exchange, American Stock Exchange, or NASDAQ) are required by the U.S. Securities and Exchange Commission to disclose any information that is deemed important and relevant to its shareholders. As described in Title 17 of the Code of Federal Regulations, that disclosure involves about 180 different forms. The most important ones for investors are annual and quarterly reports, proxy statements, and 10K and 10Q reports.

Annual report. Most companies put serious money into producing a visually impressive annual report, and many investors, rightly considering them marketing pieces, have a tendency to go over lightly at best. That is a mistake. Tucked deep inside the report, sometimes in type too small to read comfortably, some very valuable information is often hidden.

Scrutinize all footnotes, as they are often a source of information you need. Company A, for instance, shows a good profit in its report to shareholders, but a footnote reveals the source of the earnings increase: The assumed rate of return of the pension plan was revised upward, so the company was required to set aside less for workers and could drop more money to the bottom line. As another example, "certain parties" at Company B (officers or directors) have received loans from the company, and a footnote shows that the company is writing the loans off as delinquent.

Also take time to study the back of the report. Here you will find management's discussion of the company's revenues and expenses detailed more thoroughly. Pay close attention to what the company's managers say about these topics: how they decide to allocate the profits of the company; their policy on dividend and share repurchase; distribution of stock options to employees; shift in accounting policies; change in tax rates; and the company's policy on acquisitions and divestitures.

This back-of-the-book material is not as sexy as the glossy front of the report and not as warm and fuzzy as the chairman's breezy letter, but it is very revealing. Remember that you are approaching this research like an investigative reporter. You will not be seduced by the company's very expensive public relations line. Your job is to look beneath the surface, analyze, and determine if there are any inconsistencies between what the data says and what company management is saying.

Proxy statement. After studying the annual report, next look at the company's proxy statement. It reveals salaries and benefits paid to top executives, and includes biographical information on board members. If a company is considering a change in accounting firms—something you should view with suspicion—the proxy statement is where you will find this request.

Prospectus. Next review the company's prospectus. When a company seeks to raise more money by either issuing new shares or selling bonds, the prospectus is the document in which they must reveal the business risks to potential buyers, including competition and pending lawsuits that could have a material effect on the company. The prospectus also must explain what the company plans to do with the cash proceeds from the offering.

Other SEC reports. The 10K and 10Q reports (annual and quarterly, respectively) give much more detail on the company's operation than the annual report and quarterly reports provided for shareholders. The SEC also requires companies to disclose any changes in management or accountants, or any other "material events"; this information will be found in Form 8K, entitled "Current Update." Also take a look at Schedule 13D. The SEC requires any individual or institution that acquires more than 5 percent of the outstanding stock of a company to disclose the ownership. Also, they must disclose whether they plan to do any significant buying or selling of shares in the future and whether their intentions are to invest in the company or take control of it.

Other oversight agencies. For investors, the SEC is the most relevant federal agency, but there are others you should take note of, which investigate or regulate unfair or unsafe practices in both public and private companies. These include:

- The Federal Trade Commission (www.ftc.gov); anticompetitive and deceptive business practices

- The Consumer Product Safety Commission (www.cpsc.gov); unsafe products

- The Equal Employment Opportunity Commission (www.eeoc. gov); discrimination based on race, ethnicity, gender, age, or disabilities

- The National Labor Relations Board (www.nlrb.gov); unfair treatment of workers, whether union or nonunion

- The Occupational Safety and Health Administration (www.osha. gov); physical and health hazards in the workplace

- The Environmental Protection Agency (www.epa.gov); pollution of the land, air, and water by both individuals and companies

These are all public agencies, and the material they produce is available to all of us. They may have valuable information about the behavior of companies, and it is a good idea to contact them before you invest your life savings.

The simplest tool is your computer. All these agencies maintain searchable Web sites; granted, each will probably load you up with more than you need, but with practice you can quickly skip over the more esoteric reports and zero in on material relevant to a company's financial picture.

And don't forget the state and local agencies that play a similar role in the oversight process. Although you might think if a company had committed a major violation the matter would be recorded by the appropriate federal agency, in some cases the first regulatory investigation can start at the state level.

Also, if you are investigating a specific company, remember that agencies have been created to oversee particular industries. For example, pharmaceutical companies are regulated by the U.S. Food and Drug Administration (www.fda.gov). The Office of Comptroller of the Currency (www.occ.treas.gov) regulates nationally chartered banks. Utilities are regulated by the state in which they do business, but they are also monitored at the federal level by the National Association of

Regulatory Utility Commissioners (www.naruc.org). As with the oversight agencies listed above, you can search their Web sites for information on the company you're interested in.

Human Sources

Reporters are famous (or infamous) for their persistence in contacting anyone connected with a story they are pursuing. They manage to talk with CEOs, board chairs, senior government officials, and all manner of celebrities. You, as an individual investor without the sanction of a recognized media source behind you, will probably not be able to reach the same sources. But that doesn't mean that you have to forgo access to personal sources; it simply means you'll have to be creative and resourceful. Look again at Chapter 3, and review the suggestions for finding people with a current or former connection to the company you are investigating.

APPENDIX 2

FOR FURTHER READING

Because the creators of our three Great Detectives are major figures in literature; because detective fiction as a literary form has been analyzed, critiqued, discussed, debated, and dissected by numerous critics and historians, from both an academic and a generalist perspective; and because many books have been produced that attempt to explain the theory and techniques of mysteries to faithful readers and aspiring authors, the net result is that even a quick trip through the shelves of a good-sized library produces a dizzying array of references. The sources listed here are, therefore, by no means a complete list of possibilities; they are simply the ones I consulted and found useful, in whole or in part, while researching this book.

Appendix 2

ON EDGAR ALLAN POE AND AUGUSTE DUPIN

Grossvogel, David I. *Mystery and Its Fictions: From Oedipus to Agatha Christie.* Baltimore: The Johns Hopkins University Press, 1979. This academic examination of the work of various writers of serious literature includes one chapter on Poe.

Harrison, James A, ed. *The Complete Work of Edgar Alan Poe.* New York: AMS Press, 1965. One of many editions of Poe's stories, novels, and poems.

Hoffman, Daniel. *Poe Poe Poe Poe Poe Poe Poe.* London: Robson Books, 1973. A fanciful work of biography and literary criticism, encompassing all of Poe's stories and poems as well as his complex life; one chapter is devoted to the detective stories.

Irwin, John. *The Mystery to a Solution: Poe, Borges, and the Analytic Detective Story.* Baltimore, MD: Johns Hopkins University Press, 1996. A professor of humanities examines the many intellectual facets of Poe's fiction and the Argentinian author's stories that "double" Poe.

Silverman, Kenneth. *Eagar A. Poe: Mournful and Never-Ending Remembrance.* New York: Harper, 1991. A detailed, highly readable biography.

Silverman, Kenneth, ed. *New Essays on Poe's Major Tales.* New York: Cambridge University Press, 1993. Edited by Poe's biographer, this collection of essays by various writers addresses the full range of Poe's stories, and includes one chapter on the stories featuring Dupin.

Thoms, Peter, ed. *Detection & Its Designs.* Athens: Ohio University Press, 1998. An academic critique of detective fiction as literature; includes chapters on Poe, Doyle, and others.

ON ARTHUR CONAN DOYLE AND SHERLOCK HOLMES

Accardo, Pasquale, John Peterson, and Geir Hasnes, eds. *Sherlock Holmes Meets Father Brown and His Creator*. See bibliography section on Chesterton, below, for details on this interesting book.

Booth, Martin. *The Doctor and the Detective: A Biography of Sir Arthur Conan Doyle*. New York: St. Martin's, 1977. Comprehensive, readable biography of Holmes's creator.

Carr, John Dickson. *The Life of Arthur Conan Doyle: The Man Who Was Sherlock Holmes*. New York: Random House, 1949. A biography of Doyle, drawn largely from his many letters, that reads like a mystery—not surprising, since Carr is himself the author of many mystery novels.

Doyle, Sir Arthur Conan. *Memories and Adventures*. Boston: Little Brown and Company, 1924. Doyle's autobiography.

Eames, Hugh. *Sleuths, Inc.: Studies of Problem Solvers*. Philadelphia: J. B. Lippincott, 1978. One chapter is devoted to Sherlock Holmes.

Hall, Trevor H. *Sherlock Holmes and His Creator*. London: Duckworth, 1978. Each chapter is a self-contained essay on an aspect of Doyle's life or the Holmes character.

Hardwick, Michael. *The Complete Guide to Sherlock Holmes*. New York: St. Martins, 1986. A useful reference tool that includes summaries of all the stories, with highlighted quotes for each, and a who's who of characters.

Harrison, Michael. *A Study in Surmise: The Making of Sherlock Holmes*. Bloomington, IN: Gaslight Publications, 1984. Traces the many threads of Doyle's life that influenced the creation of his detective.

Jann, Rosemary. *The Adventures of Sherlock Holmes: Detecting Social Order*. New York: Twayne, 1995. An academic study of the tales and the social context in which they were written.

Park, Orlando. *The Sherlock Holmes Encyclopedia*. New York: Carol Publishing Group, 1994. One of the numerous reference works to the Holmes canon. Characters, locations, and objects are described in encyclopedia format.

Rodin, Alvin E., M.D., and Key, Jack D., eds. *Medical Casebook of Doctor Arthur Conan Doyle.* Florida: Robert E. Krieger Publishing Co., 1984.

Thomson, June. *Holmes and Watson.* New York: Carroll & Graf, 1995. A "biography" of the two fictional characters, drawn from the stories and historical documents of the period.

Van der Leun, Gerald. *The Quotable Sherlock Holmes.* New York: The Mysterious Press, 2000. A small book containing hundreds of Sherlock's immortal words, grouped into categories, ostensibly by Dr. Watson's great-grandson.

ON G. K. CHESTERTON AND FATHER BROWN

Accardo, Pasquale, John Peterson, and Geir Hasnes, eds. *Sherlock Holmes Meets Father Brown and His Creator: A Miscellany of Scholarship, Satires, and Literary Diversions.* New Westminster, BC, Canada: The Battered Silicon Dispatch Box, 2000. This intriguing book includes what amounts to a debate in print between the followers of Holmes and of Father Brown, as to which is the more accomplished detective. The greater portion of the book, however, is devoted to the life and times of Father Brown, in effect a biography of this fictional character.

Braybrooke, Patrick. *Gilbert Keith Chesterton.* Philadelphia: J. B. Lippincott, 1922. Written while Chesterton was still alive, this small book (by a man who was Chesterton's relative) is not a biography but a critical review of some of his best-known writings. It is especially interesting today for the descriptions of Chesterton's home life, seen through the eyes of one who was a frequent guest in his home.

Chesterton, Gilbert Keith. *Autobiography.* New York: Sheed & Ward, 1936, rev. 1954. The man who in many biographies so brilliantly recounted the lives of major literary figures here tells his own story. He called the undertaking "the morbid and degrading task of writing the story of my life," and completed it only three months before his death.

Chesterton, Gilbert Keith. *A Handful of Authors: Essays on Books & Writers.* New York: Sheed & Ward, 1953. Like many of Chesterton's book-length works, this one is a collection of short pieces written over a period of years. In this case, reviews and critical commentary on many writers past and present, covering a period from 1901 to 1931. It is of interest to us for two reasons: the easy glimpse it provides of Chesterton's writing style and way of thinking, and the fact that one of the essays is about Sherlock Holmes.

Dale, Alzina Stone. *The Outline of Sanity: A Biography of G. K. Chesterton.* Grand Rapids, MI: Fredmans Publishing, 1982. The title comes from one of Chesterton's books, also titled *The Outline of Sanity,* which was a collection of essays presenting Chesterton's views on economics, politics, and social justice. Dale's point of view is that Chesterton, often described as flamboyantly eccentric, was instead a rare point of sanity and balance in an age of extravagance.

Ffinch, Michael. *G. K. Chesterton: A Biography.* New York: Harper & Row, 1996. Although a full biography in the usual sense of the word, this book is concerned primarily with Chesterton's religious life. Ffinch was able to draw from an attic full of Chesterton's notebooks, letters, and drawings, some of which had not been published previously.

Ward, Maisie. *Gilbert Keith Chesterton.* New York: Sheed & Ward, 1943. The all-time classic biography of Chesterton, by a historian who was also a close family friend and Chesterton's publisher. Maisie Ward and her husband, Frank Sheed, established the publishing company that bears their names in 1926 in London, and expanded the company to New York a few years later. It remains today one of the industry's leading Catholic presses.

ON READING AND WRITING DETECTIVE FICTION: HISTORY, LITERARY CRITICISM, AND TECHNIQUE

Allen, Dick, and David Chacko. *Detective Fiction, Crime and Compromise.* New York: Harcourt Brace Jovanovich, 1974.

Ball, John. *The Mystery Story.* San Diego: University of California, 1976.

Barzun, Jacques, and Wendell Hertig Taylor, eds. *A Catalogue of Crime.* New York: Harper & Row, 1971.

Craig, Patricia, ed. *The Oxford Book of Detective Stories.* New York: Oxford University Press, 2000.

Craig, Patricia, ed. *The Oxford Book of English Detective Stories.* New York: Oxford University Press, 1990.

Day, Marele, ed. *How to Write Crime.* St. Leonards, NSW, Australia: Allen & Unwin, 1996. A dozen authors contribute how-to chapters on various aspects of the mystery writer's art.

Dove, George N. *The Reader and the Detective Story.* Bowling Green, OH: Bowling Green State University Popular Press, 1997. A highly academic work of history and literary criticism built around theories of reading and perception.

Eco, Umberto, and Thomas A. Sebeok. *The Sign of Three: Dupin, Holmes, Peirce.* Bloomington, IN: Indiana University Press, 1988. A challenging academic study of logic and philosophy, with each chapter written by a different author.

Freeman, Lucy, ed. *The Murder Mystique: Crime Writers on Their Art.* New York: Frederick Ungar, 1982. In their individual chapters, working writers talk about the history of the genre, the appeal of mysteries, and how they go about their writing.

Haycraft, Howard. *Murder for Pleasure: The Life and Times of the Detective Story*. New York: D. Appleton-Century, 1941. The first—and for a long time the only—all-purpose history of detective fiction, produced for the hundredth anniversary of the publication of "The Murders in the Rue Morgue." Well written and well researched, it is a classic work encompassing history, criticism, and biography.

Haycraft, Howard, ed. *The Art of the Mystery Story: A Collection of Critical Essays*. New York: Simon & Schuster, 1946. Following on the heels of his brilliant history of detective fiction, Haycraft here presented the essays about mysteries (from many writers) that he most admired.

Hillerman, Tony, and Otto Penzler, eds. *The Best American Mystery Stories of the Century*. Boston: Houghton Mifflin, 2000.

Hillerman, Tony, and Rosemary Herbert, eds. *The Oxford Book of American Detective Stories*. New Yor: Oxford University Press, 1996.

Keating, H. R. F. *Writing Crime Fiction*. New York: St. Martin's, 1986.

Kelly, Gordon R. *Mystery Fiction and Modern Life*. Jackson, MS: University Press of Mississippi, 1998.

Landrum, Larry, Pat Browne, and Ray Browne, eds. *Dimensions of Detective Fiction*. New York: Popular Press, 1976. A collection of essays on mysteries in general and specific mystery writers. The chapters, most of which originally appeared in academic journals, are by different authors.

Murch, A. E. *The Development of the Detective Novel*. London: Peter Owen, 1958. A history of detective fiction as literature, with chapters on Poe, Holmes, and others.

Nevins, Francis M., Jr., ed. *The Mystery Writer's Art*. Bowling Green, OH: Bowling Green University Popular Press, 1970. Thought-provoking essays by a wide range of commentators on the mystery novel and its creators.

Panek, LeRoy Lad. *Probable Cause: Crime Fiction in America*. Bowling Green, OH: Bowling Green State University Popular Press, 1990. A two-step survey of detection and detective fiction produced from 1840 to 1940, subdivided into three time periods. Each period is described in paired chapters: one on advances in criminalistics and general trends in detective fiction, called "the contexts"; the other on significant books published during the period, called "the texts."

Penzler, Otto, ed. *The Great Detectives.* Boston: Little, Brown, 1978.

Queen, Ellery. *Queen's Quorum: A History of the Detective Crime Short Story as Revealed by the 106 Most Important Books Published in this Field Since 1845.* Boston: Little, Brown, 1951. The subtitle says it all: the famous author's choice of the 106 most important books. Each one is given a mini-critique. Of particular interest to collectors of rare books.

Rodell, Marie F. *Mystery Fiction, Theory and Technique.* New York: Duell, Sloan, and Pearce, 1943. Although dated, this how-to by an editor of mystery books is still fascinating.

Roth, Marty. *Foul & Fair Play: Reading Genre in Classic Detective Fiction.* Athens: University of Georgia Press, 1995. An academic analysis of issues in and aspects of mystery fiction.

Stewart, R. F. *. . . And Always a Detective: Chapters on the History of Detective Fiction.* North Pomfret, VT: David & Charles, 1980. An academic work of literary history.

Symons, Julian. *Mortal Consequences: A History—From the Detective Story to the Crime Novel.* New York: Harper & Row, 1972.

van Dover, J. K., ed. *You Know My Method: The Science of the Detective.* Bowling Green, OH: Bowling Green State University Popular Press, 1994. Chapters on Poe, Doyle, and several other writers, all focusing on the detective as a hero of logical thinking.

Westlake, Donald, ed. *The Best American Mystery Stories 2000.* Boston: Houghton Mifflin Company, 2000.

Winks, Robin W. *Modus Operandi: A Excursion into Detective Fiction.* Boston: David R. Godine, 1982. A short book (or long essay) that warmly and cogently defends detective fiction while gamboling through the fields of more serious literature past and present. Written by a Yale historian who moonlights as a reviewer of mystery books.

Winks, Robin W., ed. *Detective Fiction: A Collection of Critical Essays.* Englewood Cliffs, NJ: Prentice-Hall, 1980. Chapters are written by mystery authors and by well-known literary critics, and cover a wide range of interesting topics. Includes Winks's list of 200 personal favorites.

ON RELATED TOPICS ADDRESSED IN VARIOUS CHAPTERS

Bazerman, Max. *Judgment in Managerial Decision Making,* 5th ed. New York: John Wiley & Sons, 2001.

Buchanan, Edna. *The Corpse Had a Familiar Face: Covering Miami, America's Hottest Beat.* New York: Random House, 1987.

Buchanan, Edna. *Never Let Them See You Cry: More from Miami, America's Hottest Beat.* New York: Random House, 1992.

de Burgh, Hugo. *Investigative Journalism, Context and Practice.* New York: Routledge, 2000.

Byrne, John A. *Chainsaw: The Notorious Career of Al Dunlap in the Era of Profit-at-Any-Price.* New York: HarperBusiness, 1999.

Dell, Michael, and Catherine Fredman. *Direct from Dell: Strategies That Revolutionized an Industry.* New York: HarperBusiness, 1999.

Dygert, James H. *The Investigative Journalist: Folk Heroes of a New Era.* Englewood Cliffs, NJ: Prentice-Hall, 1974.

Goleman, Daniel. *Emotional Intelligence.* New York: Basic Books, 1995.

Greenwald, Marilyn, and Joseph Bernt, eds. *The Big Chill: Investigative Reporting in the Current Media Environment.* Ames, IA: Iowa State University Press, 2000.

Fischer, David Hackett, Ed. *Historian's Fallacies: Toward a Logic of Historical Thought.* New York: Harper & Row, 1970.

Rappaport, Alfred, and Michael Mauboussin. *Expectations Investing:*

Reading Stock Prices for Better Returns. Boston: Harvard Business School Press, 2001.

Schiller, Robert J. *Irrational Exuberance.* Princeton, NJ: Princeton University Press, 2000.

Stocking, Holly S., and Paget H. Gross. *How Do Journalists Think? A Proposal for the Study of Cognitive Bias in Newsmaking.* Bloomington, IN: Clearinghouse on Reading and Communication Skills, 1989.

Wilson, Edward O. *Consilience: The Unity of Knowledge.* New York: Knopf, 1998.

NOTES

CHAPTER 1

"Batting Averages for Brokerages," Investars.com, May 29, 2001. Also reported in *The New York Times* (Patrick McGeehan, "Study Questions Advice
from Brokerage Firms," May 29, 2001) and the *London Financial Times*
(May 31, 2001).

CHAPTER 3

1. Matthew Schifrin, "Chain Saw Al to the Rescue?" *Forbes*, Aug. 26, 1996, p. 42.
2. Thomas Petzinger Jr., "Does Al Dunlap Mean Business, or Is He Just Plain
   Mean?" *The Wall Street Journal*, Eastern ed., Aug. 30, 1996, p. B1.
3. Gail DeGeorge, "Al Dunlap Revs His Chain Saw," *Business Week*, Dec. 2,
   1996, p. 40.
4. Andrew Osterland, "Sunbeam," *Financial World*, Dec. 16, 1996, p. 26.
5. Junius Ellis, "Forget About Sunbeam, You Should Invest Instead in Rival
   Black & Decker," *Money*, Jan. 1997, p. 29.
6. Herb Greenberg, "Short-Order Request: Sunbeam Is Toast," *Fortune*, April
   28, 1997, p. 398.
7. Jonathan R. Laing, "High Noon at Sunbeam," *Barron's*, June 16, 1997,
   pp. 29–32.

8. Ibid., p 31.

9. Interview with Jonathan Laing, Aug. 7 and 22, 2001.

10. John Byrne, *Chainsaw: The Notorious Career of Al Dunlap in the Era of Profit-at-Any-Price* (New York: HarperBusiness, 1999), p. 160.

11. Jonathan R. Laing, "Dangerous Games," *Barron's,* June 8, 1998, pp. 17–18.

12. Ibid, p. 18. On the very same date that Laing's article appeared, another journalist, Patricia Sellers, suggested in *Fortune* that Dunlap's job was in jeopardy. Patricia Sellers, "Exit for Chainsaw?" *Fortune,* June 8, 1998, pp. 30–31.

13. "Sunbeam Corporation Denounces False Accusations in *Barron's* Article," Sunbeam press release dated June 8, 1998, 11:56 a.m.

14. "Bad Company," *CFO Magazine,* July 2001, p. 84. Dunlap denied any wrongdoing. In a statement released to the media by his attorney the following day, and widely quoted in the financial press, Dunlap declared, "I am outraged that the SEC has chosen to bring these baseless charges against me."

15. Interview with Linn B. Washington, June 27, 2001.

16. Steve Weinberg, *The Reporter's Handbook: An Investigator's Guide to Documents and Techniques,* 3rd ed. (New York: St. Martin's, 1996).

17. Interview with Laing.

18. Interview with Edna Buchanan, Sept. 28, 2001. All quotations in this section were taken from this interview.

CHAPTER 4

1. The story summarized here is "The Resident Patient." Oddly enough, the initial episode, in which Holmes stuns Watson by responding out loud to his unspoken thought, appears in two different stories. It was originally intended as a prelude to "The Cardboard Box," which was written first but published later. It is an interesting commentary on nineteenth-century manners that "The Cardboard Box" was initially rejected for publication because the plot revolved around adultery. Later editions of Holmes's work included the story, with the mind-reading episode intact.

2. Arthur Conan Doyle, *The Hound of the Baskervilles.*

3. Doyle, "The Greek Interpreter."

4. Doyle, "A Case of Identity."

5. Doyle, "The Crooked Man."

6. Doyle, "A Case of Identity."

7. Doyle, *A Study in Scarlet.*

8. Doyle, *The Sign of Four.*

9. Ibid.

10. Doyle, "The Reigate Puzzle."

11. Doyle, *Memories and Adventures*, p. 26.

12. Doyle's remark is included in an audio recording made in the 1920s. Cited in Martin Booth, *The Doctor and the Detective* (New York: Thomas Dunne Books/St. Martin's, 1997), p. 111.

13. Quoted in Michael Hardwick, *The Complete Guide to Sherlock Holmes* (New York: St. Martin's, 1986), p. 49.

14. Interview with Irwin Braverman, M.D., Nov. 13, 2001.

15. Dr. Braverman's experiment is described in "Use of Fine Art to Enhance Visual Diagnostic Skills," *JAMA*, Sept. 5, 2001.

16. Braverman interview.

17. Doyle, "The Adventure of the Blue Carbuncle."

18. *The Valley of Fear.*

19. Doyle, *The Sign of Four.*

20. Doyle, "The Adventure of the Priory School."

21. Doyle, "A Scandal in Bohemia."

22. Doyle, "The Five Orange Pips."

23. Doyle, "Silver Blaze."

24. Doyle, "The Adventure of the Six Napoleons."

25. Doyle, *A Study in Scarlet.*

26. Doyle, *The Valley of Fear.*

27. Doyle, "The Naval Treaty."

28. Doyle, "The Reigate Squires."

29. Doyle, *The Sign of Four.*

30. Doyle, "The Naval Treaty."

31. Doyle, "The Boscombe Valley Mystery."

32. Doyle, "The Adventure of the Copper Beeches."

33. Doyle, "The Disappearance of Lady Frances Carfax."

34. Doyle, "Silver Blaze."

35. This is the story of "The Boscombe Valley Mystery."

36. Doyle, *The Sign of Four.*

CHAPTER 5

1. I am indebted to my colleague Mitchell Penn at Legg Mason for this insight.

2. Michael Dell, "Michael Dell's Plan for the Rest of the Decade," *Fortune,* June 9, 1997.

3. Rahul Jacob and Rajiv Rao, "The Resurrection of Michael Dell," *Fortune,* Sept. 19, 1995.

4. Dan McGraw, "The Kid Bytes Back," *U.S. News & World Report,* Dec. 12, 1994, p. 70.

5. Andrew E. Serwer, "The Hottest Stock on Wall Street," *Fortune,* Aug. 4, 1997, p. 236.

6. John Heuy, Jr., "Hottest Stock of the '90s," *Fortune,* Sept. 8, 1997, p. 16.

7. Stanley W. Angrist, "Entrepreneur in Short Pants," *Forbes,* Mar. 7, 1988.

8. C. Poole, "The Kid Who Turned Computers into Commodities," *Forbes,* Oct. 21, 1991, p. 318.

9. Julia Pitta, "Why Dell Is a Survivor," *Forbes,* Oct. 12, 1992, p. 82ff.

10. Bob Scheier, "Dell to Post Strong Numbers for First Fiscal Quarter," *PC Week,* May 18, 1992, p. 201.

11. Darrell Dunn, "Dell Surprises Naysayers with Higher Sales, Earnings," *Electronic Buyers' News,* Nov. 27, 1995, p. 2.

12. Author's interview with Vadim Slotnikov, Sanford C. Bernstein & Co., April 4, 2002.

13. A New York management consulting firm, Stern Stewart & Co., codified the concept into a proprietary management approach, and has registered "EVA" as a term. In this chapter, the shorthand phrase EVA refers to the concept of economic value added in its broadest sense, not to Stern Stewart's specific management program.

14. Shawn Tully, "The Real Key to Creating Wealth," *Fortune,* Sept. 20, 1993, p. 38ff.

15. Doyle, "The Red-Headed League."

16. Doyle, "His Last Bow."

17. All quotes from Laurie King are taken from author's interviews with Ms. King on Nov. 8, 2001 and Jan. 2, 2002.

18. Laurie King, *The Beekeepers Apprentice* (New York: St. Martin's, 1994), p. 188.

19. Ibid., p. 205.

20. Ibid., p. 24.

CHAPTER 6

1. All quotes in this opening episode are from Chesterton, "The Blue Cross."

2. Chesterton, "The Paradise of Thieves."

3. Maisie Ward, *Gilbert Keith Chesterton* (New York: Sheed & Ward, 1943), p. 42.

4. G. K. Chesterton, *Autobiography* (New York: Sheed & Ward, 1954), p. 75.

5. Ibid., pp. 96–7.
6. Quoted in Ward, *Gilbert Keith Chesterton,* p. 205.
7. Ibid., p. 92.
8. Ibid., p. 257.
9. Quoted in Contemporary Authors Online, part of the Literature Resource Center.
10. Patrick Braybrooke, Gilbert Keith Chesterton (Philadelphia: J. B. Lippincott, no official publication date but probably 1922), pp. 99–104.
11. Chesterton, *Autobiography,* p. 337.
12. Ibid., pp. 337–8.
13. Ibid., p. 338.
14. Ibid., p. 339.
15. Ibid., p. 334.
16. Ibid., p. 334.
17. Ibid., p. 334.
18. Ibid., p. 339.
19. Ibid., p. 339.
20. Chesterton, "How to Write a Detective Story," *G. K.'s Weekly,* Oct. 17, 1925.
21. Chesterton, "A Defence of Detective Stories," originally in Chesterton, *The Defendant* (London: R. B. Johnson, 1901).
22. "The Tremendous Adventures of Major Brown," featuring a detective named Basil Grant.
23. Chesterton, "The Mirror of the Magistrate."
24. These displays of Father Brown's detective skills appear in, respectively, "The Secret Garden," "The Three Tools of Death," "The Vanishing of Vaudrey," and "The Strange Crime of John Boulnois."
25. Chesterton, "The Wrong Shape."
26. Chesterton, "The Queer Feet."
27. Chesterton, "The Man with Two Beards."
28. Chesterton, "The Mistake of the Machine."
29. Chesterton, "The Honour of Israel Gow."
30. Chesterton, "The Sins of Prince Saradine."
31. Steven Miller, "For Father Brown," in Pasquale Accardo, John Peterson, and Geir Hasnes, eds., *Sherlock Holmes Meets Father Brown and His Creator* (New Westminster, BC, Canada: Battered Silicon Dispatch Box, 2000), p. 35.
32. The stories referenced here are, respectively, "The Sign of the Broken Sword," "The Hammer of God," and "The Queer Feet."
33. Chesterton, "The Mistake of the Machine."

34. Chesterton, "The Mirror of the Magistrate."
35. Chesterton, "The Absence of Mr. Glass."
36. Chesterton, "The Song of the Flying Fish."

CHAPTER 7

1. Chesterton, "The Mask of Midas."
2. Accardo, Peterson, and Hasnes, eds., *Sherlock Holmes Meets Father Brown and His Creator.*
3. Hagstrom, Robert, *The Warren Buffett Way* (New York: John Wiley & Sons, 1994).
4. Michael Maubossin, "Let's Make a Deal—A Practical Framework for Assessing M&A Activity," April 27, 1998.
5. Los Alamos National Laboratory, news release, Nov. 6, 2001, "The Origin of Universal Scaling Laws in Biology from Molecules and Cells to Whales and Ecosystems," by Geoffrey West.
6. Ibid.
7. Los Alamos National Laboratory, news release, Jan. 25, 1999, "From Cells to Whales: Universal Scaling Laws in Biology."
8. Unless otherwise noted, all Michael Mauboussin quotes come from an interview with the author on April 4, 2002.
9. Michael Mauboussin, "The Consilient Observer: An Introduction," Jan. 15, 2002.
10. For a complete discussion of this concept, see Robert Hagstrom, *Latticework: The New Investing* (New York: Texere, 2000).
11. Chesterton, "The Secret of Father Brown."
12. Alden M. Hayashi, "When to Trust Your Gut," *Harvard Business Review,* Feb. 2001, p. 63.
13. Gary Klein, *Sources of Power: How People Make Decisions* (Boston: MIT Press, 1999), p. 31.
14. William David Spencer, *Mysterium and Mystery: The Clerical Crime Novel,* quoted in Accardo, Peterson, and Hasnes, eds., *Sherlock Holmes Meets Father Brown and His Creator.*
15. Rosemary Herbert, ed. *The Oxford Companion to Crime and Mystery Writing* (New York: Oxford University Press, 1999), p. 421.
16. Stephen Kendrick, *Night Watch: A Long-Lost Adventure in Which Sherlock Holmes Meets Father Brown* (New York: Pantheon Books, 2001).
17. All quotes from Stephen Kendrick here are taken from the author's interview with Mr. Kendrick on April 2, 2002.

CHAPTER 8

1. "The Murders in the Rue Morgue."
2. "A Study in Scarlet."
3. "The Adventure of the Red Circle." "A Case of Identity."
4. "The Mystery of Marie Roget."
5. "The Adventure of the Blue Carbuncle."
6. "The Valley of Fear."
7. "The Sign of Four."
8. "The Valley of Fear."
9. Ludwig Wittgenstein, *Philosophical Investigations* (Englewood Cliffs, N.J.: Prentice Hall, 1957, 3rd ed., p. 200; originally published 1953). I am indebted to Bill Miller for this insight.
10. "The Oracle of the Dog."
11. "The Sign of the Broken Sword."
12. "The Stockbroker's Clerk."
13. Up to this point, all Wolfe's conversation has been created by me. But this final sardonic remark about brain capacity is Wolfe's own, from *Might As Well Be Dead*, originally published in 1956.
14. "The Man with the Twisted Lip."

ACKNOWLEDGMENTS

If it were not for Maggie Stuckey's hard work, dedication, writing talent, and love for a good mystery story, you would not be reading this book. This is not an overstatement but an accurate description of someone who put her best efforts, talents, and soul into making *The Detective and the Investor* possible.

A few years ago, when Maggie and I were working on a book called *Latticework* (later titled *Investing: The Last Liberal Art*), about the valuable cross-fertilization that comes from studying various disciplines, I wrote a section in the chapter on literature suggesting that investors could learn many important lessons from well-written mystery stories. Specifically, I argued that Holmes's method of solving mysteries—collect information, analyze it, use good logic to reach a conclusion—was in effect what investors do, or should do, when choosing their investments. Following a detective's methods, I suggested, could give investors new ways of thinking about investing. But it was Maggie who said we should expand this idea and write a book about the Great Detectives: analyze their methods for solving cases, then align those methods with the steps investors should take when analyzing stocks. So you see, without Maggie's enthusiasm and her expert knowledge of detective fiction, this book would never have been written.

I would also like to thank three booksellers whose specialized knowledge of the mystery genre has been of great value in researching this book: Carolyn Lane of Murder by the Book in Portland, Oregon; Bob Nissenbaum at Mystery Books in Bryn Mawr, Pennsylvania; and Otto Penzler at The Mysterious Bookshop in New York City. On my many visits to his wonderful bookstore, Otto always made time for my countless questions and offered several thoughtful suggestions for this book.

I am deeply grateful to Edna Buchanan, Laurie King, and Stephen Kendrick, three talented writers who generously gave their time and shared their personal insights about their books and characters and offered suggestions on how mystery stories could in fact help individuals become better investors.

I would also like to thank Jonathan Laing at *Barron's*, Professor Lin Washington at Temple University, and Michael Mauboussin at Credit Suisse First Boston for their outstanding contributions to this book. Each individual spent valuable time helping me to connect the methods we learned from the Great Detectives into practical lessons investors could use.

Several other individuals contributed their time and insights for this book. At Legg Mason Funds Management I have benefited greatly from the lessons I have learned from Bill Miller, Mitchell Penn, and Randy Befumo. Thanks also to Vadim Slotnikov at Sanford C. Bernstein & Company for his insights on Dell Computer.

A special thanks to Dr. Irwin Braverman at Yale University and Dr. Geoffrey West at Los Alamos National Laboratory for their invaluable research.

Myles Thompson, publisher, president, and friend, has, in a few short years, done an outstanding job of bringing together a diverse group a very talented writers. I am privileged to be a part of Texere and I thank all those who work tirelessly on our behalf.

I am deeply grateful and indebted to Laurie Harper at Sebastian Agency. Laurie is an author's perfect agent. She supports me unquestionably and helps me navigate the complexities of starting a book, writing a book, and then getting it published. With so many distractions and difficulties over the past year, Laurie has been a true champion and I thank her for her professionalism, integrity, honesty, and, at the end of a long day, her good humor. Thank you, Laurie.

A special thanks to Ericka Peterson and Cathy Coladonato for their support and hard work at Legg Mason Focus Capital. Ericka worked extra duty researching several ideas for me while Cathy meticulously prepared the manuscript for delivery.

When a writer becomes absorbed in a project, it is not uncommon that the family gets less attention. I am truly fortunate that my wife, Maggie, is a constant source of love and support. With all the demands of raising a family, she allows me ample opportunity to read, conduct research, and write. Although they come last in this list, Maggie, Kim, Robert, and John will always be first in my heart.

For all that is good and right about this book, you may thank the people mentioned above. For any errors or omissions, I alone am responsible.

R. G. H.

INDEX

Holmes, Sherlock (*cont.*)
  choice of name for, 83
  "The Disappearance of Lady Frances
    Carfax," 124
  "The Greek Interpreter," 75–77
  introduction of, 83
  Laurie King's books, 127–30
  summary of method of, 71, 86, 90
  see also Doyle, Arthur Conan
"How to Write a Detective Story,"
    148–49
human behavior, understanding of, 33,
    134–36, 151, 159, 160, 172–75, 193,
    213–14, 217
human sources, 49, 50, 62–63, 229
  currents, 50, 53
  experts, 50, 52–53
  finding, 54
  formers, 50, 52
humor, sense of, 154
hypotheses, willingness to examine
    alternative, 32, 129, 137, 152–53,
    155, 157, 159, 194, 216

IBM, 112
ImClone Systems, 202
Incredulity of Father Brown, The
    (Chesterton), 148
industries:
  primary materials on, 53–54
  regulatory agencies overseeing
    specific, 228–29
Innocence of Father Brown, The
    (Chesterton), 148, 165
insider trading, 200
institutional investors, 57
intangible values, cultivating an under-
    standing for, 155, 170–72, 175–76,
    211
Intel, 105, 113
Intelligent Investor, The (Graham), 173
Internet:
  Dell sales over the, 109
  distribution of visitors per site, 185–86
  as secondary source, 224–25

Internet service providers (ISPs), 186–87
Internet stocks, 174, 201
intuition, 14–15, 152, 155, 159, 160,
    192–93, 198
inventory, 116
  Dell's control over, 104, 106, 110, 112,
    114
"inventory stuffing," 40–41
Investigative Reporters and Editors Inc.,
    48
investment:
  defined, xii, 6
  skills of detectives applicable to, *see*
    individual skills and detectives
  speculation versus, xi, xii–xiii, 5–6
  trading versus, xi
investment banking, 57, 100
  Chinese Wall and, 8, 203
investor psychology, *see* psychology,
    investor
Irrational Exuberance (Shiller), 174

J. D. Power and Associates, 106
journalists, investigative, 13–14, 34–35
  qualities of successful, 46–50
  see also names of individuals
Journal of Applied Corporate Finance, 184
Journal of Finance, 174
Judgment in Managerial Decision Making
    (Bazerman), 176–77
Jung, Carl, 192
junk bond market, 200
justice, passion for, 96, 130, 145, 148

Keating, Charles H., Jr., 200
Kellogg Company, 176
Kelly, Irene (fictional detective), 60
Kemelman, Harry, 195
Kendrick, Stephen, 15, 195–97
Kennedy, Professor Craig (fictional
    detective), 126
Kersh, Russell, 40
Keynes, John Maynard, 6
Kimberly-Clark, 37
King, Laurie, 14, 127–30